Teaching Undergraduates with Archives

Edited by

Nancy Bartlett, Elizabeth Gadelha,
and Cinda Nofziger

Ann Arbor
Maize Books
2019

Copyright © 2019 by Nancy Bartlett, Elizabeth Gadelha, and Cinda Nofziger
Some rights reserved

This work is licensed under the Creative Commons Attribution-NonCommercial-NoDerivatives 4.0 International License. To view a copy of this license, visit http://creativecommons.org/licenses/by-nc-nd/4.0/ or send a letter to Creative Commons, PO Box 1866, Mountain View, California, 94042, USA.

Published in the United States of America by
Michigan Publishing

DOI: http://dx.doi.org/10.3998/mpub.11499242

ISBN 978-1-60785-556-9 (paper)
ISBN 978-1-60785-557-6 (e-book)
ISBN 978-1-60785-564-4 (open-access)

An imprint of Michigan Publishing, Maize Books serves the publishing needs of the University of Michigan community by making high-quality scholarship widely available in print and online. It represents a new model for authors seeking to share their work within and beyond the academy, offering streamlined selection, production, and distribution processes. Maize Books is intended as a complement to more formal modes of publication in a wide range of disciplinary areas.

http://www.maizebooks.org

The cover image is designed by Elizabeth Gadelha, Bentley Historical Library, University of Michigan.

The design is derived from the curvature of a folder, which is repeated and rotated twelve times around a shared point. Inspiration was found in student work from a design course, based on the Bauhaus Vorkurs, taught at the University of Michigan from 1924-1925. Similar to the Bauhaus influence on education, teaching undergraduates with archives provides students with fundamentals that support continuous learning. Teaching with archives also brings together a diverse range of individuals committed to a common cause. The design, thus, represents the shared goal of enriching the undergraduate experience through teaching with archives.

Contents

Introduction: It Began with Questions ~ 1
Nancy Bartlett and Cinda Nofziger

Acknowledgments ~ 9

CLASSROOM CASE STUDIES

Give Earth a Chance: History Undergraduates and Environmental Activism in the Archives ~ 13
Meghan Clark, Hannah Thoms, and Matthew D. Lassiter

Campus Revolution: Engaging in Critical Information Literacy through the Examination of Race, Gender, and Free Speech during the 1960s ~ 31
Holly Luetkenhaus, David Peters, and Matt Upson

What's in It for Me?: Student-Faculty Collaboration and Critical Editing ~ 48
Naomi J. Stubbs

"Decoding" with Encoding: Digital Tools in the Special Collections Classroom ~ 60
Rachel C. S. Duke and Sarah Stanley

Studying Urban Renewal through Archival Sources ~ 71
Ella Howard

SUSTAINABLE ROLES AND PROGRAMS

More than Managing a Calendar: Reflections on the Role of an Academic Archivist ~ 87
Cinda Nofziger

From the Outside Looking In: An Early Career Librarian Builds and Then Brings a Seat to the Table ~ 106
Ashleigh D. Coren

Oh, It's You Again: Increasing Archival Instruction through Sustainable Relationships ~ 113
Joshua Youngblood

Labor and Materials: Towards a Sustainable Special Collections Instruction Program ~ 129
Shira Loev Eller and Leah Richardson

EXPERIMENTS IN COLLABORATION

Discovering and Visualizing the Invisible: Identifying African American Students at the University of Michigan, 1853–1970 ~ 147
Brian A. Williams

Teaching Towards the Whole: Integrating Archives and Secondary Sources through Collaborative Instructional Design Practices ~ 162
Elizabeth Call, Kimberly Davies Hoffman, and Kristen Totleben

History Keepers: Collaboration Between the Yale Afro-American Cultural Center and the Yale University Library ~ 181
Christine Weideman, Camila Zorrilla Tessler, and Shelby Daniels-Young

Archivists and Librarians: Co-Teaching Connections with Primary Sources ~ 193
Chloe Morse-Harding and Laura Hibbler

The Archives as History Lab: The Princeton & Slavery Project ~ 203
Martha A. Sandweiss and Daniel J. Linke

PEDAGOGICAL APPROACHES

Historical Thinking through the Archives ~ 223
Caroline S. Boswell and Jonathan C. Hagel

Ethically Teaching Histories of Violence,
Racism, and Oppression ~ 242
*Andi Gustavson, Analú María López, Lae'l Hughes-Watkins,
and Elizabeth Smith-Pryor*

Active Learning with Primary Sources ~ 265
Peter Carini and Morgan Swan

REFLECTIONS AND FORECASTS

Teaching Undergraduates with Archives:
Past, Present, and Futures ~ 279
Elizabeth Yakel

Faculty Perspectives on Teaching Undergraduates with
Primary Sources: Results of an Online Survey ~ 295
Sean Noel

About "That Phone Call" and the Future of Teaching
Undergraduates with Archives ~ 309
Terrence J. McDonald

This Is Where We Go from Here: Constructing a Community
of Teaching with Primary Sources Educators ~ 320
*Anne Bahde, Heather Smedberg, Matt Herbison, Robin M. Katz,
and Marissa Vassari*

Priorities for Progress ~ 337
Robin M. Katz

Contributors ~ 347

INTRODUCTION: IT BEGAN WITH QUESTIONS

Nancy Bartlett
Cinda Nofziger
University of Michigan

Our journey to this volume began in 2017 with questions: how can the Bentley Historical Library at the University of Michigan contribute to current conversations on teaching undergraduates with archives? Could we bring the community together for a sustained conversation through a symposium? With an abundance of support from the university that would allow there to be no registration fee, what might the event yield in terms of presentations and workshops from a preferably wide variety of archivists, librarians, teaching and research faculty, students, and others who have, with energy and innovation, been advocating for a better undergraduate learning experience through primary sources? Was now the time to offer another kind of event beyond the highly successful Teaching with Primary Sources unconferences held in conjunction with annual Society of American Archivists conferences or the Librarians Active Learning Institute at Dartmouth? Those of us asking these questions did feel that we had something to share, since we were approaching the midpoint of a provost-funded, five-year research and teaching program at Michigan on teaching with primary sources. We also knew that we were more than ready to learn from the work and ideas of others, including the most recent experiences of students, if such an event were to occur. We even sensed that the idea of the symposium had urgency to it, given the times we live in.

As we contemplated our questions, we started to turn them away from hypotheticals and towards a vision and a plan of what the symposium would be. We pictured three days of plenaries, workshops, presentations, and conversations in hallways, over a full complement of meals. We saw the rubrics of collaboration, design, evaluation, and research as the framework for a program, one that would have enough space for practice, analysis, forecast, and review. We even started to anticipate what might be the afterlife of such an event; perhaps a publication? We imagined voices of veteran innovators and newcomers to the conversation—including undergraduates, the ultimate beneficiaries—would be equally valued in the symposium. We wanted to aim for a dynamic involving experience and experimentation, emerging best practices, and radical departures from expectations. We knew that institutions of undeniable privilege could dominate if not for our best efforts at inclusion. At the same time, we had an opportunity as well as obligation, we felt, to demonstrate that teaching with primary sources is not an academic research agenda exclusive to schools of information and the impressively growing number of archivists who specialize in teaching: the University of Michigan is but one example of a place where faculty in the School of Education share in the common cause of conducting studies on the undergraduate educational experience with primary sources and archives.

The first sign that the idea appealed to others was the submission of more than twice as many proposals for presentations as the symposium could possibly accommodate. Initial hopes that at least seventy-five individuals would participate in the event were also far surpassed: there were more than two hundred registrants from across the country and beyond. For three days in November 2018, attendees engaged in sessions such as "defining new roles in instruction and outreach," "sensitivity and silences in the archives," "using archives to document and inspire activism," "archivists and librarians teaching together," "faculty perspectives on primary source collaboration," "growth and sustainability for instruction programs," and "students as creators and collaborators." The intensity of interest—including by those who were unable to attend—and the quality of presentations answered a question that we as the organizers didn't really even need to ask: should the symposium lead to a publication? This University of Michigan Press volume is the result. It is our response to those who want to continue, with as little delay as possible, what the symposium offered. Like the symposium itself, the content of this volume is representative rather than comprehensive. It is offered online at no cost and as soon as possible after the symposium, all in the interest of inclusion in real time.[1]

The several themes that emerged during the symposium are represented in this volume. New and expanded instruction programs in libraries and archives call for increased professional development to create student-focused, productive, and ethical class sessions, often involving active learning. Assessment remains important, as do strong collaborations among faculty, archivists, librarians, and students. The symposium and this book reward our original hope and vision for a focused look, from many views, at where the field of teaching and learning with archival materials has come from, where it is now, and where it is heading. In their chapters, Elizabeth Yakel, Robin M. Katz, and Terrence J. McDonald offer their perspectives on that trajectory; theirs are exemplary of research faculty, teaching archivists, and teaching faculty. Other chapters delve more deeply into different themes, categorized here as one way of anticipating them but certainly open to even more understandings and sortings as evidenced by the book's section headings.

~ ~ ~

---

1. For those with a curiosity about the symposium's fuller content, the program has been archived at http://wayback.archive-it.org/5476/20181205132716/https://www.teachingwitharchives.com/schedule-of-events.

New Programs and Professional Development

In their *American Archivist* article from spring 2018, Anderberg et al. wrote that between 2014 and May 2017, 140 jobs with a "teaching" tag posted on Archivesgig.[2] As the numbers of institutions who have dedicated people who teach with primary sources increases, there's an interest in creating stronger instructional programs at an institutional level. Rather than designing individual courses in an ad hoc way, authors in this volume express a desire to think more broadly, especially as teaching archivists and librarians think about being able to manage the scale of an increased teaching load. Shira Loev Eller and Leah Richardson offer a compelling picture of what a sustainable program should include. Joshua Youngblood's chapter describes one institution's move towards a programmatic approach. Cinda Nofziger's chapter provides evidence of the impact of a holistic, collaborative, and systematic approach to instruction.

Additionally, there is strong interest in developing a wider community of practice across institutions, which would encompass archivists, librarians, curators, faculty, K-12 educators, and museum educators—anyone with an interest in teaching with primary sources. There have been some efforts at this by both the Rare Books and Manuscripts Section (RBMS) of the American Library Association and the Reference and Outreach section of the Society of American Archivists (SAA). For example, the Instruction and Outreach Committee of RBMS and the SAA's RAO Teaching with Primary Sources Committee have collaborated on some projects together, like the Teaching with Primary Sources Unconference and the Resource Bank. The SAA-ACRL/RBMS Joint Task Force on Primary Source Literacy is a great example of collaboration across professional organizations to work towards a larger

---

2. Archivesgig.org is an independent, online clearinghouse for archives related jobs run by Meredith Rowe. "About" Archivesgig, accessed October 29, 2019, https://archivesgig.com/about-2/. See also, Lindsay Anderberg, Robin M. Katz, Shaun Hayes, Alison Stankrauff, Morgen MacIntosh Hodgetts, Josué Hurtado, Abigail Nye, and Ashley Todd-Diaz, "Teaching the Teacher: Primary Source Instruction in American and Canadian Archives Graduate Programs," *The American Archivist*, 81 no. 1 (Spring/Summer 2018): 188-215, https://doi.org/10.17723/0360-9081-81.1.188.

community of practice. SAA's series of case studies on teaching with primary sources can help practitioners see the literacy goals in action.[3] In their chapter, Anne Bahde, Heather Smedberg, Matt Herbison, Robin M. Katz, and Marissa Vassari chronicle symposium attendees' desire to create a community that crosses programs and disciplines. As teaching programs increase in archives and special collections, practitioners recognize a need for additional professional development. In her chapter, Ashleigh D. Coren generously relates her experiences in seeking out ways to become a better instructor. Peter Carini and Morgan Swan provide a glimpse into what some of that professional development might look like through a description of Dartmouth's Librarians Active Learning Institute–Special Collections and Archives workshop. Several writers throughout the volume call for more teaching training for teaching as part of the graduate school curriculum.

Student-Focused Learning: Active, Productive, and Ethical

As McDonald notes in this volume, most special collections and archival instruction has moved beyond the "show and tell" as the standard for instruction, though such sessions may be designed on occasion. Instead, archives have shifted to focusing on student learning, rather than archivists' knowledge. This has led to a more pedagogical approach to teaching with special collections and archives. This approach might include different modes of active learning, greater attention to learning goals and outcomes, skill building, and more. Carini and Swan provide insight into how librarians and archivists can incorporate active learning strategies into their teaching practice. Ella Howard's chapter chronicles several active learning activities she has constructed for her engineering, architecture, and computer science students. In their chapter, Caroline S. Boswell and Jonathan C. Hagel privilege active and

---

3. "Case Studies on Teaching with Primary Sources" (Society of American Archivists). https://www2.archivists.org/publications/epubs/Case-Studies-Teaching-With-Primary-Sources. Accessed 16 August 2019.

experiential learning methods, in order to teach students to think "like historians."

At the same time that active learning has been gaining traction in archives and special collections, instructors—including teaching faculty, librarians, and archivists—have incorporated assignments into their classes that allow students to produce and share new knowledge. Rachel C. S. Duke and Sarah Stanley describe a project in which students coded papyrus using text encoding initiative guidelines (TEI) to better understand the editorial process. Naomi J. Stubbs collaborated with community college students to produce a critical edition of a nineteenth-century diary and a digital edition of the text. In an excellent example of student-faculty-archivist collaboration, Meghan Clark, Hannah Thoms, and Matthew D. Lassiter write about their public history research project and website, called Give Earth a Chance: Environmental Activism in Michigan.

The move towards active and experiential student-centered learning in teaching with archives also lends itself to a critical approach. Archivists, librarians, and faculty increasingly are either willing or feel compelled to be reflexive about archival and historical processes, which may lead to silences and gaps, and to demonstrate a critical awareness of institutional positions and privileges. Some instructors include acknowledgment of their own position and privilege as part of their teaching practice. Andi Gustavson, Analú María López, Lae'l Hughes-Watkins, and Elizabeth Smith-Pryor provide examples of three projects from different institutions that raise important questions about teaching histories that are violent, racist, or oppressive. Holly Luetkenhaus, David Peters, and Matt Upson recount a class that incorporated critical information literacy with primary sources. Brian A. Williams, Martha A. Sandweiss, and Daniel J. Linke, in their respective pieces describe archive-based projects that are designed to shed light not just on archival gaps, but also on larger university inequities and injustices.

Assessment

Assessment of learning has been on the "to do" lists of archival and special collections instructors for quite a while. In 2008, Wendy Duff and Joan Cherry started writing about the need for assessment in archival teaching; numerous other articles followed.[4] Yakel describes some of the various assessment efforts that have occurred since then, and argues for continued work to better understand the effects of learning with archives.

Collaboration

Nearly all the chapters in this volume describe instances of and recognize the need for collaboration. These collaborations can take different forms. Chloe Morse-Harding and Laura Hibbler outline efforts at archivists and librarians co-teaching at Brandeis, while at the University of Rochester, Elizabeth Call, Kimberly Davies Hoffman, and Kristen Totleben have created a program to cross-train special collections and subject area librarians to teach together, which they recount in their chapter. Christine Weideman, Camila Zorrilla Tessler, and Shelby Daniels-Young illustrate collaborations among students, librarians, and institutions. Sean Noel's research into what teaching faculty are looking for in their relationships with archivists offers useable information for creating productive collaborations, while Nofziger's chapter offers

---

4. Wendy Duff and Joan Cherry, "Archival Orientation for Undergraduate Students: An Exploratory Study of Impact," *The American Archivist* 71, no. 2, (Fall/Winter 2008): 499–529. https://doi.org/10.17723/aarc.71.2.p6l385r7556743h. The following are a sampling of additional work on assessment. Magia Krause, "Undergraduates in the Archives: Using an Assessment Rubric to Measure Learning," *The American Archivist* 73, no. 2, (Fall/Winter 2010): 507–534. https://doi.org/10.17723/aarc.73.2.72176h742v20l115; Anne Bahde and Heather Smedberg, "Measuring the Magic: Assessment in the Special Collections and Archives Classroom," *RBM: A Journal of Rare Books, Manuscripts and Cultural Heritage* 13, no.2 (Fall 2012): 152–174. https://doi.org/10.5860/rbm.13.2.380; Julia Gardner and Leah Richardson, "Beyond the Cabinet of Curiosities: Demonstrating the Impact of Special Collections Instruction," Proceedings of the 2014 Library Assessment Conference. http://old.libraryassessment.org/bm~doc/proceedings-lac-2014.pdf.

evidence of the impact of collaboration on both archivists and teaching faculty.

~ ~ ~

Together, these chapters provide a picture of the current state of teaching undergraduates with archives. They demonstrate the issues and challenges a nascent community of practice faces in building on the past to create a future that will allow them to engage and empower the undergraduate. They more than reward our original 2017 speculations of whether a symposium would attract participants on this timely and essential topic. We invite you, the reader, to join in the conversation.

Acknowledgments

The origins of this volume lie in the symposium Teaching Undergraduates with Archives, which was held at the University of Michigan on November 7–9, 2018. The event featured ninety-six speakers and a total of 225 registrants from thirty-six states, our nation's capital, and four countries. To all who participated in the symposium, we offer our immense gratitude for stimulating conversation, impressive presentations and workshops, and affirmation of our common cause in enhancing the undergraduate's learning experience in the archives. We are grateful for collaborating with Bentley Historical Library archivists Sarah McLusky and Emily Swenson on the symposium planning and program committee. We also treasure the many Michigan faculty who have demonstrated through action and word a commitment to collaborative teaching in the archives, including through their involvement in conceptualizing the symposium and presenting at it.

As editors of this volume, we realize that we set an extremely fast timeline by aiming to publish a fine representation, if not a complete record, of the symposium within one year of the event. We are indebted to the symposium presenters who contributed to this volume, especially at such a pace. Our work on the symposium and book was enriched and rewarded by the support and interest of our Bentley Historical Library colleagues, not least our director, Terrence McDonald.

In turning a symposium into a publication, we continued to benefit from the strong support of the sponsors listed below.

- The Thomas C. Jones Fund for Engaged Education
- The University of Michigan Bentley Historical Library
- The University of Michigan College of Literature, Science, and the Arts Office of the Associate Dean for Undergraduate Education
- The University of Michigan Department of Afroamerican and African Studies
- The University of Michigan Department of Film, Television, and Media
- The University of Michigan Department of History
- The University of Michigan Library
- The University of Michigan Office of the Provost
- The University of Michigan School of Education

CLASSROOM
CASE STUDIES

GIVE EARTH A CHANCE: HISTORY UNDERGRADUATES AND ENVIRONMENTAL ACTIVISM IN THE ARCHIVES

Meghan Clark
Hannah Thoms
Matthew D. Lassiter
University of Michigan

Project Overview: Matthew D. Lassiter

Collaborating with undergraduate researchers in the public engagement course that produced the Give Earth a Chance: Environmental Activism in Michigan website (http://michiganintheworld.history.lsa.umich.edu/environmentalism/) turned out to be the most ambitious and meaningful teaching experience of my academic career. In 2015, the Department of History at the University of Michigan launched the Michigan in the World initiative as a partnership with the Bentley Historical Library. This initiative would enable undergraduate students to create online multimedia exhibits about the history of U-M and its relationship to events at the local, state, national, and global levels. I codesigned the Michigan in the World program and taught its pilot seminar, Global Activism at U-M: The Anti-War, Anti-Apartheid, and Anti-Sweatshop Movements, which produced the first three digital projects created by teams of undergraduate scholars. Through 2019, this innovative collaboration among faculty, students, and archivists has resulted in the publication of nine Michigan in the World exhibits that utilize the open-source Omeka platform and combine textual narrative and scholarly analysis with the extensive reproduction of archival documents from the Bentley's collections, as well as supplemental archives and databases.[1] The projects emphasize active learning techniques, team-based research methods, student acquisition of digital media skills and career-enhancing experiences, and the significance of producing historical content for diverse public audiences and not just for the instructor. As the Michigan in the World initiative has expanded, history faculty have increasingly recognized the benefits of collaborating extensively with Bentley archivists in the design phase as well as the implementation of each project. I began planning the History 399: Environmental Activism in Michigan course during the Bentley's winter 2017 Engaging the Archives seminar to promote faculty-archivist dialogue.[2]

---

1. The Michigan in the World exhibit showcase is here: https://lsa.umich.edu/history/history-at-work/programs/michigan-in-the-world.html. Omeka is a free web publishing platform, provided by the Roy Rosenzweig Center for History and New Media at George Mason University, which enables collaborative creation of multimedia exhibits and digitized archives. See https://omeka.org.

2. In 2016, the U-M Office of the Provost's Third Century Initiative awarded a five-year Engaging the Archives grant to the Bentley Historical Library to promote greater collaboration between faculty and archivists in the development of pedagogical practices that involve undergraduates directly in archival research through course assignments. The main focus, an annual Engaging the Archives seminar, has brought five Bentley Faculty Fellows and a rotating group of Bentley archivists together each year to brainstorm course design and discuss best practices for introducing undergraduates to archivally based projects. For more on the Bentley collaboration with my Environmental Activism in Michigan course, see Cinda Nofziger and Emily Swenson, "Success in the Long Term: Learning Objectives in a Semester-Long Research Course," *Case Studies on Teaching with Primary Sources* (Society of American Archivists, 2019), https://www2.archivists.org/sites/all/files/TWPSCase_8_Success_in_The_Long_Term.pdf.

Figure 1. Give Earth a Chance exhibit, front page.

The resulting Give Earth a Chance online exhibit (Figure 1) is a public-facing history project of original academic scholarship, collectively researched and produced in History 399 during the fall 2017 semester by eight undergraduate students and me (in the hybrid roles of history professor, project supervisor, and direct collaborator). The exhibit contains fifty-four separate web pages in five thematic sections that cover the origins of the modern environmental movement in the state of Michigan and at the national level, the spring 1970 environmental teach-ins at the University of Michigan and during the first Earth Day nationwide, multiple case studies of activist campaigns in Ann Arbor and across Michigan during the 1970s, detailed analysis of the struggles for clean air and water at the state and federal levels, and a concluding segment on the legacies of this era.[3] The student researchers located, edited, and reproduced more than six hundred archival sources—including textual documents and historical photographs from nearly two dozen Bentley collections, and video excerpts from twenty documentary programs produced by the University of Michigan Television Center between the late 1960s and the early 1980s and digitized by the Bentley for our project. Following the mantra that sources always lead to more sources, the research team tracked down and conducted interviews with ten historical participants in the environmental movement and enhanced many of the exhibit pages with videotaped excerpts of these living activists.[4] A particular highlight is "Why Environmental History Matters," the final page of the Legacies section, where research team members reflect on the methods of digital humanities scholarship, relate how they found inspiration from the activists and campaigns they uncovered in the archives, and emphasize the value of creating historical content for public audiences during this time of ecological crisis.[5] The remainder of this chapter features the joint account of Meghan Clark and Hannah Thoms (Figure 2), two extraordinary students and highly productive members of the research team, to provide an undergraduate perspective on the process of directly engaging students in history courses with archives and to reflect on their experiences with the Give Earth a Chance project.

---

3. Joshua Blum, Meghan Clark, Amanda Hampton, Maya Littlefield, Julia Montag, Trent Reynolds, Hannah Thoms, Kiegan White, Matthew D. Lassiter, "Give Earth a Chance: Environmental Activism in Michigan," January 2018, http://michiganintheworld.history.lsa.umich.edu/environmentalism/.

4. The interviews are archived here: http://michiganintheworld.history.lsa.umich.edu/environmentalism/exhibits/show/interviews.

5. "Why Environmental History Matters," http://michiganintheworld.history.lsa.umich.edu/environmentalism/exhibits/show/main_exhibit/legacies/why-environmental-history-matt.

Figure 2. Hannah Thoms (left) and Meghan Clark (right) present research on citizen activist Joan Wolfe of the West Michigan Environmental Action Council, January 26, 2018. Courtesy of Matthew D. Lassiter.

The Undergraduate Perspective: Meghan Clark and Hannah Thoms

We enrolled in History 399: Environmental Activism in Michigan in fall 2017 as two of eight undergraduate students from a diverse range of majors that included history, environmental studies, public health, engineering, economics, and political science.[6] Meghan joined the research team as a junior studying history with a minor in environmental studies. Having grown up in Oklahoma, a state at the center of contemporary fracking and fossil fuel debates, she came to this project seeking a way to direct her interests in environmental law and policy into meaningful research with a public impact. Hannah, who would become her closest collaborator, was a junior studying anthropology with minors in history and museum studies. After working in the

---

6. Student biographies are included on the "About" page, http://michiganintheworld.history.lsa.umich.edu/environmentalism/about.

collections departments of several historical museums, Hannah wanted to develop archival research skills and produce a history project that would reach a broad audience.

Our class spent the first two weeks of the semester collectively formulating research questions based on historical scholarship about environmental activism in the 1960s and 1970s and on archival documents that the professor had preselected from databases and the Bentley Historical Library. In the third week, the eight students divided into two research teams of four and identified the research topics for the rest of the semester. Our group focused on four main topics: the national mobilization around the first Earth Day in April 1970, the passage of the landmark Michigan Environmental Protection Act later that year, debates about nuclear power in the state of Michigan, and activism and legislation to limit air pollution at the state and federal levels. The other team researched the ENACT Teach-In on the Environment at the University of Michigan in March 1970, the formation of the Ecology Center of Ann Arbor, and activist campaigns for wilderness preservation and clean water legislation. The scale of our research agenda initially seemed overwhelming, especially since our team had responsibility for multiple environmental campaigns at the state and national levels. For that reason, our research would require a combination of database and archival sources to find these collective and individual stories. We did not go into the archives blindly but created research plans and asked a set of questions that evolved alongside our research findings. Our team of four soon divided into pairs; the two of us were a natural fit because our research topics—the Michigan Environmental Protection Act and air quality activism—correlated and because our personalities, schedules, and levels of commitment to the project also aligned.

Together, we searched for stories about Michiganders working in their local communities to protect the environment, situated within a framework of national grassroots mobilization. As we discovered these stories in the archives, we worked to translate them into an accessible and engaging narrative for a public audience. But we needed more than just a textual narrative to suit the digital format of an online exhibit: we needed to find and reproduce documents, photographs, and videos as well. The search for each of these components drove the research process in unexpected directions, requiring creativity and resourcefulness. To illustrate how we traced issues of national significance back to individual local activists, we will explain the process of researching and creating two website pages about the Michigan Environmental Protection Act (MEPA).

Research Process: Exploring the Archives

Historians have noted that women shaped the environmental movement but have not received sufficient acknowledgment. We wanted to explore this issue in our project, especially after our class observed that grassroots female activists appeared frequently in documents we located through archival research but rarely in the leadership roles of national organizations.[7] Women's engagement in conservationism dates back to the Progressive Era, but the 1962 publication of Rachel Carson's *Silent Spring*, which dramatically exposed the dangers of toxic chemicals to the public, marked the first time a female activist took the national stage. Her revelation led to a paradigm shift in the public perception of DDT and helped to inspire a nationwide campaign to ban the chemical, largely driven by women. Through database research, we found a Kennedy administration report that sought to minimize the pesticide threat in an effort to lessen the sense of horror instilled by *Silent Spring*, and then we uncovered Rachel Carson's testimony from a congressional hearing on the issue. This national debate propelled activists, especially women, to take action across the country by forming grassroots organizations in their communities, lobbying politicians, and working to ban DDT and other toxic pesticides. In the Bentley's digital media holdings, we discovered video footage of women activists pressuring politicians in part of the series *Ecology: Man and the Environment*, produced in 1970 by the University of Michigan Television Center and the School of Natural Resources. These video sources and

---

7. Adam Rome, "'Give Earth a Chance': The Environmental Movement and the Sixties," *Journal of American History* 90:2 (September 2003): 525–554.

other Bentley collections revealed the extensive efforts of grassroots female activists, who advanced the fight that Rachel Carson had started on the national scene.[8]

In the late 1960s and early 1970s, citizen groups continued to work tirelessly to ban the sale of pesticides, often taking cases to court. University of Michigan Law Professor Joseph Sax worked on one such groundbreaking DDT case, which brought him to the attention of environmental activists across Michigan. Expecting to drown in legal jargon, we made the daunting decision to sift through Sax's records at the Bentley. Our hesitation dissipated when we discovered a letter from Grand Rapids activist Joan Wolfe, the founder of a coalition of twenty-five citizen groups, the West Michigan Environmental Action Council (WMEAC). Wolfe requested that Professor Sax write a bill to empower grassroots organizations to hold the government and corporations accountable for the harm that they caused to the environment (Figure 3).[9]

Joan Wolfe's correspondence sparked the Michigan Environmental Protection Act (MEPA), a revolutionary bill that allowed citizens to sue government agencies on behalf of the environment and gave activist groups a powerful legal weapon in the fight for environmental protection. We reproduced and analyzed these documents on the website and also asked the archivists at the Bentley to digitize a program about environmental law produced in 1970 by the now defunct U-M Television Center, which allowed us to hear Professor Sax elaborate on the importance of MEPA in his own words and brought these historical figures to life for our public audience and for us as well.[10]

We then decided to tell the story of a prominent citizen lawsuit brought under the law to illustrate MEPA's significance. The articles we read in law journals brought our attention to a decade-long land-use

---

8. "Toxic Chemicals and Citizen Activism," http://michiganintheworld.his tory.lsa.umich.edu/environmentalism/exhibits/show/main_exhibit/origins/ environmentalism-and-the-great/toxic-chemicals-citizen-activi.

9. Mrs. Willard E. [Joan] Wolfe to Dr. Joseph Sax, January 28, 1969, Folder 2, Box 1, Joseph L. Sax Papers, Bentley Historical Library, University of Michigan.

10. "Michigan Environmental Protection Act," http://michiganintheworld.history. lsa.umich.edu/environmentalism/exhibits/show/main_exhibit/1970s_activism/mepa

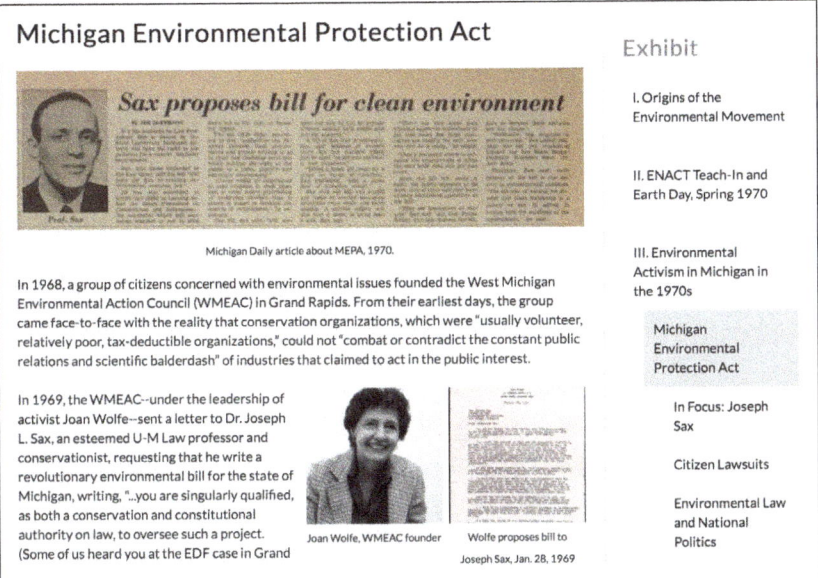

Figure 3. Grand Rapids activist Joan Wolfe envisioned the Michigan Environmental Protection Act of 1970 in a January 1969 letter to U-M Professor Joseph Sax, who received the formal credit. Excerpt from the Michigan Environmental Protection Act section of Give Earth a Chance.

lawsuit over oil drilling in the Pigeon River Country State Forest, an immense nature preserve in the heart of northern Michigan. Led by the WMEAC, the Grand Rapids-based coalition headed by Joan Wolfe, environmental organizations across Michigan mobilized to battle not just the oil corporation but also the state government, which wanted to lease the oil reserves beneath the forest. The case reached the Michigan Supreme Court and represented a rare victory for environmental activists.

A preliminary search of the Bentley's online finding aids revealed a wealth of sources about the Pigeon River controversy. In the WMEAC's records, we found memos and letters from environmental organizations that helped us identify important figures. We also found correspondence from concerned citizens in the records of Helen Milliken, the wife of Governor William Milliken, showing that saving Pigeon River mattered to people outside of the circle of environmental activists we had focused on thus far. Professor Sax consulted on the case; his correspondence illustrated Pigeon River's legal significance.

These archival sources allowed us to tell the story of the fight to save Pigeon River, but we knew we needed other sources to bring this episode to life. We searched the U-M Library database and found a 16 mm film called *Pigeon River Forum*, created in 1977 by a student activist group for a panel discussion on the controversy. We doubted that anyone had seen the film since that era and so asked the Askwith Media Library to convert the footage to a digital format so that we could feature it on the website (Figure 4). Beyond providing an interesting visual component to break up a document-heavy exhibit page, the film was valuable as an historical document. Watching it, we learned about the creation of the Michigan Natural Resources Trust Fund, returned to the archives with this lead, and featured a section about it in the exhibit. Through the film, the activists and their opponents became more than just names found on archival documents. Hearing their voices helped us understand their passion and revived the controversy for our audience in a powerful way.[11]

Contributions to Historical Scholarship

Through the research process, we learned that it is possible for inexperienced undergraduates to produce original scholarship and contribute to historical debates. The Environmental Activism in Michigan class taught us to use finding aids and databases strategically to locate leads. Documents from archival collections led us to historical actors, whom we contacted for videotaped interviews, several of which enabled us to make new and surprising discoveries in the archives. Our own research then helped to challenge and revise existing scholarship about the role of labor groups, women, and environmental justice.[12]

---

11. "Citizen Lawsuits," http://michiganintheworld.history.lsa.umich.edu/environmentalism/exhibits/show/main_exhibit/1970s_activism/mepa/citizen-lawsuits.

12. For elaboration, see the stories about African American and female activism against lead poisoning and toxic chemicals on the "Toxic Chemicals and Citizen Activism" page (http://michiganintheworld.history.lsa.umich.edu/environmentalism/exhibits/show/main_exhibit/origins/environmentalism-and-the-great/

Voices of the Pigeon River Controversy

Concern about the future of Pigeon River Country spread throughout Michigan, even reaching the campus of the University of Michigan. In 1977, the U-M Pigeon River Country Association held an event to spread awareness and produced a film featuring interviews with many of those advocating for and against oil development in the forest.

This segment features the perspectives of DNR Director Tanner and John Miller, a representative of the Michigan Oil and Gas Association, who describe their reasons for supporting the oil development agreement. Miller remarked that the recent energy crisis and decline in domestic energy production made oil development in Pigeon River Country essential. He also viewed development as the DNR's only ethical option because the state had already leased the land to the oil companies.

Director Tanner conceded that hydrocarbon development in the forest would lead to "damages to certain elements of wildlife" but said he was optimistic because the Michigan Natural Resources Trust Fund arose from the controversy. After considering the perspectives of all groups involved, Tanner had selected the plan he believed was the best option. "My principal concern is that the Pigeon River be a better place, a more beautiful place, a quieter place, a larger place, a more productive place, when we finish than when we began."

Voices of Support
DNR Director Howard Tanner and Michigan Oil and Gas Association Representative John Miller explain their support for oil development in the forest, 1977.

Voices of Opposition
Former DNR wildlife biologist Ford Kellum, U-M law professor Joseph Sax, and elk biologist Jim Knight explain their opposition to oil development, 1977.

Environmentalists did not share Director Tanner's optimism. They offer their perspectives in this segment from the same video that featured Miller and Tanner. Former DNR wildlife biologist Ford Kellum expressed the popular opinion that "the sounds and smells of industry" would ruin the aesthetic value of the forest. Jim Knight, an authority on elk, described the forest's herd as "a kind of environmental barometer" and could not guarantee that the herd could recover if development disrupted it.

Again, Joseph Sax objected to the development, which he saw as a rushed response to the country's "energy crunch." Although he

Figure 4. Digitized excerpts from *Pigeon River Forum*, a 1977 documentary film produced by a U-M student organization, enhance the "Citizen Lawsuits" page of the Give Earth a Chance exhibit.

Figure 5. The United Auto Workers hosted environmental activists and delegates from civil rights and labor organizations at its Black Lake Conference Center, July 1970. Courtesy of George Coling.

Our videotaped interviews with living sources led us to discover that the United Auto Workers (UAW) had been a critical early supporter of the environmental movement in the 1960s and 1970s, contradicting dominant historical narratives.[13] In November 2017, a research team

---

toxic-chemicals-citizen-activi), and the documentation of labor union involvement in environmental activism on the "Environmentalism and the Great Society" page (http://michiganintheworld.history.lsa.umich.edu/environmentalism/exhibits/show/main_exhibit/origins/environmentalism-and-the-great) and in the "Politics of Clean Air and Water" section (http://michiganintheworld.history.lsa.umich.edu/environmentalism/exhibits/show/main_exhibit/pollution_politics).

13. Scholars have emphasized the conflict between the jobs-and-economic growth agenda of labor unions and the environmental movement's emphasis on anti-pollution regulations, but our research uncovered significant support by the United Auto Workers during the 1960s and early 1970s for strong clean air legislation and other reforms that would now be labeled part of the environmental justice vision. See "Reforming

member interviewed Barbara Reid Alexander, the Midwest Coordinator for Environmental Action, the national group that organized the first Earth Day. She urged our class to investigate the support that organized labor groups such as the UAW had provided to the environmental agenda. At the Bentley, another member of our research team found archival documents showing that the UAW financially supported the U-M Teach-In on the Environment in March 1970, as well as photographs of UAW President Walter Reuther speaking at the event. In Environmental Action's newsletters, we learned that the UAW endorsed a radical plan to reduce air pollution, including a demand that General Motors stop producing the internal combustion engine altogether. After the first Earth Day, in further demonstration of its commitment to the environment, the UAW hosted a retreat at its Black Lake Conference Center in Michigan for environmental activist groups, labor unions, and civil rights organizations to develop strategies and form a political coalition (Figure 5).[14] This early evidence of the UAW's support of the environmental movement demonstrates that organized labor believed that strong laws and regulations could protect its workers and the environments in which they lived. These discoveries led us to conclude that labor unions, civil rights groups, and environmentalists started the discussions that shaped the environmental justice movement much earlier than mainstream scholarship suggests (Figure 6).[15]

The Give Earth a Chance website also offers a reconstruction of the narrative surrounding the efforts of women's groups and provides a broader understanding of the scope of their influence. Though historians have deservedly credited women, especially white middle-class

---

the Auto Industry," http://michiganintheworld.history.lsa.umich.edu/environmentalism/exhibits/show/main_exhibit/pollution_politics/national--air-quality/reforming-the-auto-industry; and Chad Montrie, *The Myth of Silent Spring: Rethinking the Origins of American Environmentalism* (Berkeley: University of California Press, 2018).

14. The photograph of Black Lake Conference participants, July 1970, is from the personal collection of George Coling, who provided it to the project following an interview.

15. "Reforming the Auto Industry," http://michiganintheworld.history.lsa.umich.edu/environmentalism/exhibits/show/main_exhibit/pollution_politics/national--air-quality/reforming-the-auto-industry.

Senator Philip Hart founded the Urban Environment Conference (UEC) in 1971 as part of an effort to shift the environmental movement beyond middle-class suburban issues to address the problems faced by poor, largely black populations that lived in inner-cities and suffered disproportionately from pollution. In this interview, George Coling, a member of the ENACT steering committee who later became a leader of the UEC, describes the conference as a "union-expressed environmental organization" that facilitated the creation of a "coalition of labor unions, civil rights groups, and environmental groups." By bringing together organizations including the UAW, the United Steelworkers, the Sierra Club, the Wilderness Society, and the National Welfare Association, the UEC hoped to define urban environmental issues and bring them to the forefront of the environmental movement.

George Coling describes the UAW's involvement in environmental issues and the Urban Environment Conference.

Urban Environment Conference flyer, 1975.

In the UEC's early years, the organization lobbied for changes that would benefit urban communities including improving mass transit, reducing lead in paint, and improving workplace conditions. After its first few years of operation, the UEC became a non-profit lobbying organization with branches devoted to education, outreach, and fundraising. According to Coling, "UEC's strength in the 1970s was advocacy for improvements in occupational safety and health, and in-plant pollution. We organized... comments on proposed Occupational Safety and Health Administration (OSHA) rules, organized coalitions from all over the country for increased funding for OSHA and the National Institute for Occupational Health and trained thousands of women, minority and unorganized workers on worker rights and specific in-plant work hazards."

Figure 6. Documenting the early environmental justice movement: an excerpt from the "Reforming the Auto Industry" page features an interview with activist George Coling and a 1975 flyer produced by the Urban Environment Conference, an organization that united the concerns of labor, environmental, and civil rights groups.

suburban women, for their extensive participation in the environmental campaigns of the 1960s and 1970s, their motivations are often narrowly construed as a function of gender roles.[16] The records and testimonies of women activists that we discovered in the archives offered a more complicated story. By holding politicians and corporations accountable for environmental degradation and advocating for stronger regulations, these women not only contributed to the beautification of

---

16. Adam Rome, *The Bulldozer in the Countryside: Suburban Sprawl and the Rise of American Environmentalism* (Cambridge: Cambridge University Press, 2001).

their communities but also articulated a then-radical critique about the collusion between government and corporate polluters that national leaders such as Ralph Nader underscored. The records of grassroots organizations such as WMEAC and the League of Women Voters demonstrated that public pressure from women's groups frequently drove specific local issues, such as pesticides and water quality, upward into the national arena. Such campaigns allowed women to create new and influential connections and to become informed, engaged, and resilient environmental activists. Seemingly small leads from the archives gave us new insights that reframe a story that is typically dominated by the loudest, and usually male, voices. Our website redirects the national narrative back to the grassroots, with specific stories in local archives.[17]

Personal and Public Impacts

As any undergraduate student studying history knows, "transferable skills" is a useful buzz-phrase for justifying the value of a degree in the humanities to parents and potential employers. But the skills we developed truly do transfer. We gained an understanding of the history we researched, and we also learned how to edit photos and videos, write for a public audience, and collaborate as a research team.

Students in the class uncovered, analyzed, and edited every one of the more than six hundred archival documents, images, and videos published on the website. We developed a set of strategies to photograph documents from the archives for clean and bright reproduction and learned how to convert them into PDF files. We taught ourselves to use tools such as iMovie. To support our arguments, we prepared short clips from our video interviews with living subjects and from the Bentley's digital media holdings. Editing videos and hundreds of

---

17. See, especially, "Toxic Chemicals and Citizen Activism," http://michiganintheworld.history.lsa.umich.edu/environmentalism/exhibits/show/main_exhibit/origins/environmentalism-and-the-great/toxic-chemicals-citizen-activi, and the pages in the "Environmental Activism in Michigan during the 1970s" section, http://michiganintheworld.history.lsa.umich.edu/environmentalism/exhibits/show/main_exhibit/1970s_activism.

documents took an unexpectedly long amount of time, but the finished website is engaging and looks professional because of this investment of labor. Because of this course experience, we can also list photo and video editing as skills on our resumes.

The first few website pages that we drafted proved challenging, in part because we were accustomed to writing formulaic academic papers that only our professors would read. The mission of a public history project is to make the historical record more accessible, and so the language that we used had to be accessible too. To effectively convey the content in this new way, we had to imagine a general audience, composed of people who had a slight interest in the topic but not much time to spare. Although the exhibit makes complex historical arguments, we had to distill what we learned into concise and direct language, and carefully supplement our writing with visuals from the archives to break up the text and bring the historical documents alive. The ability to write clearly is an undervalued skill that is useful in any context.

By transforming our archival research into a public website, we knew that we were creating a valuable resource that would live beyond the end of the semester.[18] We grew to care about these environmental activists and wanted to elevate their stories with this platform. At the same time, we were bringing hundreds of archival documents within reach of new audiences. Once seemingly hidden in the archives at the Bentley, the documents are now fully accessible online, available to other students and interested readers through a simple Google search.

A project of this scale would not have been possible without a sustainable system of collaboration. Reflecting on what contributed to our effective partnership, we identified four basic factors: shared interests, corresponding schedules, compatible research and writing styles, and mutual commitment to the public goals of the project. At the beginning of the semester, we both indicated an interest in researching community-based citizen activism. Though shared interests originally motivated us,

---

18. The Give Earth a Chance website is archived on the Michigan in the World public history project site maintained by the University of Michigan History Department; see https://lsa.umich.edu/history/history-at-work/programs/michigan-in-the-world.html.

corresponding availability allowed us to develop routines for meeting and working together that would sustain such extensive collaboration. This is especially true in the case of archival research because traveling to the Bentley during business hours, sifting through boxes of materials, taking detailed notes, and discussing our findings took a lot of time. As a result, we conducted most of our archival research independently, but our compatible personalities and work styles enabled us to effectively use the time we had together. We discovered that our strengths complemented one another: Meghan tends to think about the bigger picture while Hannah focuses on the finer details. These strengths proved essential to guide us through the seemingly never-ending leads that emerged throughout our research. When we wrote collaboratively, we discovered that we were both perfectionists—we endlessly revised each sentence. Through this process of researching, writing, and editing as a team, we developed great respect for and trust in each other, which motivated us to keep working when the tasks ahead seemed insurmountable. That solidarity made it possible to collaborate, to hold each other to a high standard, and to dedicate the time and energy needed for such a project.

We can attest to the impact and importance of creating engaged learning opportunities for undergraduates. It is common for our classmates in the natural sciences to do research in labs, gaining practical skills while contributing to projects that have clear public impacts. For humanities students, these experiences are far rarer. Through this class, like our peers, we had the opportunity to test our original ideas and historical hypotheses by comparing seemingly untouched archival documents to well-known scholarly sources. Professor Lassiter facilitated open discussions during class time, fielding questions and working with us to find the answers. He structured the class to respond dynamically to our interests and findings, so that we grew more confident in our skills as researchers and felt ownership over the final product. During our many trips to the Bentley, we became comfortable working with archivists and reference room assistants as well. When we had trouble locating relevant archival collections or navigating U-M's many online resources, we knew we could turn to the Bentley's team of capable archivists for guidance. As the semester progressed, we began to see ourselves as not just students and researchers but as educators and historians. We became collaborators piecing together a story that hadn't been told in the way we wanted to tell it, which gave us the motivation to tell it well.

Our collaboration didn't end when the class did. While students in the course researched local and state activism, Professor Lassiter developed a partnership with the Ecology Center of Ann Arbor to provide undergraduates with fellowship opportunities to apply their newfound research skills for the benefit of a community nonprofit organization. The two of us spent the summer of 2018 researching the Ecology Center's activism during the 1970s. Our goal is to create a digital exhibit that will be the first section of a comprehensive organizational history to be completed by future students in commemoration of the group's fiftieth anniversary in 2020.

The opportunity to participate in the Environmental Activism in Michigan course and to coauthor the Give Earth a Chance exhibit profoundly shaped our undergraduate experiences. Both of us decided to pursue independent research as seniors by writing honors theses, drawing upon the skills we developed through this project. This research also introduced us to archivists and activists and gave us a newfound appreciation for the valuable work that both groups do. As students of history and as citizens concerned about the environment, we are grateful to the archivists who made these resources available, to the professor who gave undergraduates a chance, and to the opportunities we have had to grow as researchers and share these stories with the public.

CAMPUS REVOLUTION: ENGAGING IN CRITICAL INFORMATION LITERACY THROUGH THE EXAMINATION OF RACE, GENDER, AND FREE SPEECH DURING THE 1960s

Holly Luetkenhaus
David Peters
Matt Upson
Oklahoma State University

Background

This chapter examines the use of local archival material and oral histories within the context of an information literacy assignment for undergraduates. The assignment required the use of materials related to events that occurred at Oklahoma State University (OSU) during the 1960s. Instructors asked students how gender, race, class, and identity played into the creation of information, how marginalized communities were represented within that information, and how these issues are echoed by current events. This assignment, designed by instructional librarians with support from librarians and archivists from the library's Special Collections division, was prepared as part of a three-credit-hour course at OSU, a doctoral university with a very high level of research activity and an undergraduate student population of approximately 20,000. The course (currently housed within the Honors College) was developed by two librarians within the Research & Learning Services division of the library and titled "They Wouldn't Put It on the Internet if It's Not True: Information Literacy in a 'Post-Truth' Era." The course was first offered in the fall of 2017 but had been in development since 2015. Initially, it was envisioned as a traditional information literacy course, focused on stereotypical academic research "skills" such as database navigation and source evaluation, and was intended to act as a concurrent course for high school students, potentially feeding them into the university's Freshman Research Scholars, a program of approximately 60 students that allows new students to partner with faculty mentors on advanced research projects. The departure of a colleague in the Undergraduate Research Office, who was planning the course alongside librarians, provided an opening for rethinking the direction of the course. The increasing prevalence of mis- and disinformation in the news; the continued "debate" over issues such as climate change, data privacy, and social media concerns; and the preface to and aftermath of the 2016 United States presidential election all led to a dramatic shift in the nature and intent of the course. The course morphed into an information literacy course that emphasized social justice, equity, and practical long-term utility, rather than just immediate course or research-related skills, although these are still addressed. The course description reads as follows:

> This course provides an overview of essential concepts and skills needed for success in navigating an increasingly uncertain and perilous information landscape. Awareness of, access to, and quality of information have demonstrable impacts on social, economic, academic, and political well-being. This course addresses issues of access, use, creation, and dissemination of information and how it affects particular populations of people, with an emphasis on historically marginalized and underrepresented

groups. Students learn to locate, access, use, evaluate, organize, create, and present information effectively for personal and academic research needs. Students examine biases within each of those, paying particular attention to issues of race, gender, class, sexuality, ethnicity, and other personal, political, and socioeconomic factors. Students also improve their understanding of authority and trust, value of information, the nature of scholarly conversation, and the nature of inquiry and exploration.

The learning outcomes, which were revised after the initial offering in fall 2017, reflected the course's growing focus on social issues and intersectionality with information literacy. The outcomes used for the fall 2018 course were as follows:
Students will:

- Identify personal information needs and knowledge gaps.
- Design and implement strategies for searching for, locating, and accessing information.
- Organize information strategically, professionally, and ethically.
- Critically evaluate information.
- Synthesize information to create new knowledge.
- Differentiate the information creation and dissemination process in a variety of disciplines and media.
- Articulate how access to and awareness of information has a demonstrable impact on social, economic, and political well-being.
- Connect research skills to practical, lifelong uses within personal, academic, and professional needs.

Archival and Special Collections Context

The mission statement for our university archives is to "Save, Secure, and Share the Story of Oklahoma State University." This succinct and yet broad declaration could be adjusted and adapted for any number of similar organizations. But as those who reside in the world of university archives know, these stories are diverse and complicated.

Many in our particular university community have created a simplified narrative of hearty pioneers in a new land determined to establish a land grant college on the plains of Oklahoma for the betterment of their descendants with a good-natured aspiration to outshine the University of Oklahoma in all competitive endeavors. In the OSU Archives we understand and desperately want to share a nuanced and complex story that more accurately captures our unique university experiences, our relationships with other public and private institutions, our diversity of thought and practice, and our participation in improving conditions for our state, nation, and world. We attempt to preserve and share our institutional successes, challenges, and failures so that the university and others can learn and benefit from all significant past experiences and be better prepared to make informed decisions today. There are occasions when the complexity and sometimes potentially disturbing nature of records housed in some collections may create challenges for the university if not managed and communicated responsibly when shared within and outside our academic community. This institutional "dirty laundry" may at times place the archives in conflict with university branding efforts focused on marketing the best characteristics to students and their parents, alumni, donors, and employees.

Traditionally patrons in the university archives have come from the faculty and graduate student ranks, and researchers from outside our university community. However, over the last decade, the OSU Archives has made a concerted effort to improve outreach programs to undergraduate students. Staff in the archives have worked with lower division classes in material culture, geography, art, history, English, education, and others. Archives staff especially appreciated the opportunity to collaborate with library faculty involved with Research and Learning Services to include an archives component in the honors information literacy course.

Historically, groups and individuals have a tendency to search for and accept simple answers to complex questions. Modern undergraduates frequently expect and accept the notion that all relevant knowledge can be identified in a Google search. However, the vast majority of records of enduring value housed in most archival collections are not available online. There are immense holdings preserved only in analog formats. Less than five percent of the OSU Archives' analog collections are available in digital formats, and the limited demand for the remaining documents doesn't justify the cost associated with digital conversion and discovery.

The question then becomes: how do the university archives overcome this conundrum of introducing meaningful analog content to the digital generation of undergraduate students? They will not discover most of our content through their smart phones and laptops. In many cases, university archivists must not simply hope or wait for students to "discover" the archives on their own, but must make the first contact. This initial contact should be only the first step. Archivists should take this opportunity to share information about our research services and help students discover the many layers of information available in the collections.

Archivists serve as guides on these expeditions. In the information literacy class, the students would not have time to conduct an in-depth research exploration for all available resources. For this specific instance, the archivists created artificial access points and directed the students to particular examples to address their limited research queries. The objective for the archives department and our Special Collections Division in the library was to expose undergraduate students to archival collections and services while hopefully helping them develop an appreciation for the diversity of the content discovered.

OSU was not at the forefront of the campus unrest occurring throughout the United States in the 1960s. These nationwide conflicts on college campuses generally revolved around the Vietnam War, freedom of speech, academic freedom, racial tensions, and equal rights for women. While never suffering the violence experienced at Kent State University and other campuses, there were students and staff in the OSU community who expressed their disagreement with the status quo in a variety of peaceful ways. These included inviting controversial speakers to campus, forming "radical" student organizations, participating in marches, and distributing provocative publications. Because administrators were fearful that outside "agitators" would influence

Figure 1. Oklahoma State University students began publication of the institution's first unauthorized "underground" newspaper, titled *The Drummer*, in 1967. Initially a voice supporting free expression, *The Drummer* was created in response to a controversial campus speaker's policy. The newspaper would ultimately address many of the challenges facing university communities in the 1960s related to race, gender, and war.

local protesters and lead to violence, the university collaborated with outside state authorities to reduce the possibilities for conflict. The documents and records in the OSU Archives for this turbulent time were transferred from a number of different sources, including the OSU Board of Regents, OSU Presidents Papers, the student newspaper, yearbooks, OSU Centennial Histories Series, underground newspapers, oral histories, and collections from relevant organizations and individual participants.

The second area within the library to contribute to the assignment was the Oklahoma Oral History Research Program (OOHRP). Founded in 2007, OOHRP seeks to add detail and nuance to the historical record through the gathering of firsthand experiences and perspectives. Collaborating with this information literacy class presented the

Figure 2. Cartoons have the ability to illustrate the occasional absurdity of human experience in a humorous and nonthreatening way. This cartoon, which featured an anonymous university administrator speaking to a crowd supporting academic freedom while simultaneously expressing limits on the diversity of topics, appeared in the Oklahoma State University underground student newspaper, *The Drummer*, in response to a modified campus speaker's policy that restricted controversial speakers from appearing on campus.

opportunity to engage with undergraduate students who were largely unaware of the existence of this type of resource, and allowed students to hear firsthand stories from OSU alumni, whose experiences could further deepen their understanding of the historical context of contemporary issues.

The final department to collaborate on the design and delivery of the assignment was Government Information. As a regional depository for United States government publications, the Government Information Department retains state, federal, and international government and organizational publications. Like the OSU Archives and OOHRP, part of the mission of the Government Information Department is to assist patrons with research, provide instruction, and maintain access to primary source materials. As with other special collections divisions, students often don't know what information is accessible or how to use government publications and datasets. Contributing to this project provided an outreach opportunity for government information librarians, and examining federal reports and federal and state court cases helped students to understand the national perspective on local events and issues.

Impetus for the Assignment

In the first iteration of the course, librarians invited representatives from OSU Archives, OOHRP, and Government Information to discuss not only what they do, but how their collections are shaped and curated. We wanted students to understand how decisions are made about what to collect and preserve and what gets left behind, for whatever reason. Who gets to have their story told and why? This question, paired with the opportunity to connect with local resources, encouraged us to expand our collaboration with the special collections units for the second offering of the course, which led to the addition of the archival assignment we describe in this chapter.

We wanted students to understand the importance of historical continuity and context; that today's current political and social climate closely echoes past periods of unrest in U.S. history. We hear a lot of "this is not who we are as America" in today's rhetoric when we talk about political violence, discrimination, interference with free speech, etc., but the denial of our past actions as a society only serves to perpetuate these issues. We need to confront the historical roots of contemporary social and political issues in order to fully understand and address them. Understanding the historical origins of the problems within our society is the only way to fully comprehend all the complexity within in it, which therefore provides a stronger foundation from which to dismantle the power systems that perpetuate the problems.

Specifically, we wanted students to examine OSU artifacts related to the 1960s and understand that only some stories were saved, and only some information was shared, while other stories—specifically those of women, Black Americans, pacifists, and activists—were overlooked, forgotten, suppressed, or, in some cases, misused or falsified. We wanted students to connect to local instances of these events using documents and artifacts from the archives, OOHRP, and the Government Information department. These documents and artifacts accounted for a broad range of voices, including those who were marginalized during the time period covered by the assignment (1960s).

Before we address the specifics of the assignment, it should be noted that there was a significant obstacle/opportunity with this assignment. We asked students, none of whom were history majors, to investigate the local context of a broad historical issue, using sources that we highlighted and selected, within a very short timeframe. Needless to say, this had the potential to be a precarious situation. As a way to situate students within a historical mindset, we thought it was important to offer them this quote from Jill Lepore's history of the United States. It is succinct and hits the point we wanted to make about the relationship between information and history:

> Most of what existed is gone. Flesh decays, wood rots, walls fall, books burn. Nature takes one toll, malice another. History is the study of what remains, what's left behind, which can be almost anything, so long as it survives the ravages of time and war: letters, diaries, DNA, gravestones, coins, television broadcasts, paintings, DVDs, viruses, abandoned Facebook pages, the transcripts of congressional hearings, the ruins of buildings. Some of these things are saved by chance or accident, like the one house that, as if by miracle, still stands after a hurricane razes a town. But most of what historians study survives because it was purposely kept—placed in a box and carried up to an attic, shelved in a library, stored in a museum, photographed or recorded, downloaded to a server—carefully preserved and even catalogued. All of it, together, the accidental and the intentional, this archive of the past—remains, relics, a repository of knowledge, the evidence of what came before, this inheritance—is called the historical record, and it is maddeningly uneven, asymmetrical, and unfair.[1]

---

1. Jill Lepore, *These Truths: A History of the United States*, New York: W.W. Norton & Company, 2018, 4.

Assignment Design and Outcomes

For the assignment, students were asked to examine preselected, digitized documents from special collections, including an issue of the student newspaper, an issue of an underground newspaper, and a yearbook; listen to one oral history interview; and examine one government publication (these took various forms, from a court case to a report about the Civil Rights Act, etc.). Each item was selected by a librarian or archivist, and each student group was given a set of five artifacts to examine around a common theme. The themes that we chose were the Vietnam War, women's rights, race relations/Civil Rights Movement, and free speech. These were selected because of their importance to the sociopolitical climate of the 1960s and because we see similar dialogues happening around these issues today. One of our goals for this class was to have students view issues in information literacy through an intersectional lens, considering race, class, gender, identity, etc. The 1960s provided a microcosm through which to view intersectional issues in information literacy. This intersectional approach was woven throughout the course, so students had been challenged to approach all of the coursework from this perspective. We used a variety of readings, such as *Algorithms of Oppression* by Safiya Umoja Noble, to frame the intersectional nature of the course. Our hope was that students would be able to apply what they discovered about the past to current trends in media, news, and information.

To prepare them for handling the various artifacts and for understanding the content contained within them, members of our various special collections areas (archives, oral histories, and government information) visited class to talk about their work. Additionally, a faculty member from the history department came to class and gave an overview of the 1960s and the role that college-aged students played in movements, protests, and social justice. As a deliverable at the completion of their investigation, students worked in groups (again, clustered around the four themes) to create visual representations of the narratives that were being told at the time. Throughout the class, we take a multimodal approach when discussing information—that

Figure 3. "Women's Rights" by Jace Colvin. This student-drawn comic highlights issues facing women students of Oklahoma State University in the 1960s, including concerns about job opportunities and unequal pay, women's athletics, reproductive rights, and the restriction of "women's hours."

is, we encourage students to consider the many mediums and formats through which we create and consume information today—so asking them to visually represent their findings kept with this course theme. They were asked to pay attention to whose voices were being represented and where, what stories were being told (or were not being told), and consider both the local events and national discourse at the time.

Student groups produced a variety of formats for the visualization, two of which we will examine in more detail. First, one group looked at women's rights, and produced a comic to show the various ways that women were talked about in their artifacts, and what issues stood out as important (see Figure 3). They focused on access to birth control, the difference in job ads that actively recruited men vs. women, the restrictions of "women's hours" on campus, and the state of women's athletics at the time. This group chose to take a holistic approach—they

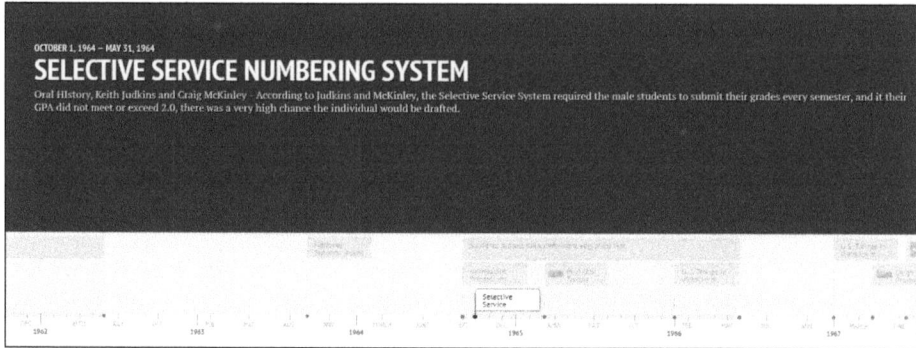

Figure 4. "Vietnam War: Optimism Over Time" by Caleb Bengs, Carson Elmore, Ashley Jeffers, and Ryan Yang (digital, 2018). This screen capture of a digital timeline depicts findings from an oral history interview with two Oklahoma State University alumni. The two men recalled having to submit their grades to Selective Service in order to delay being drafted while in college.

incorporated both local and national, and group and individual experiences in one image.[2]

The second example is from a group that examined artifacts related to the Vietnam War (see Figure 4). Rather than try to tell the entire story (which would take quite a bit of time and space), they built a timeline (using Timeline JS[3]) to track the "optimism" about the war over time, pulling from both local and national narratives. They incorporated images (though didn't do a great job of citing them) and used color to tell the story of how optimism about the war ebbed and flowed over the years covered by their artifacts.[4]

After completing the project as a group, individual students wrote short reflections on what they learned, focusing on how our current sociopolitical climate is similar and dissimilar to the 1960s and how identity impacts information creation, access, and use. Some common themes emerged. First, there was a general unawareness of archival materials, oral histories, and government documents prior to the project. Multiple students commented that they would like to make further

---

2. Jace Colvin, *Women's Rights*. Unpublished comic, 2018.
3. Knight Lab, *Timeline JS*. Available at: https://timeline.knightlab.com/
4. Caleb Bengs, Carson Elmore, Ashley Jeffers, and Ryan Yang, *Vietnam War: Optimism Over Time*, 2018. Available at: http://tinyurl.com/infolitvietnam1

use of special collections in future research assignments. Second, many students talked about the similarities between the conversations that are happening today around issues of race, gender, and free speech. They reflected on the value of being able to see and hear the perspectives of people who lived during these moments that they had previously only encountered through a history textbook, calling the experience "eye opening." Several students reflected on the value of examining voices outside of "official" university or government records, as well, by using oral histories and underground newspapers. Those who reflected on this lack of representation noted that both for our historical records and for our current information environment, the voices of women, Black Americans, and LGBTQ+ individuals are *still* largely absent from many narratives. Finally, one student commented that the project made him consider what the records we produce today will look like to people who look back 50 years from now. Will the memes, tweets, blogs, and snapchats be recorded and kept? And what will they say about *us*, and what we value?

Conclusions

Student, librarian, and archivist reactions to this new assignment were positive. The students involved in the course are not a representative sample of OSU, so it would be dishonest and unreasonable to generalize these results to a broader population, although we did have some key takeaways that we will consider as we continue to teach this course and further develop the archives and special collections section.

Exposure to diverse resources available through the archives and special collections allows current students the opportunity to examine events from five decades ago in new and innovative ways. They can question the reliability of these sources, determine the extent of outside influences, wonder about bias in the documentation and resources, consider voices that were excluded, identify significant participants, and arrive at a better understanding of the OSU experience during this pivotal era in America.

As we mentioned at the beginning of this chapter, we were worried some students might view it too much as a "history" project in a "library" course, but none expressed that concern in their assignment reflections or course evaluations. They enjoyed the visit from the history faculty member and commented that it helped them make sense of what they were looking for. Additionally, it brought more awareness to special collections, and several students commented in their reflections about wanting to engage with these collections again in future projects. Perhaps these students and their acquaintances will return to the archives in the future to assist with other research projects. Even if they do not, they hopefully will have discovered that there are places with relevant information, information with context, information with sources, and information of enduring value. There is also the aspiration that undergraduates exposed to the unique resources housed in the OSU Archives become aware that there are archives around the world maintaining valuable records and services available to assist them. During these interactions, the archives staff have the opportunity to talk to students about bias in record creation and retention, and about multiple and sometimes conflicting perspectives in records, and provide the opportunity for them to think critically, to question, and to weigh and analyze information. These are the kinds of practical skills undergraduate students will need in life.

This assignment supported the intersectional goals of the course by asking students to consider issues of race, gender, class, and identity and how that relates to what information gets shared, saved, and used. The group that worked with documents related to race relations and the Civil Rights Movement, for example, commented on the discrepancy between officially sanctioned sources—like the yearbook—and the personal recollections found in oral history interviews. Whereas the yearbook seemed to paint a picture of racial harmony and integration, personal reflections from Black men and women who attended OSU during the time indicated that being on campus during that time was much more complex. In their individual reflections, every member of the group echoed the value of having a variety of perspectives represented in the historical narrative and the importance of listening to the stories of underrepresented groups.

Similarly, the group that examined women's rights, in addition to examining the stories that were being told, paid attention to *who* was telling the stories. One member of the group, for example, reflected on the number of stories written by men that appeared in a given edition of the campus newspaper, compared to the number of stories written by women. Even articles that concerned women's issues, such as access to birth control or women's hours, were sometimes penned by men rather than women. She was able to draw disappointing, though not surprising, parallels to how many of these same issues are discussed in the media and politics today.

We were also able to identify areas where we might revise certain aspects of the instruction and assignment for this unit in order to increase student engagement with special collections. One of these potential changes is to dedicate more time to this unit. We chose, in the interest of time, to preselect the sources students used, but we would like to have more time in the future to give students space for more exploration and discovery. Secondly, all the sources provided were available digitally, which meant that the project itself didn't press students to consider issues of access as it would if we had used historical *print only* documents. This is something that could deepen the class discussions. Finally, while we did take some class time to learn options for visualization (like Timeline JS, Piktochart, and PowerPoint), we want to continue to explore other tools and options that would encourage more students to break away from text-reliant products and incorporate more information visualization techniques.

The experience of collaborating across multiple library departments has encouraged librarians and archivists to consider new ways of teaching and engaging students about primary source material and intersectionality in information literacy. This assignment can serve as a model for future partnerships: what they might look like and what might be possible. Instruction and special collections librarians and archivists can draw from their experiences to develop ways of incorporating intersectionality into the traditional "one-shot" library sessions, have new tools to draw from when supporting teaching faculty and research assignments, and use this foundation to bring issues of access, power, and narrative into other course assignments.

It has also informed our approaches to existing course/archives collaboration. For example, the First-Year Composition program at OSU has an eight-week unit within the Composition II course where students work with digital archives. In this unit, students analyze digital collections rhetorically, and are asked to consider what story is being told, what voices are absent, and if the collection is successful in meeting its purpose. Drawing on the work they did with archivists on the assignment described in this chapter, instruction librarians have gained a deeper understanding of the work done in archives, which allows them to better support students completing their Composition II assignments.

Many composition courses also incorporate multimodal assignments, such as asking students to create podcasts or infographics. The increased collaboration afforded by the development of the assignment described in this chapter has strengthened the partnerships between instruction librarians and special collections, which has translated into more collaboration in supporting these types of assignments. For example, faculty in OOHRP are better equipped than instruction librarians to help students develop the skills needed to plan, create, and store audio files. They can also help students develop an understanding of the *value* and *purpose* of creating oral documents to save and share knowledge.

Finally, this partnership has led to increased visibility throughout the library regarding opportunities for special collections instruction. This has led to a discussion about a possible new instruction space within archives and special collections to allow for the increased numbers of classes working with or creating primary source materials. Having a dedicated instruction space could help alleviate potential issues with the scalability of this type of collaboration.

Overall, the work described in this chapter has provided a framework from which librarians and archivists can continue to build paths for engagement with undergraduate students. While we reached only a small number of undergraduates through this single course, we have strengthened partnerships and developed strategies we can deploy to create similar opportunities in other courses. It has impressed upon us the value of exposing undergraduate students to the range of documents and voices they can encounter through special collections, and it will continue to inform the work that we do for years to come.

Bibliography

Bengs, Caleb, Carson Elmore, Ashley Jeffers, and Ryan Yang. *Vietnam War: Optimism Over Time*. Knight Lab, 2018. http://tinyurl.com/infolitvietnam1.

Colvin, Jace. *Women's Rights*. Unpublished comic, 2018.

Lepore, Jill. *These Truths: A History of the United States*. New York: W.W. Norton & Company, 2018.

Timeline JS. Knight Lab. https://timeline.knightlab.com/.

WHAT'S IN IT FOR ME?: STUDENT-FACULTY COLLABORATION AND CRITICAL EDITING

Naomi J. Stubbs

LaGuardia Community College

Engaging undergraduate students in faculty research is widely recognized as a valuable goal for students; how it might benefit junior faculty members beset with high teaching loads, copious administrative service, and ever-present tenure demands has been given far less attention. As a faculty member in the humanities at a community college, I have found that the scholarship demands of tenure compete with teaching time (I have a 5/4 load); that I have little time for one-on-one mentorship of students and their research projects; and that I am in disciplines where collaboration in publications is not championed (English and theater), so there is little room for combining scholarship with mentoring undergraduates. As an untenured member of faculty, collaborating with my students on my research agenda did not initially seem like a wise move. However, in the case study I present here, I share how I invited students to collaborate with me on my scholarship by taking a class with me for college credit (a six- or twelve-week internship class offering hands-on experience) or by being hired as interns (part-time positions of six to twenty-four months). In these various capacities, we worked collaboratively to produce a printed critical edition of selections from a nineteenth-century diary, along with a digital edition of the complete text, to great success. Working with teams of primarily undergraduate students, I identified different kinds of tasks and contributions so students at a variety of academic levels were able to contribute in valuable ways. Most surprising and rich were the collaborations with community college students—a population not typically granted access to faculty-student collaborative research in the humanities.

The Harry Watkins Diary

Actor, manager, and playwright Harry Watkins (1825–1894) worked in the theater for a full forty years. Despite his clear awareness of celebrity and his attempts to mimic the career choices of actors who were famous, Watkins never achieved stardom and consequently is largely forgotten today. Yet his career was impressive: he penned more than twenty plays, enjoyed successful tours in England and the United States with his own theater company, and collaborated with the most celebrated performers and producers of the day, including P. T. Barnum, J. B. Booth, and Edwin Forrest. His intimate knowledge of the theatrical profession is revealed through his variously pensive, comical, and often-blunt accounts of contract negotiations, traveling conditions, and reflections upon the talent of his peers (or lack thereof). These industry-related entries are interspersed with tales of his love life, family dramas, and political aspirations. Because of the range and depth of the topics covered, his diary, maintained from 1845 to 1860, provides a revealing glimpse into the theater, politics, and day-to-day life in the US during the nineteenth century.

In order to make this valuable and fascinating resource available to a wider audience, Amy E. Hughes (Brooklyn College) and I created two critical editions of the diary—a traditional printed critical edition of selections of the diary, complete with introduction, annotations, and indices, as well as a digital edition of the complete text freely available online and equipped with advanced searching features. At the base of both complementary editions was an XML file containing the entirety of the diary text, encoded using a custom schema conforming to the Text Encoding Initiative (TEI) guidelines. From this single file, we extracted the text needed for the print edition (with the tags providing assistance in constructing the indices, among other things) and generated the base text for the digital edition.

In order to ensure the academic integrity of these editions, we sought to adhere to the best practices of the Association for Documentary Editing (ADE) as well as the TEI, thus allowing future scholars to have confidence in the products we created. Indeed, by using more universally understood (TEI-conforming) XML tags, we were able to allow future users to export our XML file and manipulate it in whatever way they desire (creating interactive maps of his travels, studying corrections in Watkins's spellings, etc.). Yet to follow such recommendations would mean that each of the 1180 manuscript pages would have to go through eight stages,[1] and that each of the two rounds of proofreading would be performed by two people (tandem proofreading, involving one person reading aloud from the manuscript while the other person marks any errors on a printout of the transcription, being one of ADE's best practices). This presented challenges of scale, meaning we needed to seek support from others in order to complete this project in a timely manner.

We enlisted Scott Dexter (Brooklyn College, City University of New York) as our technology director to assist with the development of the schema and to create a workbench to manage the numerous files (one file per page) as each moved through the various stages of transcribing and proofreading. We also recruited Shane Breaux (then a PhD candidate at the Graduate Center, City University of New York) as our editorial associate to assist with transcribing, encoding, and proofreading. However, while we made tremendous progress in the first year, the process was still slow and our high teaching loads meant it was hard to carve out time during the semester to devote much time to this work.

---

1. Draft transcription (including encoding), tandem proofread 1, revision 1, tandem proofread 2, revision 2, editorial consult, final approval, and published.

In order to expand our team further, I decided to explore the option of engaging undergraduate students at my home campus on the project.

Community College Students and Humanities Research

Although research in the humanities is still thought of as a solitary endeavor that is "necessarily more individualistic than research in the social or natural sciences," requiring years of training and immersion,[2] several scholars have found ways to productively collaborate with students in their research.[3] Aside from student-led independent studies, and beyond simply having students undertake repetitive and mundane tasks that help with a faculty member's project (collecting and copying articles, compiling indices, etc), various faculty have found that undergraduate students can contribute to their work in meaningful ways. In addition, more than assisting the faculty member in their academic endeavors, students can benefit tremendously from such work by developing a host of valuable skills (such as critical thinking, communication skills, and how to apply academic knowledge). Where there are published results (such as books, articles, exhibits, and reports), students can boost their confidence, identify real-world applications for academic work, and build their resumes. Finally, students engaged in such work benefit from being closely mentored by a faculty member.

One of the main objections leveled at such possibilities is that students do not have enough knowledge in the field and that training them takes too long. At LaGuardia, we have the additional "obstacle" in that many of our students aim to graduate in two to three years, so we have a still-smaller window of time in which to develop the skills

---

2. Mark S. Schantz, "Undergraduate Research in the Humanities: Challenges and Prospects," *Council on Undergraduate Research Quarterly* 29, no. 2 (Winter 2008): 27.

3. See for example: Naomi Yavneh Klos, Jenny Olin Shanahan, and Gregory Young, *Creative Inquiry in the Arts and Humanities: Models of Undergraduate Research* (Washington, DC: Council on Undergraduate Research, 2011); and Todd McDorman, "Promoting Undergraduate Research in the Humanities: Three Collaborative Approaches," *Council on Undergraduate Research Quarterly* 25, no. 1 (September 2004): 39–42.

and knowledge required. In addition, as an untenured faculty member, I was presented with a further challenge: collaboration is not a hallmark of humanities scholarship, and I had to consider how my publication might be received as part of my promotion and tenure applications. Despite this, I am one of many who have seen the benefits of working with undergraduates firsthand; my first foray into working with community college students on my research yielded very positive results, academically, pedagogically, and professionally.

I began by recruiting students to work with me as editorial assistants; with funding from grants and federal work study opportunities, I was initially able to work with a total of six students over four years. I had planned on training them to transcribe and encode some of the pages of the diary that would then be read by Hughes and Breaux, and then I, in turn, would proofread pages transcribed by Hughes and Breaux with my editorial assistant. This allowed for distinct teams of editorial staff to tandem proofread work they had not transcribed or encoded themselves, leading to greater consistency across transcribers and more rigorous and effective proofreading. In cases where I had students work with me who were not able to stay on the project long, or had to work with less supervision, I found other tasks for them that added to the project. For example, one student looked through images of playbills for performances held at Oakland University. The playbills contained a wealth of information about the various productions Watkins was involved in, including the titles of plays, names of theaters, and complete cast lists. When it came to the annotation phase of the project, these images were especially helpful but were not easy to use (1,333 images with no index or keyword searching available). To remedy this, the student assistant tagged each image for dates, geographic places, names of theaters, titles of plays, roles, and actors, allowing us to search these images more effectively when we needed to do so. Another assistant input lines from the diary into Twitter, allowing us to generate a Twitter feed for Watkins and help publicize the project (@WatkinsDiary). Beyond simply performing rote tasks, the students brought new opportunities to my attention and then engaged with the material in deep ways. The tagging project led to the student learning about nineteenth-century printing and theatrical contexts, and the Twitter project required the student to identify the most relevant and compelling snippets from each entry.

Seeking to expand the involvement of students and to address the issues of workload that had kept me from devoting more time to the project, I then led two class sections in consecutive semesters at LaGuardia with students working on the project for course credit. As LaGuardia has an interest in offering internship opportunities to our students whenever possible (including in the humanities), we have several courses providing college credit to students engaging in hands-on experiences. In the English department, ENG288 "The Internship" allows students to "design and complete, or complete a significant portion of, a major scholarly, research, creative, or social project with the intent to publish, present, or otherwise make available to the public the results of the project."[4] In many instances, this means students working on the school newspaper or magazine, but recently this has expanded to include students working with faculty as editorial assistants on academic journals, for example.

In winter and spring 2014, I ran two sections of ENG288 with a total of thirteen students dedicated to this project. In week one, we examined what critical editing entailed, drawing on texts they had encountered in earlier classes for examples. We moved then to paleography and they had their first experience trying to decipher the (reasonably clear) writing of Watkins. I was surprised to realize how unfamiliar students were with cursive, but they rose to the challenge. We then discussed XML-encoding, and they quickly picked up the basics of coding. From there, they transitioned into transcribing and encoding one page of the manuscript (all working on the same page) to put into practice what they had learned and identify inconsistencies in how they (and indeed, how we as a team) were applying the schema. Many of the questions they asked about how to decide when one tag applied but not another pushed me

---

4. "LaGuardia Community College Catalog," LaGuardia Community College, 2018-2019: 124, https://www.laguardia.edu/uploadedFiles/Main_Site/Content/Academics/Catalog/PDFs/2 018-2019-Catalog.pdf.

(and consequently our team) to be more consistent and transparent. After that, students were assigned ten pages each, and they transcribed and encoded these, assisted by one of my editorial assistants. We then demonstrated the practice of tandem proofreading, and students were assigned pages to proofread in pairs. Each page was proofread twice by two different pairs of students and the edits were made accordingly. These pages were then proofread by the Brooklyn College team, meaning these pages had an additional (third) level of proofreading applied.

Throughout this process, students were enamored of different aspects of the project to varying degrees: some found the deciphering of his handwriting to be fascinating while others found it frustrating; some enjoyed the beautiful simplicity of XML while others struggled to comprehend it; some became enthralled with Watkins's perspective on what had formerly seemed esoteric topics, while others found him to be arrogant and dismissive. All of them, however, were especially drawn to the fact that what they were doing was new work. That is, this was not a project with predetermined results known by their professor, but rather, they were part of a team of scholars reading and preparing manuscript pages that had previously been read by very few people. It was clear that contributing to an academic publication through their work with little-known material was a great source of pride and pleasure to them all. I saw this to an even greater extent in the final projects they developed.

For their final course project, each student was required to develop a product with an outside audience in mind. Students pursued the element of the project they found most interesting and connected it to their skills and abilities. The students' final projects were wide-ranging and surprising, including:

Creative works
Creative writing majors in the internship class saw the Harry Watkins diary as a treasure trove of source material. After becoming familiar with his style of writing, one student wrote a fictional (and comical) entry. Another composed a song about Watkins. Still another revealed the rhythms of Watkins's writing in a poem about him, which was published in the school magazine. In each of these instances, the students

demonstrated their firm understanding of Watkins's character and style, and produced engaging and creative pieces, to be appreciated by people not affiliated with the project. These works made still more clear to us (the editors) how rich a resource this diary is.

Pedagogical
Several students observed the frustrations experienced by some of their classmates and desired to create materials that would assist future students working on the project—one created a guide to Watkins's handwriting, isolating each letter in lowercase and as a capital letter as well as common deviations from the standard form (when at the end of a word, for example). Another did something similar, but with XML-encoding, creating a short video about how XML operates and how to use the software we were using for the transcriptions. In both of these instances, students used the knowledge and skills they had developed within the course to help future interns and assistants.

Research
Several students had aspirations to graduate-level study and saw this project as an opportunity to test out research skills and explore questions to which answers were not yet known. One researched Watkins's family tree to see if he could locate descendants and assist with the introduction of the book. Another student was interested to learn more about theatrical touring circuits and extracted tagged place names from the XML files to track Watkins's movements over a six-year period, creating an interactive map of his tours.

Publicity
Stemming in part from their pride in the project, several students wanted to do more to help publicize the project. One student decided that we should not be handing out business cards at conferences, but rather, should have something more memorable and connected to the project; she created postcards with the first page of the diary on one side and our contact information on the other (see Figure 1). Another student wrote a blog post for our website to alert our followers to their

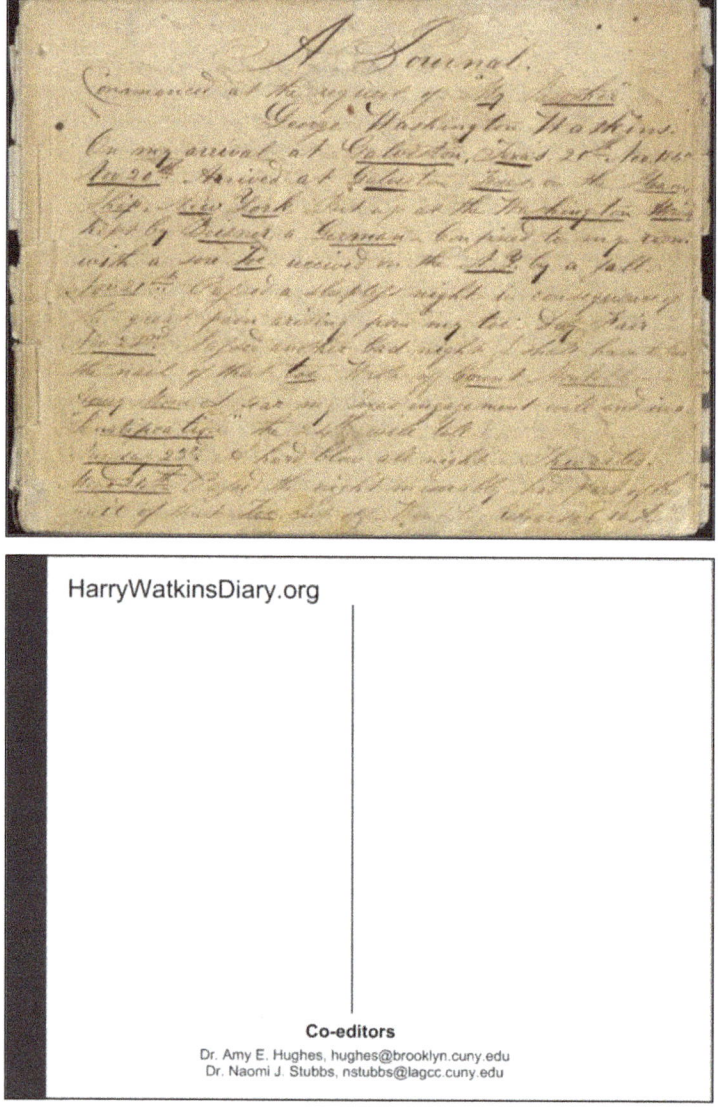

Figure 1. Postcard created by a student intern as part of their final project, publicizing the project, front and back.

involvement, while another wrote an article for the school newspaper.

In addition to these products, students who had worked on the project (as interns or editorial assistants) were able to contribute to the project in additional ways: two students co-led a workshop at New York University on uses of XML in theater scholarship; one student co-presented at a conference with me; and one student presented our project at an event attended by the chairman of the National Endowment for the Humanities and the president of LaGuardia Community College.

The students developed a wide range of skills by participating in this project; skills that helped prepare them for graduation, transfer, and employment. Students learned about critical editing, editorial interventions, XML encoding, proofreading practices, and historical context, and each developed an original product. The public audiences for their work helped them gain confidence, improve their communication skills, and enhance their abilities as independent learners, while they also learned about academic methods and publishing (especially important for those who have since gone on to study at the graduate level). They had access to networking opportunities, were able to mentor other students, and added to their resumes. Historical topics gained new life for them as the diary connected them to primary documents and historical subjects. And, of course, they were part of a scholarly process leading to two published products (they are listed in the acknowledgements of both)—something they take great pride in.

But what was more surprising to me was how much I gained from the experience. I went into this thinking that working with students might provide me with assistance in the transcribing and proofreading processes, but in fact this was the least of the benefits. Indeed, in the transcribing and encoding stages, I had to supervise them very closely and take time to explain basic aspects, meaning their involvement took more time than if I would have undertaken the work myself. However, as I continued to work with them, I discovered many surprising benefits to their involvement. From a practical perspective, I was able to direct some of my teaching time to research through internships as classes. In addition, I gained access to funding sources through engaging students in my work that I would not have otherwise had access to. The academic rigor of my research project was greatly enhanced by having to clearly articulate what I was doing and why, and to have my methods questioned by the students. Their "outsider" perspective brought new clarity to our work and greater consistency to the development of the schema and transcribing guidelines. Their insights and especially their final projects helped me to see new venues and new uses for our work. In terms of publicity, their ideas helped us spread the word of our project to a much wider audience through the Twitter feed, through the use of postcards, through on-campus events and publications, and through the blog. In addition, my students were developing the very same research skills, critical thinking abilities, and capacity for independent learning that I aim to draw out in my students in all of my classes. In sum, working with them helped me to achieve both my pedagogical and scholarly goals.

There is a widespread hesitancy towards including undergraduate students in our research, but this dismissal may be a missed opportunity. The practice can be productive in surprising ways. Writing a monograph within the humanities does require detailed knowledge and years of study, but outside perspectives can provide us with new directions and nuances in our arguments. While my project was not a traditional monograph, discussing my ideas about the purpose and future use of the critical edition led me to take it in different directions than I might have otherwise, and I would certainly consider working with students on my next project. There are also some very practical benefits, from assistance with academic work, to access to additional funding avenues, to opportunities to direct some teaching obligations towards research. Indeed, student engagement in a faculty member's scholarship should be considered an indication of an effective collaborator and should be encouraged. And since it is clear that students also benefit when they engage in faculty research, such work should be acknowledged and rewarded as part of faculty members' pedagogical work.

Undergraduate research should be more present in the humanities—not just in student-led independent studies, but in collaboration with faculty-led projects. As the examples in this volume attest, we are already training our students in the necessary research skills to engage in such work; as faculty, we just need to be better (on both individual and institutional levels) at valuing that work and aligning our professional goals with theirs.

"DECODING" WITH ENCODING: DIGITAL TOOLS IN THE SPECIAL COLLECTIONS CLASSROOM

Rachel C. S. Duke
Sarah Stanley
Florida State University

In an effort to provide more interactive, experiential learning in class visits, Florida State University libraries have been working with faculty to develop and deploy assignments and activities that position students as researchers. Originally, these assignments focused on the physical collections held in FSU's Special Collections and Archives, but as the program grew, it became advantageous to incorporate the library's Office of Digital Research and Scholarship. The libraries were able to enhance students' understanding of technologies of text by supplementing historic study with modern-day digital scholarship technologies. In this chapter, we will share one assignment in its two iterations: fall of 2017 and fall of 2018. In both cases students in the course titled History of Text Technologies practiced transcription of Greek characters from papyrus fragments—a simple activity, but one that lent itself to both the course objectives of the English department and the active-learning instructional goals of FSU libraries. The first iteration of the assignment engaged students with hand transcription and digital transcription of the papyrus fragments, and the second iteration built upon this framework to encourage students to engage with digital technologies of editorial intervention and textual transmission. This chapter outlines an implementation of digital technologies in the archives instruction room to encourage students to understand how both digital and analog media impact the production, transmission, and reception of text.

The authors are both librarians at Florida State University. Rachel C. S. Duke is the rare books librarian in FSU Libraries' Special Collections and Archives (SCA). She co-leads SCA Instruction and Outreach, organizing class visits, collaborating with faculty to select materials, and developing assignments for student interaction. Her primary interests are incorporating experiential learning into special collections class visits and enabling historically underserved populations in special collections spaces.

Sarah Stanley is the digital humanities librarian in FSU Libraries' Office of Digital Research and Scholarship. In her role, she conducts instruction, training, and research consultations related to the implementation of digital tools in research and pedagogy. She focuses on humanities data analysis, text analysis, and the representations of text in digital media.

In addition to prioritizing active learning in the History of Text Technologies classroom, we wanted to foreground digital technologies of text in this assignment. One obvious reason for expanding upon the digital methods in this assignment was that it introduced our students to yet more technologies of text, which they could use to enrich their knowledge of textual production and media of dissemination. Additionally, the course centered around teaching students about how texts are (re)mediated through the editorial process. The students completed assignments that demonstrated how editing modifies text and read articles about how transmission impacts reception.[1] The second version of

---

1. For example, the students began the course by reading Robert Darnton's "What Is the History of Books?" (*Dædalus*, 1982) which outlines the sociological import of codicological materiality (i.e. the physical characteristics of books) in his "communications circuit."

the assignment focused on how the editorial process is enacted through a digital medium, and the immediacy of digital "publishing" allowed us to demonstrate how the editorial process transforms texts over the span of only three classes.

Through each iteration of the assignment, we ensured that the digital instruction was paired with interaction with the physical materials and some nondigital activity. We followed the principles of what Paul Fyfe refers to as "Digital Pedagogy, Unplugged." In his article of the same name, Fyfe argues that digital work "too frequently seems transparent, or so flattened that students fail to notice its own critical topologies" and argues that "[b]y unplugging [. . .] or doing preliminary exercises with analog collections, one might help students to appreciate, by contrast, their active mediation of similar work in the digital field."[2] We intentionally constructed assignments that allowed the digital and papyrus-based components to inform each other pedagogically.

The physical materials we chose for this assignment have historically only been useful in the "show and tell" approach to special collections instruction. Students can learn a great deal about the materiality of our papyrus fragments by examining them alongside a brief introduction to papyrus as a substrate (i.e. writing surface). However, the script, language, and amount of wear to the materials limit possibilities for in-class assignments. The collection of papyrus fragments held by Florida State University includes twenty-six fragments sandwiched between panes of glass, cushioned on four sides with foam, and laid flat in a box. The papyrus fragments once served as banknotes, c. 87–84 BCE. In past instruction sessions, the glass panes often were not removed from their boxes, as students were merely observing them from a distance.

One class that regularly makes use of these fragments in Special Collections and Archives is ENG 3803: History of Text Technologies (HoTT). This course is required for the editing, writing, and media major in the English department, and is meant to provide an overview

---

2. Paul Fyfe, "Digital Pedagogy Unplugged," *Digital Humanities Quarterly* 5, no. 3 (2011): par. 11, http://www.digitalhumanities.org/dhq/vol/5/3/000106/000106.html.

of major text technologies throughout history. The department-provided course objectives for ENG 3803 are as follows:

- Question how technological innovations influence the creation and reception of texts
- Develop skills for working with, analyzing, and writing about rare materials
- Innovate new ways to present research
- Employ relevant vocabulary for analyzing print and digital literature

The course description places emphasis on the three phases of textuality, stating that classes will examine case studies that "demonstrate how literary production, transmission, and reception are shaped by the materiality of texts themselves."[3] In past years, HoTT courses visited Special Collections and Archives for exposure to various forms of textuality, usually in a large, chronological spread of materials hitting major shifts in textual reproduction. The specific focus of this course, and the instructors' investment in introducing the students to diverse physical materials year after year, made this the perfect course to design an innovative assignment for.

To that end, we created the first iteration of the assignment in the fall of 2017 to get students interacting with FSU's papyrus fragments in ways that would raise questions about intervention in the transcription and translation of primary sources. In preparation for the visit to Special Collections and Archives, students read a chapter of their textbook on the history of papyrus as a substrate.[4] The fragments (still between panes of glass) were removed from their boxes and spread out throughout the room so groups could gather around them. Students were asked to attempt to transcribe any characters they saw, to participate in group discussion when opinions differed, and to confer with

---

3. From the Editing, Writing, and Media program website: https://english.fsu.edu/programs/editing-writing-and-media/ewm-course-descriptions.

4. William Proctor Williams and Craig S. Abbott, *An Introduction to Bibliographical and Textual Studies*, 4th Edition (New York: Modern Language Association, 2009).

group members if a character was impossible to make out. The groups then rotated, and the class session ended with groups that had transcribed the same fragment comparing their transcriptions and noting points of departure. The small group conversations led to a wider class discussion about who makes decisions when it comes to an authoritative transcription of a text.

Next, we wanted to introduce the concept of digital work with primary texts. In the following class session, students were asked to bring their laptops or to check one out from the library. As a class, we navigated to Zooniverse.org, a website that once housed the University of Oxford's Ancient Lives project, a massive effort to transcribe around 500,000 papyrus fragments by crowdsourcing identifications of individual characters, which were then converted into a digital consensus transcription.[5] Using the Ancient Lives interface, students were able to click on a letter and identify it within the Greek alphabet. This resulted in a fruitful class conversation on the merits of in-person vs. digital work, on digital humanities and the breadth of possible projects in the discipline, and on the virtues and vices of knowledge production by consensus.

In 2018, the opportunity arose to attempt another iteration of the papyrus transcription assignment when Lindsey Eckert joined the English Department as an assistant professor. Eckert was open to this collaboration, and she committed both of her sections of ENG 3803 to the three visits to the library required in our enhanced version of the assignment. While the first iteration was successful in many ways, there were drawbacks to the digital portion of the original approach that required modification. The in-person work that students completed with papyrus fragments did not connect to the digital work, due to the fact that the Ancient Lives project used different fragments from the ones viewed in FSU Special Collections. While participants felt that they had contributed to a knowledge community, they did so in a

---

5. The Ancient Lives project currently has its own site (https://www.ancientlives.org/), but at the time of the first version of the assignment, the transcriptions were crowdsourced at https://www.zooniverse.org/. The Ancient Lives project still uses Zooniverse for its crowdsourced transcription software.

vacuum: solo, at a computer, and without any feedback or discussion as they made transcription decisions. Most frustratingly, the students' work disappeared into the Zooniverse, where it was silently corrected by consensus, without the opportunity to explore their relationship to the editorial process.

As we rethought the structure of this assignment for the fall 2018 iteration of the History of Text Technologies class, we decided it would be best to move away from external, web-hosted platforms for saving and sharing student work. Especially with the ephemerality of the Zooniverse project, we thought it would be best to have students use technologies that they could work with locally on their computers, rather than web-based platforms. We also knew that this would allow the students to do digital transcription and editing of materials that we housed in FSU's Special Collections and Archives, rather than working with digitized materials from other institutions. Using our materials during each stage of the assignment would provide students with a more cogent understanding of how the papyri were mediated at every step of the editorial process.

We decided to design the assignment using the Text Encoding Initiative (TEI) guidelines for the digital transcription and editing portion of the assignment.[6] The TEI guidelines are an open source standard for describing text objects for machine readability. Unlike web publication languages like HTML, the TEI provides tools for describing the appearance *and* semantics of text, rather than just instructions for rendition. For example, HTML provides tools for displaying struck-through text. The TEI takes this a step further, allowing an encoder to describe text that was struck through in a manuscript, along with information about the agent who crossed out the text, when in the editorial process the strike-through occurred, and the replacement for the deleted text. The TEI allows users to move beyond the mere rendering and appearance of text to make editorial assertions that are embedded in the transcription itself.

The redesigned assignment used the TEI to allow students to make

---

6. http://www.tei-c.org/release/doc/tei-p5-doc/en/html/index.html.

notes on the process of editing the papyrus fragments as they completed their digital descriptions. We encouraged the students to focus on four specific TEI elements in their transcription and encoding, which would allow them to make statements of uncertainty and indecision (for a look at a sample encoding, see Appendix 1):

- `<unclear>` - Wrapping this element around a string of characters allowed the students to indicate when they were uncertain about their reading of a given text segment. Students were also allowed to assign these elements certainty attributes (`@cert`) to indicate if they had a "high," "medium," or "low" level of certainty about their reading.
- `<choice>` - The students were divided into groups for encoding. They would occasionally disagree about what a given character was. The students were allowed to put multiple `<unclear>` elements inside of `<choice>`, to indicate that there were many possible readings to choose from. They also could use the `@resp` (responsibility) attribute to indicate who agreed with which reading.
- `<gap>` - This element allowed them to indicate when they were omitting characters from their transcription that they suspected were in the original fragment. They were given the ability to indicate how many characters they thought may be missing from their transcription with the `@extent` attribute, and the `@reason` attribute to indicate *why* they couldn't read those characters (e.g. the page was burnt or torn or the character was smudged).
- `<damage>` - This element allowed students to indicate when there was damage to the physical text. They had the option of stating the extent to which the damage impacted the text (`@degree` with "high," "medium," and "low") and the cause of the damage (`@agent`).

The students were given minimal instructions for encoding using these elements and were directed to some of the guidelines provided by the TEI. Even though they had access to these guidelines, they were largely encouraged to describe the texts according to their interpretations, and they were encouraged to discuss encoding decisions with their fellow group members.

After the students completed their transcriptions, we wrote a script that transformed the TEI (which is rich in information, but not renderable in a web browser) to HTML (which contains less information, but can be displayed easily). We decided on a few display features that would render their editorial interventions as display information. For example, we made all text that the students were certain about black, but put uncertain text in gray, with "high" certainty being in dark gray and "low" certainty being light gray. We also put all possible readings from `<choice>` elements in curly brackets, with each option separated by a vertical bar ("{option a | option b | option c}") so the students could see where a group disagreed.

With two sections of the class working on the same papyrus fragments, we were given the opportunity to show how each group transcribed and encoded the documents slightly differently. Some groups made heavy use of <choice> and <unclear> to indicate their uncertainty about their readings, while other students working with the same texts were much more decisive in their readings. We showed the classes both versions of the displayed encoding to demonstrate how two people could come away from the same document with entirely different readings and perceptions of the content contained therein. Of course, the documents were in ancient Greek, and were frequently illegible due to damage or wear, which impacted overall readability. However, the exercise underscored lessons that the students had been learning in other parts of the class, such as the impact of editorial interventions on how readers understand text.

Before the class meeting in which we rendered and transformed their transcriptions, the students read W.W. Greg's "The Rationale of Copy-Text," which discusses the choices editors make when selecting an authoritative text to base an edition on, and the circumstances in which editors should supplement readings from other versions of the text. Although Greg's article primarily focuses on printed works and exclusively deals with texts for which there are multiple editions, the students were able to make connections between the arguments made in that piece and the work they did transcribing and encoding the papyrus fragments. Greg discusses editorial choice within the context of selecting a "copy-text," saying, "[i]t is impossible to exclude individual judgement from editorial procedure."[7] The students were able to see through the display of their encodings how their decisions affected their "editions" of the fragments. The insights they gained through this exercise of hands-on editing helped frame discussions about how the transmission of texts through different technologies and by different agents impacts how the text is read.

While this assignment led to many fruitful discussions that complemented the objectives of the course, we largely designed the assignment in the absence of a completed syllabus, as our conversations about this activity began before Lindsey Eckert arrived at Florida State. In the future, we hope to revise the assignment to more intentionally incorporate the student readings and course objectives. While the readings guided the students to understand the "why" of the project, the course readings could more specifically prepare students for engaging with digital technologies of text. Ultimately, this will require further collaboration with Eckert to determine how to frame the assignment and when to deploy it in the arc of the semester.

As previously discussed, the History of Text Technologies course requires students to understand three phases of textuality: production, transmission, and reception. In preparing and piloting this assignment we came to recognize a missed opportunity for elucidating the complicated relationship between these phases. In the editorial process, production, transmission, and reception collapse in on themselves, and all occur simultaneously. The editor is at once receiver, transmitter, and producer of text, and a thorough understanding of editorial intervention requires an awareness of this complexity. We wish to adapt future versions of the assignment in ways that deliberately call attention to these connections. The original version of the assignment did not intentionally incorporate this theorization of textuality, and we are curious to see how the assignment could be enriched by explicitly raising students' awareness of this process and its implications.

---

7. W. W. Greg, "The Rationale of Copy-Text," *Studies in Bibliography* 3 (1950): 26.

Additionally, we hope to expand the assignment to include more familiar and approachable texts, such as printed texts in English. Designing the assignment using illegible Greek papyrus fragments was useful for demonstrating the impact of the transcriber in an extreme, but the same principles still apply for more modern, and even well-known texts. A possible future version of the assignment could include multiple different versions of a well-known text, such as a Shakespeare play. Having the students choose a "copy-text" and other texts to draw readings from would encourage them to engage with questions of what makes an "authoritative text." A version of the assignment using a more familiar text could also give students the opportunity to provide justifications for their editorial decisions or write editorial statements.

The flexibility of this assignment lends itself to remixing and adaptation in other institutional contexts. While our version of the assignment benefitted from the extensive holdings of FSU's Special Collections and Archives, under-resourced institutions could feasibly enact this assignment with digitally available materials. Ultimately, the driving force behind the project is to demystify the process of textual production for students. Using the framework of history of text technologies, we are able to introduce students to the concept of "information creation as a process." Media of dissemination are selected intentionally and have an impact on the way readers interact with the information they receive.

Appendix 1 - Sample Encoding of Fragment

```
<choice>
  <unclear cert="high" resp="#student1 #student2 #student3" reason="illegible">I</unclear>
  <unclear cert="low" resp="#student3" reason="illegible">ζ</unclear>
</choice>
<damage agent="demummification" degree="high"><gap extent="4 characters" reason="damage"/></damage>
```

Appendix 2 - Image of Transformed Text

{T | Π}*[Gap: ill-formed character]* λ *[Gap: damage]* Μο
{Ε | Σ}ονι *[Gap: damage]*
τε*[Gap: damage]* χ*[Gap: damage]*π
χιχο Επινε *[Gap: damage]*
χ*[Gap: ill-formed character]* Π{χ | λ}Νπ Κ*[Gap: damage]*
ΙΦ *[Gap: bad handwriting]*

A sample version of the text, created by the authors, as rendered in HTML. Unclear text is rendered in gray; damage and its extent (high, medium, low) is indicated in square brackets; and multiple potential readings are indicated in curly brackets.

Bibliography

Fyfe, Paul. "Digital Pedagogy, Unplugged." *Digital Humanities Quarterly* 5, no. 3 (2011). http://www.digitalhumanities.org/dhq/vol/5/3/000106/000106.html.

Greg, W. W. "The Rationale of Copy-Text." *Studies in Bibliography* 3 (1950): 19–36.

STUDYING URBAN RENEWAL
THROUGH ARCHIVAL SOURCES

Ella Howard

Wentworth Institute of Technology

In recent decades, the learning objectives for college courses have become more specific. Seeking heightened student engagement, many instructors have developed hands-on learning activities to take the place of classroom lectures.[1] Fueled by student preferences and data from the study of teaching and learning, educators and administrators have increasingly emphasized applied skills over memorized knowledge. Employers, too, often describe their desire to hire workers skilled in problem solving and creative thinking.[2] For all of these reasons, many history professors are creating assignments asking students to use digital tools to analyze materials found in archives on and off campus. This chapter surveys some of the archival assignments I have developed and discusses the challenges and opportunities presented by each. Working with students majoring primarily in engineering, architecture, and

---

1. Jennifer L. Faust and Donald R. Paulson, "Active Learning in the College Classroom," *Journal on Excellence in College Teaching* 9, no. 2 (1998): 3–24.

2. Casey Fabris, "College Students Think They're Ready for the Work Force. Employers Aren't So Sure," *Chronicle of Higher Education*, January 20, 2015.

computer science, I create assignments that allow students to do more than just engage superficially with archives: they must wrestle with archival material and probe the gaps in our disciplinary knowledge.

Archives present inherently fragmentary pieces of evidence. Such sources require students to read texts closely and examine images carefully, rather than rely on narratives written by subject experts. Assignments grounded in analyses of archival documents empower students to synthesize information from both primary and secondary sources to answer questions of their own design. Through such projects, students fulfill in meaningful ways the core learning objectives of the undergraduate history course.

Universities that maintain their own archives offer incredible laboratories for student work. Those teaching at universities without such resources can form useful partnerships with area municipal archives and other local, public organizations. Such projects help students learn about the nature and structure of public archives and allow them to experiment with their collections.

In my Boston History class, we study the development of the city and its broader area from 1630 until the present day, focusing on housing, the built environment, and immigration. At the center of the course is the Boston: Then and Now digital project, done in partnership with the Municipal Archives of the City of Boston. The city of Boston has digitized more than 13,000 photographs, which archivists have posted online in a Flickr stream.[3] These photos form an amazing resource, documenting architecture, neighborhoods, politicians, and community events. Due to schedule constraints, my students are not able to visit the archive in person, but they use the digital resources to carry out research projects.

Students choose three historic photographs from this collection, recreate them by taking an image of the same view with their phones, and use Juxtapose JS, a very simple free online tool, to create a digital

---

3. Boston City Archives, Flickr Stream, accessed January 31, 2019, https://www.flickr.com/photos/cityofbostonarchives/.

slider that shows change over time.⁴ Students then post these sliders on the main project website I maintain, sharing their work with the public.⁵ Myths surrounding digital humanities convince many that grants and extensive resources are required to carry out meaningful projects. However, Boston: Then and Now is one of several projects that I administer through an inexpensive website hosted by Reclaim Hosting.⁶

This simple project achieves several learning goals. Students become aware of archives and begin to understand their purpose, as well as their structure. The assignment requires students to spend significant time exploring the archive's digital holdings. In completing the project, they collect and record specific metadata for each image, such as the date the photograph was taken and the identity of the creator of the image. For many students, this is their first exposure to the structure of databases. Students majoring in computer science, who have previous experiences with databases, begin to see the connections between their more theoretical class assignments and practical applications of data management.

Students analyze the changes they see depicted in their photos. Those changes provide the basis of a scholarly research paper explaining the political, economic, or social factors at stake. Students turn to scholarly books and articles, as well as historical newspapers, seeking answers to their own questions. Their work on this assignment has exceeded my expectations. They have pursued innovative lines of inquiry, formulating specific research questions and seeking out relevant sources and information.

The second project comprises the core of my digital studio course, where students spend a semester studying the federal program of urban renewal using various types of technology to analyze and visualize data. Most undergraduate history courses cover a broad swath of material. This course structure allows us instead to focus narrowly on

---

4. Knight Lab, Juxtapose JS, accessed January 31, 2019, https://juxtapose.knightlab.com/.

5. Ella Howard, "Boston Then and Now," accessed January 31, 2019, http://explorebostonhistory.org/ThenAndNow/.

6. Reclaim Hosting, accessed January 31, 2019, https://reclaimhosting.org.

our subject. Students become confident in their knowledge of federal urban programs, then spend much of the semester critically analyzing relevant data. The project is done in partnership with the archives of the Boston Planning and Development Agency (formerly the Boston Redevelopment Agency, or BRA).[7]

This project is possible due to the expertise of the archivists who work for the City of Boston. I approached Marta Crilly, the Archivist for Reference and Outreach at the Boston City Archives, inquiring about documents related to the Great Fire of 1872. My initial plan was to have students use 3D modeling software to depict the area of Boston that was destroyed in the fire. In this sense, 3D modeling is of two main types. In one variety, users stitch together thousands of photographs of an existing structure, thereby creating a digital model of the building or set of buildings. Alternately, one can choose from a wide range of drawing tools to create something from scratch. This second approach is especially useful when recreating buildings that are no longer extant. The technique has been used in everything from gaming technology to major digital humanities projects that recreate aspects of the ancient world.[8] As a historian of the twentieth-century United States hoping to have students create 3D models, I was looking for an area of Boston that was no longer standing and was of some historical interest. Crilly politely informed me that not enough photographs had been taken of Boston prior to the fire of 1872 to pursue the type of project I envisioned, given the relatively recent advent of photography. She suggested that I instead pursue the West End files, housed in the collections of the Boston Redevelopment Authority, overseen by Chief Archivist Nathaniel Smith.

The topic was definitely of historical interest. The West End urban renewal project, announced in 1953 and carried out in 1958, is infamous among urban planners, historians, and Boston residents for its lack of sensitivity toward the displaced population.

Funded by the federal government, urban renewal projects at

---

7. Boston Planning and Development Agency, accessed January 31, 2019, http://www.bostonplans.org.

8. Urban Simulation Team, University of California at Los Angeles, "The World's Columbian Exposition of 1893," accessed January 31, 2019, http://www.ust.ucla.edu/ustweb/Projects/columbian_expo.htm.

Figure 1. Photograph of West End Project Area Looking Northeasterly, 1959, Urban Redevelopment Division, Boston Housing Authority photographs in Boston Redevelopment Authority photographs, Collection # 4010.001, City of Boston Archives, Boston. Image available at: https://www.flickr.com/photos/cityofbostonarchives/9322028822/in/album-72157634708439390/

mid-century set out to upgrade downtown neighborhoods, razing slums and replacing them with mixed-use developments. The project in the West End was carried out with poor planning and even worse communication.

The first step of urban renewal was for city officials to commission a study of the neighborhood in question. In the case of the West End, that study took into account Scollay Square, Boston's skid row neighborhood, which contained SROs—single-resident occupancy hotels. Those structures were, not surprisingly, dilapidated and in poor condition. These results ensured that the West End would be branded a slum and subsequently approved for redevelopment. The residential neighborhoods in the area were often described by residents not as slums, but as working-class and lower middle-class housing.[9]

---

9. Thomas O'Connor, "Trial and Error," in *Building a New Boston: Politics and Urban Renewal 1950 to 1970* (Boston: Northeastern University Press, 1993), 113–149.

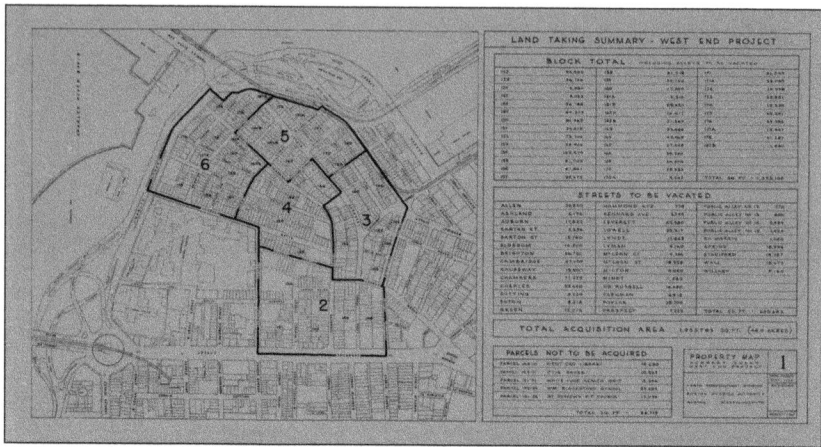

Figure 2. West End Project Property Map, 1954. Boston Planning and Development Agency Archives. Image available at: https://bpda.app.box.com/s/womas92t5fjatlsn2j7ouj4i7rioi7qi/file/350785679587

As the urban renewal project continued, residents were given false assurances that their neighborhood would not be leveled. They were provided inadequate notice that they needed to find new homes prior to the demolition of the neighborhood. Psychologists have discussed the demolition of the West End as a traumatic event in the lives of area residents, similar to the loss of a loved one.[10] The urban renewal of the West End is taught in classrooms across the country and beyond as a textbook example of inappropriate implementation of public policy with destructive results for a community.

The Boston Planning and Redevelopment Agency Archive houses the surveys carried out by the BRA prior to purchasing the West End buildings from their owners. Each building was assigned a file folder, containing a completed survey form detailing the building's exterior and interior and the condition of each. Many of the files also contain a photograph of the building's exterior. Supplemental boxes of files contain detailed legal and financial documents pertaining to the sale of each building. University funding paid for the digitization of the three

---

10. Marc Fried, "Grief and Adaptation: The Impact of Relocation in Boston's West End," in *The Last Tenement: Confronting Community and Urban Renewal in Boston's West End*, eds. Sean M. Fisher and Carolyn Hughes (Boston: The Bostonian Society, 1992), 80–93.

Figure 3. Photograph of West End, 91-93 Green and Leverett, Block 123, Parcel 06. West End Urban Renewal Acquisition Photos, Boston Planning and Development Agency Archives. Image available at: https://bpda.app.box.com/s/vnf7vclgflssrjibt4vdjskhaygjkycl

core boxes of survey files and photographs. When processing is complete, these historic survey forms will be available to the public and to scholars through the BDRA Archives (http://www.bostonplans.org/about-us/archives).

Students in the course use the digitized documentation to recreate a model of one or more buildings that were destroyed. They record relevant metadata about the building, such as year built and building materials, in an Omeka database.[11] They also screenshot the photograph of the building and enter that into the database.

Students then use Sketchup, the 3D modeling software currently suggested for beginners, to create a rendering of the building.[12] They recreate the shape, features, and appearance of the structure that was

---

11. Roy Rosenzweig Center for History and New Media, Omeka, accessed January 31, 2019, https://omeka.org/.
12. Trimble, Inc., Sketchup, accessed January 31, 2019, https://www.sketchup.com/.

Figure 4. Photograph of West End, 194 Merrimac, Block 122, Parcel 01. West End Urban Renewal Acquisition Photos, Boston Planning and Development Agency Archives. Image available at: https://bpda.app.box.com/s/mgrp5j8czjsw15suoxl3qcu3nnupaujp

destroyed. Once several blocks have been recreated, I hope to import these models to gaming software, enabling a robust walkthrough of the neighborhood.

Although I hope to create a public-facing digital project from the models, the focus of the course is very much on process, not product. Architecture majors who take the course often bring extensive experience in 3D modeling. They serve as our class experts during this unit, fielding some student questions and demonstrating best practices. Other students have never before tried to use these tools, and their work is that of a beginner. The assessment focuses on effort and thoroughness, rather than technical proficiency.

Students also work with archival evidence in other assignments for the course, both before and after this midterm project on the West End. Early in the course, students learn how to use National Historic

Figure 5. View of Class Model of Lynde Street in Progress, Spring 2019. Created with SketchUp 2018, from records courtesy of the Boston Planning and Development Agency Archives.

Geographic Information Systems (NHGIS) archival census data.[13] They also learn how to use Quantum Geographic Information System (QGIS) software to create historical maps of the census data.[14] This exercise gives them a detailed understanding of how the census works as a source of data and as a source of historical analysis. They wrestle with the methodological differences between measuring data at the national level, the state level, the county level, the tract level, or the block level. With racial segregation, for instance, measurements at the block level yield lower segregation rates than those calculated at the neighborhood or city level. Students also learn about the shifting types of data that have been collected in various census years. Government documents themselves form another type of archival source to be explored.

Students also learn to use Tableau, data visualization software currently free to teachers and students, to search for data trends.[15] The course uses a range of tools, rather than focusing on a single method of

---

13. National Historic Geographic Information Systems, accessed January 31, 2019, https://www.nhgis.org/.
14. Quantum Geographic Information System, accessed January 31, 2019, https://qgis.org/en/site/.
15. Tableau, accessed January 31, 2019, https://www.tableau.com/.

analysis. This range is highly intentional. The course is by no means an introduction to GIS or Tableau, for instance. Such tutorials and courses are widely available in many formats. Instead, this course teaches students how to use various technologies to answer research questions that are vital to the study of history and sociology.

For their final project, students work in teams on specific urban renewal projects in New York and Boston. Teams study digitized urban renewal reports available through the Internet Archive, using them as source materials to understand the projects that were carried out. The scaffolding of assignments earlier in the course has given students the skills they need to pursue these less structured projects.

Students use QGIS and NHGIS census data to answer geographic questions of their own design, about topics such as change over time in race, income, and education level of residents in their area of study. They use Tableau to create charts and graphs depicting key data trends. Using such findings in conjunction with secondary sources, such as newspaper articles and the work of historians, sociologists, and economists, students develop a strong understanding of the neighborhood they are studying before and after it underwent urban renewal.

Using a 3D modeling tool of their choice, students also create a model of some aspect of the project, whether a single building or a block. This could result in the digital rendering of a neighborhood or the printed 3D model of a single building. Students are free to use digital tools creatively to research, analyze, and share information.

These projects have been successful and remarkably well received by students, even though they require a significant amount of work both inside and outside of the class. They are designed to move general education students as close to the top of Bloom's taxonomy as possible, toward the creation of new knowledge.[16] The course design facilitates this, in part, by refusing to start with the written narratives that historians have produced. Instead, students are forced to wrestle with real, fragmentary pieces of history, such as those professional historians use

---

16. Lorin W. Anderson et al., *A Taxonomy for Learning, Teaching, and Assessing: A Revision of Bloom's Taxonomy of Educational Objectives* (New York: Longman, 2001).

in archival research. Some of this evidence is purely visual, which forces students to rely on their own powers of observation and analysis—skills few have developed in prior history classes. While these projects are tailored specifically to students of digital and urban history, the core principles are widely applicable. The built environment serves as an excellent laboratory for undergraduate students, who are often eager to understand the relationship between the past and the present. By guiding them to primary and archival sources, educators can help students find their own analytical power and voice.

Learning here takes place in the gaps remaining in our established bodies of scholarly knowledge. Primary source analysis has provided the core of history education at many educational levels for decades. These assignments vary from the "document-based question" and other traditional models that ask students to analyze primary sources. With archival projects, educators are leading students into less-curated collections, exposing them to data in its less-processed form, and allowing them to share in the excitement of true discovery through data analysis. As a result, students are forced to draw their own conclusions. Whether they are starting from photographs or from building surveys or from census data, they work from the ground up, building a framework of evidence and only then looking outside that small model for supplemental secondary sources to understand and interpret the results they have found. This model resembles in some aspects the method of material culture analysis made famous by Jules Prown. In Prownian analysis, students analyze objects before considering their broader cultural, economic, and political contexts.[17]

These projects also bring the history classroom closer to the STEM (science, technology, engineering, and math) model of laboratory education, in which students carry out experiments and then analyze their findings, rather than simply trying to use data to confirm existing theories. Inspired by these connections, I have shifted some of the writing assignments in these courses to tasks akin to a lab report. For each

---

17. Jules David Prown, "Mind in Matter: An Introduction to Material Culture Theory and Method," *Winterthur Portfolio* 17, no. 1 (Spring 1982): 1–19.

analysis carried out, students answer a series of specific questions. They explain their method, describe their findings, and articulate further research goals. These assignments have kept students focused on the analysis at hand, allowing them to sharpen their writing on a specific topic.

Slowing the pace of undergraduate instruction, narrowing to a specific topic, and embracing a laboratory model of education allows instructors to meet students where they are while helping them develop new skills. The ability to read quantitative and qualitative data with interest, and the ability to analyze it with confidence, represent highly transferable skills that serve students well in diverse professions.

Opportunities for partnerships between university teachers and archivists abound. At a previous position in Georgia, my students worked closely with Luciana Spracher, Director of the Research Library and Municipal Archives of the City of Savannah. Spracher gave my classes guided tours of the archives, where she allowed them to peruse key historic documents. Students then pursued research topics based on the city's collections, scheduling appointments for later research visits. This sustained research guidance led students to develop projects by drawing on materials they would otherwise never have been able to access.

Caroline Hopkinson, University Archivist at Georgia Southern University's Savannah Campus (then Armstrong State University), also provided focused instruction in several courses. Most notably, for the First Year Seminar, I had students work in teams to research university alumni, writing short biographies and recording narrated slideshows of their achievements. Hopkinson hosted student researchers in the campus archives, introducing them to research protocols and helping them to locate suitable source materials.

Such projects benefit immensely from true collaboration with archival partners. Historians and other scholars too often struggle with authority, clinging to our titles, degrees, and sense of ourselves as experts, when cooperating with archivists and librarians. In my experience in these and other projects, when historians can approach archivists with curiosity and humility, we can benefit from archivists' subject expertise, creativity, and interest in outreach. The projects resulting from such rich collaborations provide students with unparalleled opportunities.

SUSTAINABLE ROLES AND PROGRAMS

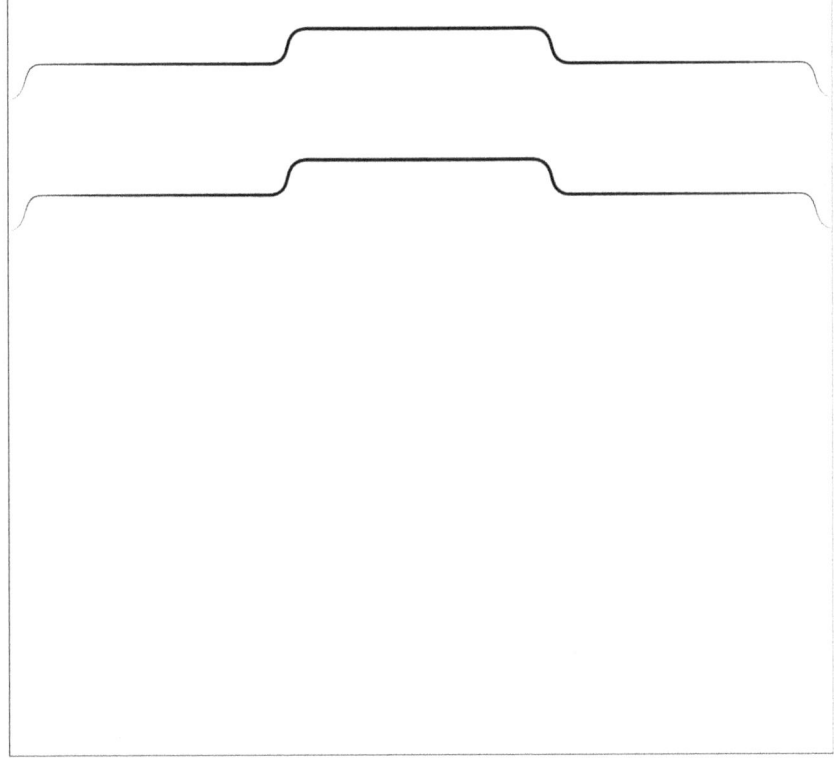

MORE THAN MANAGING A CALENDAR: REFLECTIONS ON THE ROLE OF AN ACADEMIC ARCHIVIST

Cinda Nofziger
University of Michigan

When people ask me what they need to know about me to best work with me, I tell them that I live by my calendar. If something isn't on my calendar, it doesn't exist. Attending meetings, coordinating classes, finding open rooms, and managing prep time all make my calendar a very important tool. Some, looking at what instruction archivists and librarians do, might see our primary work as calendar management. Others might see what we do as simply finding materials. For example, one faculty member answering a prompt about his experiences with archivists in the past indicated that archivists had been "consultants, where you go along . . . doing your own thing and then you ask them if you . . . have a problem. Then they disappear until you need them again."[1] But what we do as instruction archivists and outreach librarians

---

1. This quotation comes from an interview in 2016, which is part of a research project in which the Bentley is involved. The project is described in greater detail in the text below. The names of the respondents are anonymized throughout this chapter for their privacy. Interviews for the project have been conducted by University of Michigan

is much more than scheduling, and we can do more than help find materials. Like many other aspects of working in archives, the work of instructors is about relationships—with other archivists, with teaching faculty, and with students. Some of the relationship-building we engage in can help to change expectations about the kinds of skills and knowledge archivists and special collections librarians can add to the classroom. We can teach students skills of archival intelligence, primary source literacy, and more. Our teaching efforts at their best can be transformative to teaching faculties' understandings of archives, special collections, and the people who work in them. Our teaching can also help transform student learning. It can help students think in new ways—critically, historically, and creatively—with new questions and perspectives. The goals then are not only to provide students with an opportunity to create new knowledge or complete a project, but to help them build skills, confidence, and ways of approaching all sources that will help them throughout life. These are all important investments of time and effort, strategically enabled by a very mindful use of the calendar in the interest of new goals and new roles.

A reality in the archival profession is a trend toward more instruction, and I welcome it. A recent article in *The American Archivist* stated that there has been an increase over the last five years or so in archival jobs requiring teaching.[2] The archival and special collections professional literature has seen a similar increase in articles and books about instruction. These publications are just recent examples; this literature has been growing for years. The interest in the symposium on teaching undergraduates with archives, held at the University of Michigan

---

School of Information Assistant Professor Patricia Garcia, as well as University of Michigan School of Information graduate students, who are Research Experience Master's (REMS) students, and part of the Engaging the Archives research team (https://www.si.umich.edu/research/research-experiences-masters-students). The student interviewers have been Joseph Lueck and Tori Culler.

2. Lindsay Anderberg, Robin M. Katz, Shaun Hayes, Alison Stankrauff, Morgen MacIntosh Hodgetts, Josué Hurtado, Abigail Nye, and Ashley Todd-Diaz, "Teaching the Teacher: Primary Source Instruction in American and Canadian Archives Graduate Programs," *The American Archivist* 81, no. 1, (Spring/Summer 2018): 188–215. https://doi.org/10.17723/0360-9081.1.188.

in 2018, demonstrates how teaching has come to the forefront of the archives and special collections landscape.

Since 2015, the Bentley Historical Library has prioritized a programmatic approach to push teaching with archival materials forward at the University of Michigan. The Bentley established a new position, Archivist for Academic Programs and Outreach, to lead these efforts. They hired me to fill that position.[3] Hallmarks of our approach include intensive collaboration with faculty and archivist colleagues through a faculty-archivist teaching seminar, and research. Though we are only four years in, the approach has been quite successful. Our efforts have revealed data about the impact of teaching with primary sources on faculty, archivists, and students. This chapter examines the Bentley's approach to teaching, in which the academic archivist plays a significant role.

Engaging the Archives Grant, Seminar, and Research Project

In 2016, the Bentley received a grant from the University of Michigan's Provost Office. The grant was part of the university's Third Century Initiative, a project to develop "innovative ideas for enriching student learning."[4] The grant funds five years of a semester-long seminar that brings faculty and archivists together to collaborate on the development of course syllabi and individual course assignments, which draw on Bentley materials. The goals of the seminar are ultimately a more successful teaching and learning experience for Michigan students,

---

3. I hold this position, having come to the archives field after earning a PhD in American studies and a master's degree in information. My background provided me with undergraduate teaching experience and course design, which helped make me comfortable and confident in this position. Not everyone who comes to this work has the same background, and I believe that we can do more to support new teachers. I strive to learn to become a better teacher. Some of the other chapters in this book propose ideas about how to do that.

4. Laurel Thomas Gnagey, "Six Projects Get Major Grants through Third Century Initiative," *The Record*, May 15, 2015, https://record.umich.edu/articles/six-projects-get-major-grants-through-third-century-initiative. Accessed April 26, 2019.

faculty, and archivists. It is based on collaboration with faculty, in which archivists, faculty, and research scientists think together about how to best teach with archival materials, recognizing that archivists are not necessarily experts in teaching and faculty are not necessarily experts in archives. At the Bentley, we believe that together we can advance pedagogical uses of the archives. Archivists and faculty should collaborate more intentionally to develop common teaching goals and approaches in order to maximize student learning.

The Bentley has run three semesters of the seminar, and it has had a positive impact on how classes using the Bentley's materials are constructed and implemented. Each semester, five or six faculty from different disciplines participate in the seminar. The seminar's planning committee—which consists of the Bentley's Director Terrence McDonald,[5] Associate Director Nancy Bartlett, and myself—invite the faculty, who receive a stipend for their participation. The seminar also includes a selection of archivists from all areas of the Bentley. The seminar group spends about 1.5 hours together each week throughout a semester, learning about historical thinking, archival intelligence, and best pedagogical practices for teaching with archival materials. The schedule includes guest speakers who are researchers at the University of Michigan in the areas of historical learning, archival literacy, assessment, and cognition. These include School of Education Professor Chauncey Monte-Sano, who emphasizes planning, including the need for learning objectives and outcomes, and the significance of modeling for students how experts think. School of Information Professor Elizabeth Yakel discusses archival intelligence and archival literacy to highlight the skills students need to excel at archival research. School of Information Assistant Professor Patricia Garcia describes archival instruction assessment, and cognitive psychologist Bill Gehring, a professor in the Department of Psychology, provides an engaging interactive session about student cognition. Selected readings from archival,

---

5. Terrence McDonald's background as a professor and Dean of the College of Literature, Science and the Arts led him to prioritize undergraduate learning when he came to the Bentley in 2013. He continues to hold an academic appointment in the History Department as Arthur F. Thurnau Professor of History.

educational, and psychological literature provide supplemental information for the discussions from week to week. Past participants return to share with current members how their teaching has changed because of the seminar. Individually, faculty meet for intensive sessions about potential sources, first with all the archivists participating in the seminar, and then with fewer, based on the archivists' interests and expertise. These sessions are deliberately staged after the halfway point of the seminar to help demonstrate the need for initial planning. Additionally, faculty then have time to work with material on their own in the reading room. Throughout the semester, the participants workshop syllabi and specific assignments, so that when the seminar is finished, faculty walk away with tangibles that they can use in upcoming classes.

Sixteen faculty members have participated in the seminar. Because one of the goals of the seminar is to expand the disciplines that use the Bentley and test the applicability with a wide variety of academic disciplines, faculty come from departments across campus. These include African American studies; American culture; architecture; art and design; art history; history; Judaic studies; music, theatre, and dance; philosophy; television, film, and media; and women's studies. Fifteen archivists have also participated; the seminar planners choose them from various areas of the Bentley because of their knowledge of collections and archival processes, as well as their interest in how faculty think about teaching. This includes archivists and project archivists[6] from curation, university history, and reference. Nearly all archivists at the Bentley have participated in the seminar. The seminar has generated eleven iterations of classes.

A related research project titled Engaging the Archives: Researching Best Practices for Student Success in the Archives investigates the

---

6. The Bentley's Project Archivist Program provides opportunities for early career archivists to gain skills and training across various areas of the Bentley, while participating in term limited positions of one to two years. Project archivists are assigned to specific areas of the library, but they learn about the wider library through various opportunities for professional development. Some project archivists have worked with the Archivist for Academic Programs and Outreach to develop, design, and teach class sessions.

seminar's impact on archivists, faculty, and students. An MCubed project funded by a grant from the University of Michigan,[7] this project seeks to understand the initial expectations and the subsequent impact of the Engaging the Archives Seminar on faculty and archivists as well as the effect that working with archival materials has on students. Patricia Garcia is the lead investigator and the project is guided by an interdisciplinary team of researchers at U-M: Terrence McDonald, Elizabeth Yakel, and Chauncey Monte-Sano.[8] The project's research methods consist of a series of interviews with faculty and archivists who take part in the seminar, as well as a pre- and post-course survey for students in courses taught by seminar faculty.

Garcia, or a School of Information graduate student under her supervision, conducts the pre- and post-seminar interviews with archivists and faculty. The questions for faculty ask about attitudes toward and impressions of archives and archivists; the faculty member's motivations and goals for participating in the seminar; and their views about learning. Faculty participants answer questions about how their ideas, attitudes, teaching methods, syllabi, and assignments have changed after the seminar and again after they have taught their course. Archivists answer questions about their perceptions of faculty expertise, collaboration between archivists and faculty, about student learning, and their motivations and goals for seminar participation.

Faculty provide students with the pre- and the post-course surveys, which attempt to measure any increase in transferable skills: intercultural engagement, creativity, ethical reasoning, communications, and self-agency. The research team wanted the survey to include questions about a primary source. In selecting the source, the team looked for a source that was not too long but rich enough to allow for thoughtful answers. The team also wanted the primary source to reflect an underrepresented voice. The team used an individual sample of a University of Michigan alumnae survey from 1924. The Alumni Association

---

7. "Engaging the Archives: Researching Best Practices for Student Success in the Archives," MCubed. https://mcubed.umich.edu/projects/engaging-archives-researching-best-practices-student-success-archives, accessed May 15, 2019.

8. This author is also a member of the research team.

had sent surveys to all identifiable women who had attended since the admission of women in 1870. The alumnae surveys asked about their experiences, their memories of Michigan, and their post-university endeavors. The student subjects responded to questions about the content of the alumnae survey, as well as questions about where they might find additional information on the topic of female student experiences at the university.[9]

Findings: Faculty and Archivists

Post-seminar interviews consistently include mention of the seminar's value in providing faculty with a welcome opportunity to talk and think about pedagogy with colleagues. Faculty also frequently acknowledged that the seminar led them to reconceptualize their relationships with archivists and recognize them as partners in planning and executing courses. This prompted them to include archives and archivists in their courses to a greater degree than they previously had. They also recognized the value of shifting expectations and planning in a way that allows for a slower, deeper engagement with archival processes and materials, even as they planned some very ambitious final projects.

In their post-seminar interviews, archivists also reported changes in perception. They indicated a deeper understanding of how faculty understood and prepared for teaching. The seminar caused archivists to think in new ways about how their own areas of specialization affect students and instructors. At the same time, archivists recognized their own strengths, sometimes with deep content knowledge that faculty relied on, but also with extensive knowledge of archival practices and systems that faculty could also draw on.

---

9. More extensive treatments of the findings from the student surveys and interviews with archivists and faculty will be forthcoming from Garcia and the research team.

Talking pedagogy

Faculty expressed great appreciation for the opportunity to talk and think about pedagogy during the seminar. One recalled, "I think just having the opportunity to talk to your colleagues about teaching in a sustained, relaxed way. I just love that part about it. It pushed me to think about things in different ways."[10] Faculty indicated that they don't often have the opportunity to talk with colleagues within their own departments about teaching, much less across disciplines, as they could in the seminar.[11] They found benefit in hearing about other people's syllabi and assignments as well as in learning from other fields. One faculty member stated in his post-seminar interview, "I was completely oblivious to the literature on archival intelligence and for that matter, the way in which the literature in K-12 education was actually relevant and useful for college teaching."[12] The seminar helped some faculty think very broadly about pedagogy. One explained,

> [I]t made me think of maybe a more ambitious way is to change the course that went beyond really the archival project itself . . . Teaching people how to learn, teaching people how to think, teaching people how to analyze, teaching people to communicate that analysis. And so, in a sense, the breaking down of archival thinking into its component parts inspired me to think about the course in a broader way . . . breaking its skills down into component parts and the think-aloud process of what I wanted students to do. I would say it emboldened me to think more ambitiously about ways to transform things that wouldn't be involved with archival projects . . . [13]

Though the seminar is designed to help faculty and archivist think specifically about teaching with archives, the chance to think beyond that aspect to pedagogy more generally is one of the important outcomes of the seminar.

---

10. Faculty member, interviewed by Patricia Garcia, Ann Arbor, MI, 2016.
11. Faculty member, interviewed by Joseph Lueck, Ann Arbor, MI, 2017.
12. Faculty member, interviewed by Patricia Garcia, Ann Arbor, MI, 2016.
13. Faculty member, interviewed by Tori Culler, Ann Arbor, MI, 2019.

Increased contact

The interviews have indicated that, as a result of the seminar, there have been some important changes in faculty perceptions about archivists and archives. The first types of changes are related to the design of classes. The seminar has encouraged faculty to think differently about how students would benefit from spending more time with archivists and in archives. One faculty member noted that she had changed the structure of her class so that "students feel more comfortable contacting the archivist and the work of the archivist is built in to the core structurally in a way that it wasn't before."[14]

A goal of the academic program at the Bentley is to aim for flexibility in approaches to archivists and archives. Classes might come to the Bentley more than once, so that the teaching archivists don't need to teach all the skills the students will need in a single class session. Bentley archivists might visit classes elsewhere on campus. For example, in a class on Jewish experience at the University of Michigan, a colleague and I spent about an hour during their first day of class talking about what primary sources are and how to begin to interpret them. Sometimes faculty have their students present drafts of their final projects with Bentley archivists in the audience. The archivists provide feedback and guidance to the students. The Bentley has also placed an embedded archivist in two courses. As the embedded archivist, I attended almost all class sessions, read course material, and participated in class discussions. This additional time with students allowed them to form a deeper relationship with me than students in other classes could. Spending more time with students allows archivists to get a better sense of how students are thinking about and using archival material; this in turn allows us to intervene in a more helpful way in the moment, and to better plan for future classes. An important reason why we have been able to increase contact between archivists and students is that we have a designated person who can help facilitate those connections.

---

14. Faculty member, interviewed by Joe Lueck, Ann Arbor, MI, 2017.

More process, better product

At the Bentley, we have worked with faculty to embrace an approach to class structure that places as much emphasis on the process of learning from and about archival materials as it does on the final product. One faculty member in the seminar reflected, "For those of us who've done doctoral dissertations and had to do that kind of research, we weren't taught it in a systematic way, we were taught by example and sort of by the process of writing papers . . . So I was not even aware of my own skill use, it was more of a habitual learning, and so breaking that down again makes me think a little bit more about the skills that are inherent to the humanities that we sort of take for granted by doing it."[15] Though the final product can still be very important, motivating to students, and exciting to produce—the chapter by Clark, Lassiter, and Thoms in this volume illustrates that—by encouraging faculty to recognize the various steps and skills needed for students to excel at archival research, we can help students achieve results that better match faculty goals.

While scaffolding and skill building are important components of teaching the process of archival research, so too is teaching students to recognize the idiosyncratic nature of archival research. Sometimes, students may not find what they are looking for, but they may find something else that takes them in a wonderful new direction. The potential for unpredictability is an important component of working with archives. Part of the Bentley's programmatic approach to teaching includes encouraging faculty to think about rewarding students for the process of working in the archives, not only for the final product. This is often simply a reflective component in which students write about their experience working in the archives, and the challenges and achievements they encountered. Another example of what this might look like has occurred in a history methods class. The professor, who was a member of the Engaging the Archives seminar, wanted to restructure the final project in the class. In previous years, she'd brought her class to the Bentley to look at student scrapbooks. The students were then in three weeks supposed to do research about the scrapbook's creator and write

---

15. Faculty member, interviewed by Tori Culler, Ann Arbor, MI, 2019.

a mini biography. She was frustrated because the results tended to be superficial and unsupported. The subjects were not necessarily famous students, but people who attended the University of Michigan in the early twentieth century, whose scrapbooks had made their way to the Bentley. The archival information about them varied. During the seminar, the group talked about the goals for her class, and it turned out that she was most interested in having students learn about doing research in an archive. We suggested then that instead of a research paper, the students write a process paper, in which they wrote about what they found but also reflected about how they had researched, where they hit dead-ends, what their "a ha" moments were, and how, if they had more time, they would continue their search. These papers, the faculty member reported, were much more successful.

Archivists as faculty collaborators
Other perceptual changes emerging from the seminar relate to ways that archivists and faculty can collaborate. After the seminar, faculty more clearly articulate the various roles archivists can play in their classes. For example, they see the contributions archivists can make in terms of syllabi timelines and topics, including when it makes the most sense for students to encounter the archives. One faculty member noted that after the seminar that she would "work much more closely . . . with archivists at the Bentley in constructing the syllabus and be much more deliberative about tapping on them . . . at different touchpoints . . ." Another stated, "getting the archivist involved when you're planning the course is more important than anything they may do once the course starts."[16]

The seminar demonstrated to faculty that archivists had expertise that could be put to pedagogical purposes, and that other archivists—in addition to the archivist for academic programs and project archivist who also teaches—could be tapped for teaching. For example, one faculty member has requested the Bentley's Michigan Historical Collections field archivist come to her classes to talk about how the Bentley

---

16. Faculty members, interviews by Joe Lueck, Ann Arbor, MI, 2017.

is currently collecting material in Detroit. One curation archivist has participated in another class because of her expertise on audio and visual copyright, which students needed to understand to create the course website. In their post-seminar and post-class interviews, faculty members focused as much on the relationships they had with archivists as on the materials held in the archives. One of the roles I play as Archivist for Academic Programs and Outreach is to bring faculty together with archivists from within the Bentley. Connecting archivists whose primary functions may be far removed from outreach or instruction with faculty and students enriches everyone's experiences.

Archivists learning and teaching

At the same time, archivists have gained a deeper understanding of pedagogy. One reference archivist stated, "I think the biggest part is really understanding that I've never made a syllabus. And understanding all the work that goes into it and how they're thinking about where the visit falls within the semester. And how they know their students learn and how their students work and just seeing that deeper level of everything it takes to plan a class, to come to the Bentley."[17] As this archivist learned more about what it takes to create a course, she gained a better understanding of how bringing a class to visit the Bentley fit into a class's overall plan.

The seminar also gave archivists a chance to demonstrate their expertise. This happened in a couple of ways. First, in terms of knowledge about the collections. One stated in his post-seminar interview, "Just being familiar with the library's collections was probably the biggest asset I brought to it. We had some good discussions in the seminar itself, with [two professors] in particular. I would say we offered them a lot of good suggestions that I think will be useful for them."[18] Archivists also demonstrated their expertise in terms of knowledge about archival processes and related policies that could be brought into classes, such as field work and copyright.

---

17. Bentley archivist, interviewed by Joe Lueck, Ann Arbor, MI, 2017.
18. Bentley archivist, interviewed by Joe Lueck, Ann Arbor, MI, 2017.

Archivists also became more aware of what faculty and students need to best make use of the archives. They have learned in the seminar how faculty use or do not use finding aids with their classes, for example, and this informs how archivists think about adapting and making accessible description tools. "I think more about my end users," one stated.[19] The seminar has helped broaden archivists' perspectives on the impact of their work, reaffirming its importance. At the same time, providing archivists who don't ordinarily teach an opportunity to get involved creates another set of advocates who can help argue for the significance of teaching with archival materials as one of the fundamental public services in archives.

The seminars and subsequent classes have brought Bentley archivists and Michigan faculty together for sustained conversations, and in doing so have increased our understandings of each other's work. Faculty have recognized a need to change some of their teaching strategies: to work with archivists more deliberately before classes begin and provide ways for students to engage with them throughout the class. The Bentley has advocated for attending as much to the process of teaching and learning about archives as to the final product. Archivists have also learned more about pedagogical practices, have felt their expertise validated, and have recognized a need to attend to faculty and students as users.

Why Teaching with Archives Matters

The response of faculty and archivists to the seminar has been very positive, but the ultimate goal of the seminar is not just to transform faculty and archivists, but also to improve the ways we are—collectively and in collaboration—teaching with archival material, so that students can better learn with them. This is important for a number of reasons. Students need to understand how to use archives and special collections to become competent researchers, but also to become competent citizens who think critically and creatively. This is of course the goal of

---

19. Bentley archivist, interviewed by Joe Lueck, Ann Arbor, MI, 2017.

all liberal arts education. Specifically, archival materials force students to ask critical questions—who wrote this, why, who was the audience, what was their perspective, what was the context?—with an urgency that other sources don't. Students can't escape these questions when they are in an archive. Working with archival material also allows for creativity, as students gain additional perspectives as they encounter different documents from the past.

I want to delve into one particular class that exemplifies the reach and scope teaching undergraduates with archives can have, especially when staffing and resources allow for prioritizing engagement. This class, Visual Identity and Branding, in the University of Michigan Stamps School of Art and Design, brought together university students and community partners and combined creative and critical thinking. It was a learning experience for me because the process of the course and the work the students produced were different than most of the classes I had worked with.

From its beginnings, this course came together in ways that were unusual for the Bentley. We approached a faculty member who teaches a class about art and design with a specific idea about creating a partnership around bicycle safety. When our Associate Director approached me about doing this class with an emphasis on some kind of bike safety campaign, I honestly wasn't sure what role the Bentley could play. Though the professor had brought students to the Bentley before, we don't really have a lot of materials about bikes and bike history, much less bike safety. At the first meeting with the faculty member, it became clear that there would be more to this class than showing students our materials. He was keen on the idea of doing something with bikes but because the course was client based, he needed help connecting to community members who might actually have a project and could be the client. My husband is involved in several local bike education and advocacy organizations in Ann Arbor and its surroundings. Mining his connections, we came up with three "clients": three different bike advocacy groups from the county. That was one way I could help, but I still wasn't sure how the archives would fit into the class.

The purpose of the course was for students to design a logo and a coherent visual identity for the client. The faculty member had taught similar classes before and the semester was carefully staged to provide opportunities for students to get feedback and reflect on their creative design process. The clients met with the students three times through the course of the semester, under the thoughtful eye and ear of the instructor. In the first interaction, the clients provided information about their backgrounds and needs. Students listened and asked questions, practicing skills that will help them elicit the kinds of information they will need to work with clients in the future. The next two meetings with clients were opportunities for the clients to see what students developed and to provide feedback. In these sessions, the students offered brief explanations of what they were attempting, and the clients provided feedback on what was successful in their specific context. As students worked, they wrote blog posts, which the clients could access, and in which the students described their creative processes. The students each created a logo and then a series of "applications" using the logo, in order to create an associated visual identity. The applications included letterhead, business cards, posters, a web landing page design, and more. Finally, the students each produced a book: a curated final project of their work. The books showed the development of their ideas, changes the visual identity had undergone, and final products. The clients then had the option to negotiate with any student to use their material.

So where did the archives fit? I learned that even in such a class, archival materials help provide context, and they also provide crucial inspiration. My preparation for the students' visit was a bit different and more intense than for other classes. Before the semester began, I met with the instructor three times for an hour or so each time. Our first meeting consisted simply of learning about the structure and goals of the class. I also attended two meetings with the faculty member and the clients and one of the first class sessions, in which the students met the clients. During that session, the clients introduced their organizations and provided background about bicycling broadly and in the area. They then took questions from students, both about background and about the mission and purposes of the three different organizations.

Attending these meetings helped me better understand the clients' needs and the kinds of questions the students were asking. That understanding helped me think about Bentley material that might be useful for them. The materials I pulled contained bike-related content—photographs of the Michigan Wheelmen from the nineteenth century, personal papers of bicyclists describing tours, papers of bike groups, photos of twentieth-century University of Michigan students riding, photos and text from university offices trying to plan for and contain bicycles on campus, road maps, and bike-specific maps. Because the students weren't using materials to do research in a more traditional way, I wanted to provide them a space to interact with the materials and each other in a useful way. I didn't think a traditional worksheet—asking students to think about sourcing, context, and corroboration—would work with these students. Instead, I tried to provide them with as much time as I could to interact with the materials in a way that made sense to them. During their visit to the Bentley, I introduced students to the library, to archives more generally, and to the materials, by telling them a bit about who created each collection, what types of material it had in general, and what I had specifically brought out for them to look at. Then, the students spent two hours looking through this material. While there was no requirement that the students use historical images in the application portion of their projects, most of them took photographs that could be used for inspiration or as part of their design.

A few weeks after their visit to the Bentley, the clients and I attended a critique session with all the students, and it was there that we saw the first impact of their visits to the archive. After the course was over, one of the clients stated, "It would've been easy to ask the question, 'why are we going to the Bentley?'" But as the process unfolded, it was impressive to see how inspiration took shape and drew from—in ways both direct and indirect—the historical documents."[20] At that mid-point critique and at the end of the semester, the students demonstrated how the visit to the archives had affected their designs.

---

20. Truly Render, "Designing for Change: Bike Advocacy Branding," News and Features, Vice President for Communications, Arts and Cultures, University of Michigan, June 14, 2017, https://arts.umich.edu/news-features/designing-for-change-bike-advocacy-branding/, accessed May 23, 2019.

More than Managing a Calendar 103

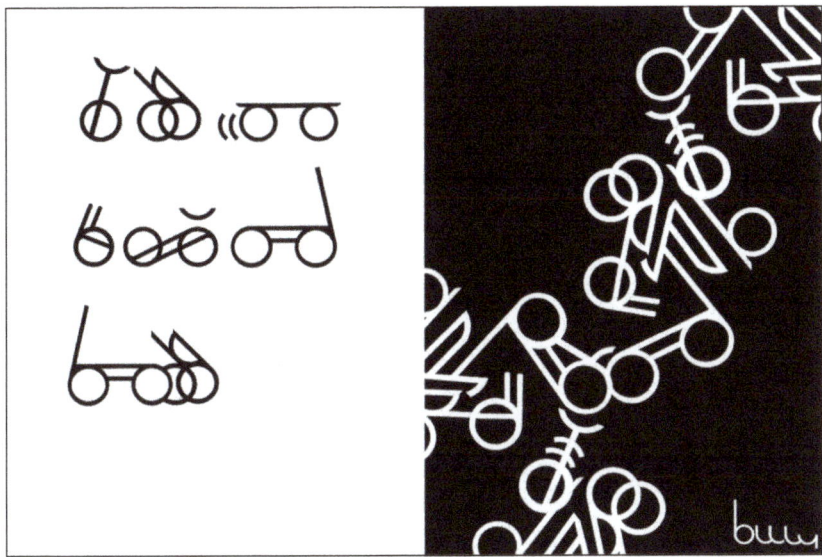

Figure 1. A student's design prior to visiting the Bentley. Anna Brooks, Design Update: Finding Solutions over Simplicity, February 19, 2017.

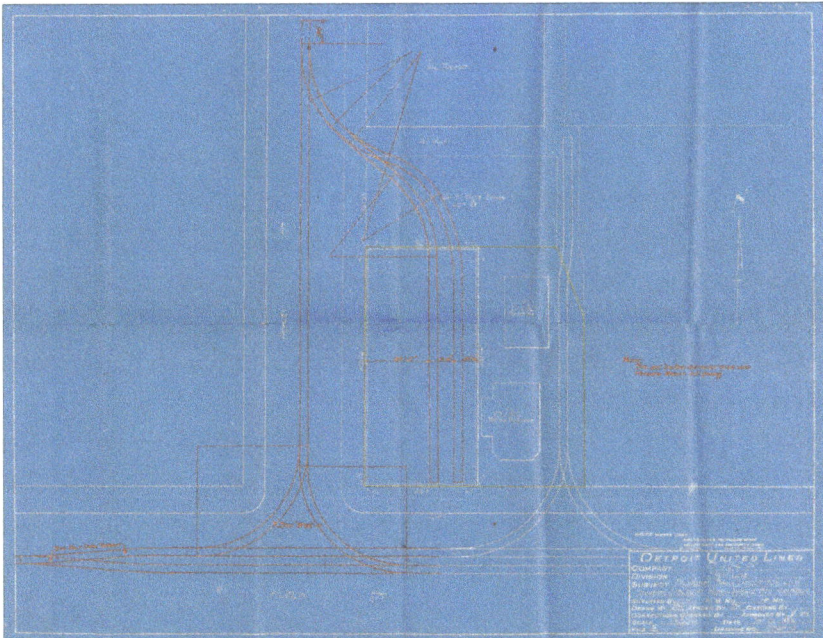

Figure 2. A sample of material a student looked at while at the Bentley. Anna Brooks, Design Solutions from Local History, March 14, 2017. Proposed track layout for Ann Arbor, Michigan Interurban, 1913. Records, Box 2, Bentley Historical Library, University of Michigan.

Figure 3. Student design after visiting the Bentley. Anna Brooks, Design Solutions from Local History, March 14, 2017.

One student took inspiration from the Bentley's materials in an abstract direction (Figure 1). After viewing the street and rail maps during the session at the library (Figure 2), this student incorporated a very abstracted map into her logo (Figure 3). In her blog she wrote, "The city maps in particular seemed like strong visual direction because of their colors, ties to motorists and non-motorists alike, and the fluidity of their design."[21]

Their visit to the archives gave students an opportunity to learn more about the history of bicycles. Even though they were not history students, nor was the class aiming to teach them about the past, the students recognized a broader bicycling world, connected to but bigger than that which they encountered through their clients or even through their own experiences biking. The lesson for them was larger

---

21. Anna Brooks, "Design Solutions from Local History," March 14, 2017, https://muser751.wixsite.com/adylanb/single-post/2017/03/14/Design-Solutions-from-Local-History, accessed September 10, 2019.

than one about bikes or about what one learns in the archives. The lesson for these design students is that they need to look beyond their own experiences, and even perhaps beyond their clients' experiences, to really create their best work. I learned from this class as well. I learned that archives can teach students much more than content, or even context, and that additional content and contextual knowledge can greatly enhance creative work. I also saw the impact of student reflection on their works in progress throughout the semester. This class also demonstrated quite clearly that collaborating with faculty to create effective courses using archives can be a resource-intensive undertaking, but one that can be rewarding for everyone involved.[22]

~ ~ ~

I began this chapter by suggesting that the work instruction archivists and special collections librarians do moves beyond managing a calendar—though that is certainly a component. Positions like the one I hold at the Bentley, in which most of my time is devoted to course plans, prep, and teaching, can serve as a bridge between instructors outside our libraries and archives and the materials and staff within. My position, additionally, affords me time to think, read, and write about this work. There is great potential for transformative teaching with archives. Archivists, librarians, faculty, and students can recognize instruction as more than providing access to materials and managing a calendar. Teaching with archival material is an opportunity to create true partnerships between instructors in archives and libraries and those outside of them. The more these partnerships are understood as vital to the education of undergraduates, the greater the opportunity archivists and special collections librarians will have to teach students to use the past to better understand the present and knowledgeably shape the future.

---

22. One of the advocacy groups, The Bicycle Alliance of Washtenaw, contracted with a student to use the logo she had created. https://www.bikewashtenaw.org/, accessed May 24, 2019.

FROM THE OUTSIDE LOOKING IN: AN EARLY CAREER LIBRARIAN BUILDS AND THEN BRINGS A SEAT TO THE TABLE

Ashleigh D. Coren
University of Maryland, College Park

Introduction

How can early career librarians prepare for a career in instruction? This question is difficult to answer and becomes even more complicated for those interested in a career in archives. In this academic personal essay, I share parts of my career trajectory, briefly address the lack of theoretical and practical pedagogical training in archival programs, and discuss how to build a community of practice in a library. Lastly, I explore my new role as a teaching and learning librarian in special collections, and I offer suggestions for library managers or administrative staff interested in developing similar positions at their institutions.

Background

At the University of Maryland, College Park, I am the special collections librarian for teaching and learning in Special Collections and University Archives, which is a completely new role for the library system. As a member of the Instruction & Outreach unit of Special Collections, I lead instruction sessions, serve as a resource for my colleagues in best practices in information and primary source literacy, manage our assessment program, and collaborate with various campus partners and units to promote the discovery and use of our collections for personal and scholarly research.[1] Other responsibilities include acting as a liaison to our Teaching and Learning Services department and representing special collections on committees and advisory bodies related to instruction in the library. My position exists as a response to the department's need to restructure its education program and provide in-house instructional support to staff. Unlike some of my peers in similar positions, I am not affiliated with public services, and I do not develop or assess collections, or lead major outreach efforts. The teaching and learning librarian position job at the University of Maryland was created to make instruction its own separate area of expertise within special collections.

My goals as an instructor, particularly one who works in special collections, are to create a learning environment that is a safe space for intellectual exploration, curiosity and debate, and to preserve the uniqueness of special collections. At the University of Maryland Libraries, our instruction program is student-centered, and we believe students should be active participants in their own learning experiences. As an instructor, my role is to act as a critical thought partner to our users both inside and outside of the classroom.

---

1. On the College Park campus of the University of Maryland, the Instruction & Outreach unit in Hornbake Library Archives is separate from the Teaching and Learning Services Department of McKeldin Library.

What's the Problem, and How Do We Fix It?

In 2015 and 2016, a group of archivists conducted a survey on archival education and confirmed a long-standing deficiency in our graduate archival programs. They wrote, "Archivists should be exposed to teaching with primary sources in their graduate programs so they may explore ideas and practice techniques under the guidance of an instructor over an extended period of time."[2] My own training as an instructor reveals, as the quote points out, the lack of exposure many archival students have to primary source literacy or pedagogical practices in our master of library science (MLS) programs. It's clear that information schools and archival programs should be more intentional about integrating how to teach primary source and information literacy into the curriculum. However, as Nicole A. Cooke points out, the purpose of graduate education is "To a certain extent . . . to teach the basics, the foundation. It becomes impractical to think we can teach students all the dimensions of their jobs."[3] While it may be beneficial to introduce graduate students to primary source literacy, we should not put the onus on archival professors to train graduate students to be teachers. Introducing students to existing initiatives like the Libraries Active Learning Institute at Dartmouth College or groups like Association of College and Research Libraries' Rare Books and Manuscripts Section's Instruction and Outreach Committee can provide aspiring teachers ways to connect with practitioners. For anyone interested in learning about teaching, I highly suggest they reflect upon and be able to answer these two questions: what are your values, and what are your benchmarks of success in the classroom?

It takes much time and energy to become an effective instructor, and it's a continuous process that cannot be completed in a graduate

---

2. Lindsay Anderberg, Robin M. Katz, Shaun Hayes, Alison Stankrauff, Morgen MacIntosh Hodgetts, Josué Hurtado, Abigail Nye, and Ashley Todd-Diaz, "Teaching the Teacher: Primary Source Instruction in American and Canadian Archives Graduate Programs," *The American Archivist* 81, no. 1 (2018): 203.

3. Anne Ford, "Other Duties as Assigned," *American Libraries Magazine*, (January 03, 2019), accessed January 31, 2019, https://americanlibrariesmagazine.org/2019/01/02/mission-creep-other-duties-as-assigned/.

program. I've spent six years learning how to properly define what information literacy is and be able to critically reflect on the value of teaching it. After graduating from my MLS program, I gained foundational knowledge in instructional design from both research and teaching librarians, and also school librarians, which has benefited me greatly. Archivists have much to learn from collaborating with school and research librarians, particularly in the areas of engagement and integrating technology in the classroom. Additional experiences, like participating in a residency program and teaching for-credit undergraduate courses, helped me to discover different communities and practitioners in the field. Other opportunities that helped me grow as an instructor included attending conferences and participating in the Association of College and Research Libraries' Information Literacy Immersion Program.

It is imperative to point out that a great contributor to my success has been the financial support I've received from various institutions and associations since starting my first full time academic position in 2015. It costs money to nurture new and existing areas of expertise, and having access to professional development funds has been a great benefit. Traveling to symposia and visiting different research libraries to discover new software and tools, identify collaborators, and observe different teaching styles is an important part of the training process. My ability to fully immerse myself in my practice without distraction is a privilege, and a very expensive one. In the last year there has been an influx of new archival instructional positions in higher education[4], and while I am optimistic about the trend, I am concerned about the possible lack of support these individuals may experience.

---

4. Since fall 2017, over a dozen archival positions with the words "teaching" and "instruction" in their job title have been featured on ArchivesGig, an employment website. Meredith Lowe, ArchivesGig, accessed April 1, 2019, https://archivesgig.com/.

Developing a Community of Practice

I've been in my position for more than a year and it's been extremely fulfilling to support the work of faculty and graduate students on campus, particularly those who are committed to highlighting the voices and stories of underrepresented communities. At the University of Maryland Libraries, I work within a community of instructors (both in and outside special collections) who are committed to promoting and providing access to our collections to foster research, discovery, and community building at both the campus and local level. Library initiatives created by our teaching and learning services staff, like the Peer Teaching Observation Program and the Fearless Teaching Institute, create a space for librarians from different departments to exchange ideas and unpack the siloed mentality that can prevent transparency and collaboration in academic institutions. These initiatives are opportunities for me to demonstrate, through my work, how the Guidelines for Primary Source Literacy complement both the ACRL framework[5] and the shared vision for instruction in the University of Maryland Library system. Participating in these library-wide programs can connect archival staff to teaching and learning and research services departments. They are our key collaborators and allies in our efforts to increase the use of our collections.

Some of the most important contributors to our community, however, are our exceptional undergraduate and graduate student workers, interns, and volunteers. One of the ways in which I've attempted to address the "pedagogy problem" in our archival programs is through mentoring and offering opportunities for both archival and nonarchival students to learn about primary source literacy and be included in our group of instructors. I co-lead classes with information science graduate students and work with UMD Libraries' research and teaching fellows to develop teaching collections and online learning modules for various courses. I also try to encourage and create opportunities for our graduate

---

5. "Framework for Information Literacy for Higher Education," Association for College and Research Libraries, accessed April 1, 2019, http://www.ala.org/acrl/standards/ilframework.

assistants in special collections. They may be interested in learning about instruction or want to feel better prepared for the job market.

Support and Retention

Institutions that are interested in creating or supporting existing instructional positions should create realistic and flexible expectations for success. The original set of goals for my position, which included increasing the yearly number of instructional sessions and serving as in-house support for special collections staff, quickly needed be reevaluated. My work also affected our access and researcher experience teams, who had to accommodate the increase of students in our reading room and their requests for both processed and unprocessed collections. After nine months, it became clear that I needed to work with my colleagues to develop shared goals for our instruction program. In hindsight, there should have been an initial assessment of the existing educational program to create best practices. This would have enabled the department to identify long- and short-term needs and to construct two or three specific and achievable goals that follow a timeline. The assessment should have involved considering the following questions: do we want to focus on increasing the number of classes we teach every semester? Should we place more energy into creating connections with underserved disciplines and campus units or focus on strengthening our current partnerships? Are there existing department-level learning outcomes and workflows for managing instruction requests and educational outreach? Any archive or special library interested in making their instruction program a strategic initiative must understand that these are very different job responsibilities, and they require the utilization of different kinds of expertise—outreach, instructional design, community building, and vision planning. At the start, instruction librarians should work with their colleagues and administrative team to define manageable teaching loads and recognize possible examples of scope creep. Without a well-defined vision, institutional support, and periodic goal-setting, there is the risk of failure. At the present I still wrestle with the weight of managing different priorities.

My status as a contingent employee with a renewable one-year contract also affects my ability to both perform my job duties and pursue creative prospects that may enhance our menu of services. The lack of job security drives me to take a more project-based approach to my work, and this prohibits me from thinking programmatically, especially if the underlying problem reveals that the issue is cultural or involves improving communication.[6] Also, the emotional labor involved in developing trust with one's colleagues to achieve shared goals takes a considerable amount of time, which needs to be accounted for when creating temporary or contract positions. People in contingent positions or similar staffing categories can only consider short-term opportunities and easy wins, which can affect the sustainability of any library instruction program.

Conclusion

In this chapter I've shared a number of factors that have contributed to my success as an instructor and that will influence the success of current or future instructional librarians in the archival profession. These factors include building a community of practice, fostering relationships with instructional librarians and subject specialists, and opening our teaching spaces to offer information science students a chance to learn about instruction. However, we must contend with how a lack of financial support for professional development, unfocused organizational planning, and precarity can prevent long-term success for these librarians. Until then, we must continue to affirm the work we all do in our spaces and challenge each other to do and be better every day.

---

6. Myron Groover, "On Precarity," Bibliocracy (blog), January 6, 2014, http://bibliocracy-now.tumblr.com/post/72506786815/on-precarity, and Adena Brons, Chloe Riley, Crystal Yin, and Ean Henninger, "Catalog Cards from the Edge: Precarity in Libraries," presented at the BC Library Conference, Vancouver, BC, May 10, 2018, https://osf.io/sqvcm.

OH, IT'S YOU AGAIN: INCREASING ARCHIVAL INSTRUCTION THROUGH SUSTAINABLE RELATIONSHIPS

Joshua Youngblood
University of Arkansas

This chapter addresses a strategic approach to increase an instruction program within limited parameters and offers techniques that worked for the special collections of the University of Arkansas Libraries. It highlights the positive outcome of significant growth in both classes and students in the collections, which was achieved through strengthening relationships and taking opportunities for change. This chapter also discusses capacity concerns and efforts to balance growth in the instruction program with other institutional priorities and duties. With rapid growth in an instruction program comes the added challenge of providing opportunities for in-depth engagement for every student. Although deeper learning and use of the collections by students were goals, the strategy discussed here embraces the entire spectrum of outreach possibilities on a growing campus as part of a staged approach to gradually expand.

The sustainability suggested here is twofold. First, sustainability refers to growth that can be maintained without negatively impacting other aspects of the "environment" of a special collections operation, such as the quality of research services and individual relationships with students. That connotation of being able to support positive growth is influenced by the second meaning of sustainability: collaborative relationships that feed (or sustain) each other and create continuing opportunities going forward between special collections and programs and teaching faculty on campus.

The special collections under discussion here at the University of Arkansas Libraries has grown its instruction program successfully over seven years of outreach and responsive design. The strategies and approaches that have proven successful include:

- Collaborative assignment and curricula design
- Encouraging honest feedback, redesign, and regular follow up
- Incorporating a variety of materials and utilizing promotional opportunities to sow the seeds for future projects
- Aligning other outreach activities to reinforce instruction
- Focus on values and relationships . . . but acknowledging limits and advocating for more

None of these approaches would have worked on its own, and none of them entailed abandoning the nascent instruction program in place in 2011 or the traditional approaches (such as show and tell tours or one-off sessions) being practiced. Instead, the instruction and outreach services gradually built upon existing relationships, adjusted the design and level of instruction sessions, and grew until reaching capacity, while accumulating sufficient evidence of achieving the targets established by the libraries' administration.

Sustainable Growth—A Stepwise Process Using All Techniques to Increase Instruction Opportunities

In 2011, I was hired as a new faculty member. The position was as the Research and Outreach Services Librarian, a tenure-earning appointment as an assistant librarian. I was replacing a longtime faculty member who retired after providing the department's instruction services for decades. At the same time I was hired, the university undertook an aggressive plan to dramatically expand the student population. Beginning in 2011, the university expanded from 19,000 to 28,000 students in five years. My position in special collections was not a part of the university-wide expansion, although the libraries recognized that a new emphasis on outreach in special collections was needed. As a faculty position it required scholarly publication and professional service, along with far-reaching professional duties, including supervising two full-time staff members in the reading room of special collections. The position of research and outreach services librarian was not a new one, but the position was now modified to include outreach. Even as the campus was growing rapidly, special collections added no other full-time positions. None of the other faculty positions—head, assistant head, and head of manuscripts, university archivist, and special projects librarian—had duties that included instruction or research services. And none of the five full-time nonfaculty positions included instruction.

As part of the University Libraries' gradual restructuring of the department, I was charged with implementing a new emphasis on outreach, while also managing the research services unit for the department. The instruction program in our special collections was active, but in a nascent state. As with many special collections that have relied on existing relationships with faculty already familiar with the collections, we worked for many years reliably with the history department, in addition to a few other programs on campus. I inherited an expectation that I would introduce students to curated archival collections and essential printed sources. This agreement was primarily with professors of Arkansas history, the history of the South, and Civil War and Reconstruction, with ad hoc opportunities in topical areas such as the New Deal in America or projects on political culture with classes from the communications department.

The Directive to Expand

Beginning in 2012, the administrative directive for special collections outreach could be summarized as "do more": more exposure, more classes, and more disciplines. The dean's office asked research services and the new faculty member (me) to grow an instruction program that had been limited in students and class visits. My duties also included continuing to tend to other relationships, such as with nonstudents on campus, distance researchers, and other faculty and staff on campus. The research services unit included a reading room supervisor, a reading room assistant, and two part-time student workers. But with limited staff availability, no classroom, and intense research services commitments, including instruction sessions and nearly 1,000 visiting patrons per year in a space with only nine tables, there were inevitable challenges to meeting these expectations.

Teaching with Archives

The special collections at the University of Arkansas reflect strengths in local history and the donations of prominent individuals associated in some way with the university. Some of those strengths include civil rights in Arkansas (particularly the Little Rock Central High School desegregation crisis), the United States Civil War in the trans-Mississippi Theater, and Arkansas politics, which in our case includes the senatorial papers of J. William Fulbright and Dale Bumpers, among others.

These collections represent an opportunity to encourage research beyond the historical strengths and take available resources—such as the papers of longtime governor and controversial Democratic power broker, Orval E. Faubus—in new directions. Faubus is notorious in the history of the Civil Rights Era for his obstruction of integration. Consequently, his papers are most often consulted by students because of their relevance to the Civil Rights Movement in Arkansas. He was governor for fourteen years, so his political archives touch every aspect of social and political life in Arkansas in the 1950s and 1960s. The Faubus papers represent an opportunity to work with students and professors to approach research assignments creatively by exploring socioeconomic and cultural issues and materials available in complex political collections, even if we are revisiting "old friends": archives often used but taken for granted.

As the flagship university of the State of Arkansas, the University of Arkansas has a high proportion of first-generation students and students from economically diverse backgrounds. The actions of the libraries, like the rest of the work of the university system, must show a demonstrable benefit to the state with a focus on student success. This success is measured in various ways, from higher retention rates and undergraduates finishing in under six years to moving toward national achievement across the university's disciplines and placement in top-tier graduate schools.

Outreach by the Numbers

"How many of you have been to special collections?" I ask this question of almost every class or outreach event audience I have on campus, or even in the community. In one particular class—I visited their regular classroom to provide a preliminary session early in the semester before they came to the library—every hand was raised. Eighteen students, and every single one had worked in special collections. Their familiarity with special collections provided evidence of the success of my intentional stepwise process to grow stronger relationships with students over the entirety of their time at the university, while also scaling up the types of service offered to the teaching faculty in whose classes those students are enrolled. That process included:

1. Introductions through show and tell, class visit, or tours
2. Co-taught or multi-visit active-learning classes
3. Variety of instruction sessions and subject areas over years
4. Integration of one-on-one consultations and encouraging long-term relationships with every student.

Having an established relationship with every senior history major in a capstone class is evidence that the process is working. It has been so effective that it seems like you can see the phrase, "Oh, it's you again," pass over the students' faces as they once again begin to research and consider primary sources with the special collections librarian.

The strategy developed early on in response to the directive to grow instruction had three key components:

- Move established relationships forward in deeper ways
- Embrace new campus programs and priorities, foregrounding the potential for collaboration
- Innovate with new partners to meet objectives, theirs related to curricula and ours related to qualitative and quantitative improvement

Targets for expansion included capitalizing on what was in place already and leveraging those pieces into sustainable future opportunities. Special collections could reach beyond the history department, but in a way that allows for repeat sessions and deeper use rather than a high proportion of one-off introductory sessions. As the campus evolved, we responded to new programs, such as the campus-wide University Perspectives, a required course providing an overall introduction to college life for freshmen. Other programs, such as medieval and renaissance studies, were rejuvenated with additional faculty and funding. The university also recently christened a School of Art, and special collections responded by expanding the number of art classes we work with to four per semester.

Between 2012 and 2018, special collections experienced a 400% increase in instruction even as staffing levels remained the same, even declining temporarily due to attrition. In 2011, the department recorded only eleven instruction sessions, almost all of them with history classes, serving fewer than 170 undergraduates. For 2017–2018, special collections provided instruction to at least forty-seven sessions, including more than six hundred students from more than eight units on campus. During the 2018–2019 academic year we held nearly seventy instruction sessions, including multiple classes working in the department during intersession periods between regular semesters and classes working in the reading room on multiple occasions, resulting in nearly 1,000 student visits to the department. Over that same time span, 2011–2018, the number of research patrons increased from 1,200 to more than 1,400 per year. The department is now largely at capacity for instruction in the reading room. A recent shift in roles within the department has allowed more staff to be involved in instruction, and a new position has been created specifically for instruction. New strategic priorities to incorporate include navigating service models related to changes in offsite storage and a large-scale renovation of the central library building, where special collections occupies a third of the basement level.

Moving Established Relationships Forward

Using the Libguides platform, and in collaboration with the library subject specialist, our special collections department produced resource suggestions and descriptions of assignments for students, in order to direct them to required archives and secondary sources. We also encouraged more regular follow-up class visits, built in and structured consultation times, and offered class study sessions without guidance—or "lab time"—that students were required to attend.

More significant was the co-development of new class projects and research assignments with professors willing to change their methods and challenge their students in new ways. For instance, through work with Jeannie Whayne, a distinguished faculty member who has worked with the department for years, we challenged students to transcribe and digitize plantation records in order to better understand agricultural history. I also partnered with the history librarian at the time to work more closely with regularly scheduled classes that are required for history majors. Meanwhile, together with the history librarian, we began to more aggressively solicit instruction in emerging areas of strength for the history department, including sub-Saharan and Caribbean studies.

In an effort to improve the collaboration of the history librarian and special collections, some history librarian duties have been assigned to me (the special collections instruction librarian). This consolidation of duties has created additional capacity issues, even as it has helped achieve other goals, including increasing the number of research consultations with undergraduate students and incorporating more special collections resources in introductory information literacy sessions. Another way the department has tried to increase instruction opportunities is by incorporating special collections into the orientation for new graduate students. The students get a detailed overview of collection strengths and tours of the facility, and we offer to collaborate with teaching assistants on designing assignments and introducing research to their students.

Collaborating with New Campus Programs

Even students who arrive on campus with strong research skills and experience with databases and research in digital environments can learn something different through the tactile interaction with materials in special collections. As Nancy Cervetti states, "Working on a flat screen in one's office or study, as important and efficient as it may be, cannot replace embodied experience."[1] Hands-on interaction with primary material in special collections augments the learning experience of students. They see the materials within the context of related collections and experience the materiality of objects with unique histories, from their provenance to the evidence of use by generations of students and researchers over years. The desire of teaching faculty and students for the visceral experience of learning provides an opportunity for closer collaboration with campus programs and the chance for innovation.

Special collections wanted to work with more than just history

---

1. Nancy Cervetti, "Bodies in the Archive," *RBM: A Journal Of Rare Books, Manuscripts, & Cultural Heritage* 15, no. 2 (2014): 124–134, Library & Information Science Source. For a closer discussion of need for physical access to special collections materials to achieve literacy goals, see Todd Samuelson and Cait Coker, "Mind the Gap: Integrating Special Collections Teaching," *portal: Libraries and the Academy* 14, no. 1 (2014): 51–66.

classes, and the Honors College provided a potential partner for further growth. There was a previous, noninstructional relationship with students from the Honors College in the form of processing internships in special collections, which lasted from 2010 to 2016. While those internships offered great work experience and good hands-on introductions to one aspect of archival work, they were one-dimensional, as they didn't allow students to pursue independent research projects.

Through seizing opportunities to work with newly arrived junior faculty and soliciting instruction opportunities available because of unique course offerings, we have grown from teaching one Honors College class per semester to four. Part of this growth has been in response to the College's innovations. For instance, we have supported the University's implementation of intersession classes (two-week for-credit classes positioned between semesters) and offered an embedded librarian with classes that require extensive research on focused themes. Integrating with the Honors College also entailed focusing on their suite of new course designs. The college's Signature Series features outstanding teaching faculty tailoring unique course offerings around unusual aspects of their own research, such as the history of soccer in Africa, or Manuscripts, a semester-long look at the creation of texts. The Retro Readings series allow distinguished faculty on campus to provide interdisciplinary courses built around significant works of literature or thinkers with remarkable legacies of letters. Special collections has partnered with these courses on topics as varied as a student-led redesign of the building the Honors College occupies and the published works of Charles Darwin. The Manuscripts course, for example, entailed numerous visits to special collections to access a wide array of materials, from medieval folios and early print books to literary archives and artist books.

The closer partnership with the evolving program of courses in the Honors College has resulted in new internships in the research and outreach areas of special collections and has demonstrated a significant return on investment, even including collection development opportunities. The manuscripts students moved from studying the context of books as artifacts and the material study of manuscripts, to actually making vellum and creating their own versions of medieval manuscripts. Through an assignment I co-developed with the teaching faculty member, students had to apply their enhanced understanding of the complex origins and meanings of manuscripts to select and recommend new acquisitions for the special collections. The course led to financial support from the Honors College to actually purchase the items recommended in one of the assignments; these are now available in special collections.[2]

Mutual Innovation and Responsive Design

Expanded and innovative work with the music department demonstrates special collections' further success at taking pre-existing relationships and using the collections to enhance learning beyond artifactual evidence and historical context, including helping performance and theory students gain information literacy skills as researchers. Using archives, regional print collections, and rare books resources such as hymnals and folk music anthologies, the special collections has moved from working with one or two music faculty per semester to four or five faculty, as well as visiting lecturers. In the process, we have gradually evolved from quick introductions to semester-long projects. Students are learning about music history, but they are also using both marquee and lesser known collections to practice music bibliography, score analysis, and other discipline-specific skills. Through conversations with new faculty about their previous experiences and effective teaching practices at other institutions and graduate school, we have implemented new-to-us projects. Semester to semester we collaboratively assess and review previous assignments—sometimes assignments they inherited as pieces of core curriculum— transitioning past collaborations to better serve new faculty covering required courses. In the process we are able to leverage unique and remarkable—and provincial—collections to meet teaching objectives. For instance, the

---

2. "Honors Student Selects Key Acquisitions for Special Collections," *University of Arkansas News*, October 23, 2018, https://news.uark.edu/articles/45208/honors-student-selects-key-acquisitions-for-special-collections.

department holds two of the most significant archives of African American composers, both originally from Little Rock, Arkansas: William Grant Still and Florence Price. Through exercises such as score analysis, students utilize world-class music manuscripts to learn composition techniques and bibliographic context.

For three consecutive years, we have collaborated with a musicology professor. We incorporate folk and regional music archives, rare print holdings, and archives related to international cultural exchange and the work of the United States State Department into this professor's instruction on music bibliography and research methods for music majors. We are now incorporating digital humanities components, such as GIS layers, for digital exhibits. These digital exhibits build upon student research related to the international cultural exchange records and the papers of the Fulbright Scholars program.

Reaching Capacity

Teaching relationships with classes such as the musicology students conducting GIS research represent the value-rich opportunities that special collections is striving for. That sort of hands-on, collaboratively designed teaching also requires a significant amount of time and investment from special collections staff, including those in research services, who are involved with activities such as digital duplication. With the 400%+ increase referred to above, the department has now approached the limit of how much instruction we can handle, if we are to continue to offer deeper teaching and high-quality research services.

The successful growth has occurred with recognition of limitations. Logistical and physical space issues limit the capacity for continued scaling for years to come. The department only has one reading room to host visiting classes, with only twelve tables for researchers and one fourteen-seat meeting table. Those classes visit concurrent with forty-nine open hours per week. The instruction has expanded from one or two sessions in that space every two weeks in 2011 to five to ten a week during the spring semester of 2019. Meanwhile, the department consistently serves more than 1,000 nonstudent researchers per year.

A second limitation is retrieval of collections. In 2018, there was a change in service models across the libraries system. About 80% of archival collections that were previously onsite, readily accessible by the reading room and instructors, are now held offsite. Now it takes longer to get materials onsite for instruction and researchers. It's also more complicated to track wide varieties of collections as they are being held on reserve or used by the array of patrons sharing the research space, including staff, visiting scholars, undergraduate students, and K-12 students. Given these limitations, the focus on relationships has allowed the instruction program to modulate and move toward slower expansion. That flexibility is currently focused on gradually increasing from the current level of sixty sessions per semester in the reading room and not outstripping capacity at the expense of other core service responsibilities.

Strategic Growth and Sustainability

Since I was hired as the Research and Outreach Services Librarian in 2011, I have provided nearly all of the instruction for the department. But recently, and due in part to the increased instruction portfolio that I developed, the Special Collections Department has undergone another restructuring of duties. There are now five other staff and faculty integrated into the instruction program. That growth in staffing resulted from demonstrating the success of the instruction program, a focus on collaboration across units in the department, and new leadership in the department emphasizing continued expansion of instruction, including allocation of available positions. A new, entry-level faculty position added to the department in summer 2019 includes instruction duties.

To create integrated and sustainably scaled instruction, we have leveraged closer relationships with interdisciplinary classes and professors: we offer material, space, and services to inspire new course designs.

Instruction librarians and outreach archivists looking to increase the volume of their offerings can use familiar, common strategies and approaches, but implementation of these techniques does not always result in more active learning. Examples of common strategies include reaching out directly to new faculty through cold-calling or using campus press releases as excuses to contact more established faculty; soliciting programs to participate in their non-library campus events to grow awareness of available resources; and tabling at student orientation sessions and campus life events. Scholars of teaching with primary sources have in recent years increasingly emphasized hands-on practice instead of increasing the numbers of student visits through "show and tell" classes and other outdated instruction techniques.[3] However, embracing a broad range approaches to diversify and augment a nascent teaching program can be coupled with hands-on work by students and focused learning.[4]

Our department's strategic growth has manifested in several ways. Teaching with primary sources is now taking place with departments that might not have previously thought of special collections, including graphic design, agricultural business and science, and mathematics. The challenge remains to reach even more programs in a sustainable fashion, allowing the full use of staff resources without creating strain on shared spaces or the workflows related to regular research services. The department's outreach program (outside of seeking instruction opportunities), is increasingly tailored so that events and communications make the department's availability for teaching collaboration apparent. Challenges we still face include an uncertain time frame for expanded classroom space and integrating new technology. We are meeting these challenges through increased use of available spaces across campus and partnerships with programs outside of our libraries with established technology labs, as well as further coordination with our libraries' evolving Digital Services Department. We also want to do more before semesters begin to help teaching faculty develop skills and curricula that incorporate special collections materials.

---

3. There are many examples of the discussions of the shift away from "show and tell." For one example that looks at learning outcomes in particular, see Peter Carini, "Information Literacy for Archives and Special Collections: Defining Outcomes," *Portal: Libraries & the Academy* 16 (1), 2016: 191–206.

4. Anne Bahde, "Taking the Show on the Road: Special Collections Instruction in the Campus Classroom," *RBM: A Journal of Rare Books, Manuscripts, and Cultural Heritage* 12, no. 2 (2011): 75–88. http://rbm.acrl.org/index.php/rbm/article/view/354/354.

Our instruction program grew from twelve sessions per year in 2011 to more than sixty in 2018. That growth was accomplished through building on existing relationships, offering a variety of approaches, gradually scaling up the depth of instruction with teaching faculty and programs, and nurturing ongoing relationships with new faculty and students. The growth in the instruction program is now reflected in the restructuring of duties for staff and faculty across the department to include instruction and the addition of a new faculty position focused on teaching with archives. The department is currently seeking ways to use alternative spaces in order to accommodate more and larger classes, as visiting researchers and special events continue to stretch the capacity of the department's space. Challenges for the future include the need for additional teaching space: currently, the department still must limit the number and size of sessions, as well as the depth of teaching that can be done with each class. We also continue to seek ways to extend the outreach to the rapidly growing STEM (science, technology, engineering, and math) programs on campus. Overall, the growth in the instruction program and the relationships developed with teaching faculty and students reflects significant success. We have found that meeting teaching faculty and students where they are creates a culture where students are ready to learn and comfortable with the archives and staff members waiting to work with them.

Bibliography

Anderberg, Lindsay. "STEM Undergraduates and Archival Instruction: A Case Study at NYU Polytechnic School of Engineering." *The American Archivist* 78, no. 2 (2015): 548–566.

Bahde, Anne. "Taking the Show on the Road: Special Collections Instruction in the Campus Classroom." *RBM: A Journal of Rare Book, Manuscripts, and Cultural History* 12, no. 2 (2011): 75–88.

Brett, Jeremy, and Jasmine Jones. "Persuasion, Promotion, Perception: Untangling Archivists' Understanding of Advocacy and Outreach." *Provenance: The Journal of the Society of Georgia Archivists* 31, no. 1 (2013): 51–74. Library & Information Science Source. Accessed September 9, 2015.

Brown, Amanda H., Barbara Losoff and Deborah R. Hollis. "Science Instruction Through the Visual Arts in Special Collections." *portal: Libraries and the Academy* 14, no. 2 (2014): 197–216. https://0-muse-jhu-edu.library.uark.edu/, Accessed January 31, 2019.

Carini, Peter. "Information Literacy for Archives and Special Collections: Defining Outcomes." *portal: Libraries & the Academy* 16, no. 1 (2016): 191–206.

Germek, George P. "Starting almost from scratch: Developing special collections as a teaching tool in the small academic library." *College & Undergraduate Libraries* 23, no. 4 (2016): 400–413.

Harris, Valerie A., and Ann C. Weller. "Use of Special Collections as an Opportunity for Outreach in the Academic Library." *Journal of Library Administration* 52, no. 3, 4 (2012): 294–303. Library & Information Science Source. Accessed September 9, 2015.

Horowitz, Sarah M. "Hands-on Learning in Special Collections: A Pilot Assessment Project." *Journal of Archival Organization* 12, no. 3–4 (2015): 216–229.

Hubbard, Melissa A. and Megan Lotts. "Special Collections, Primary Resources, and Information Literacy Pedagogy." *Communications in Information Literacy* 7, no. 1 (2013): 24–38.

Lawrimore, Erin. 2014. "Mission Critical: Effective Internal Advocacy for Your Archives." *Journal for the Society of North Carolina Archivists* 11, no. 1 (2014): 2–18. Library & Information Science Source. Accessed September 9, 2015.

Mazella, David, and Julie Grob. "Collaborations between Faculty and Special Collections Librarians in Inquiry-Driven Classes." *portal: Libraries and the Academy* 11, no. 1 (2011): 467–487.

Reynolds, Matthew C. "Lay of the Land: The State of Bibliographic Instruction Efforts in ARL Special Collections Libraries." *RBM: A Journal of Rare Book, Manuscripts, and Cultural History* 13, no. 1 (2012): 13–26.

Samuelson, Todd, and Cait Coker. "Mind the Gap: Integrating Special Collections Teaching." *portal: Libraries and the Academy* 14, no. 1 (2014): 51–66.

Theunissen, Yolanda. "Developing and Promoting Outreach Services for Elementary and Middle Schools: Case Study of a Rare Map Library at a Public University." *Journal of Map & Geography Libraries* 3, no. 2 (June 2007): 5–22. Library & Information Science Source. Accessed September 9, 2015.

Tomberlin, Jason, and Matthew Turi. "Supporting Student Work: Some Thoughts about Special Collections Instruction." *Journal of Library Administration* 52, no. 3–4 (2012): 304–312.

Totleben, Kristen, and Lori Birrell. *Collaborating for Impact: Special Collections and Liaison Librarian Partnerships*. Chicago: Association of College and Research Libraries, 2016.

Yaco, Sonia, Caroline Brown, and Lee Konrad. "Linking Special Collections to Classrooms: A Curriculum-to-Collection Crosswalk." *The American Archivist* 79, no. 2 (Fall/Winter 2016): 417–437.

Youngblood, Joshua. "Always be Teaching: Reading Room Exhibits and Displays as Instructional Tools." Poster presentation. Society of American Archivists Annual Meeting. Portland, Oregon, July 23–29, 2017.

Youngblood, Joshua. "Academic Archives and Public Engagement: Connecting Collections with the Communities They Serve." Conference paper. International Council on Archives Annual Conference. Reykjavik, Iceland. September 28, 2015.

LABOR AND MATERIALS: TOWARDS A SUSTAINABLE SPECIAL COLLECTIONS INSTRUCTION PROGRAM

Shira Loev Eller
Leah Richardson
The George Washington University

Introduction and Institutional Context[1]

Faculty, students, library leadership, donors, and colleagues all have ideas about what is important when it comes to special collections instruction. These ideas commonly focus on participants, objects, and pedagogy, but the work of librarians and archivists[2] may not come immediately to mind. This chapter is about special collections

---

1. A note about the works cited in this chapter: In keeping with our commitment to open access (OA), we only cite articles that have an OA version available. In some cases, when we were unable to locate an OA version, we have reached out to authors directly and asked that they consider making a copy available in an institutional or disciplinary repository. We cite the publication of record and link to the OA version in these cases. Moreover, we have only linked to OA platforms that are truly open and do not require the creation of an account.

2. We use the terms librarians and archivists broadly throughout this chapter to include all library workers.

instruction from a labor perspective—not explicitly about pedagogy or class assignments or outreach, which are important and have been addressed elsewhere by our colleagues.[3] We will discuss our effort to reimagine our special collections instruction program in a way that allows us to scale up meaningful learning experiences, while scaling back unproductive aspects of our teaching. In this chapter, we distill our theoretical and idealistic professional values into a set of practical applications of collaboration, communication, and documentation that we have operationalized in the service of a sustainable and visible special collections instruction program. We will be conspicuously practical and grounded in the specifics of work such as maintaining spreadsheets, calendars, and email, and schlepping book cradles to and from classrooms.

At the heart of this discussion and our collaboration is an insistence on articulating and acknowledging the labor behind special collections instruction. It is our position that making labor visible and centering the people doing the work is necessary in order to fully incorporate the pedagogical innovations in primary source literacy of the recent past. We must reiterate that this is a local approach, meaning it works for us and does little to dismantle the larger systemic issues around labor in academia. It does, perhaps, gesture at the potential of locally focused efforts to affect larger change.

We work at a private research university located in Washington, DC, and are based in two departments within the university's main campus library. Leah is the Instruction and Outreach Librarian in the Special Collections Research Center (SCRC) and Shira is the Art and Design Librarian in the Research and User Services (RUS) department. SCRC and RUS have shared goals of providing collections, research assistance, and instruction to the students, faculty, and staff of the university. SCRC functions as a blended special collection that maintains the university archives, manuscript collections, and rare book collection.

---

3. See the Society of American Archivists, Teaching with Primary Sources - Bibliography; live version Zotero group: https://www.zotero.org/groups/76402/teaching_with_primary_sources/items/collectionKey/2BKBRTH8/

Literature Review

Our profession has evolved from one that encourages the integration of special collections into the broader research library, to one that demands the leveraging of special collections to support and expand the teaching and research mission of the institution. This literature review will briefly cover the professional histories that have shaped our current labor conditions and will take a more expansive look at the recent literature around labor issues in the library and archives profession.

Discussion abounds about the placement and potential of special collections within academic research libraries; this narrative and vision have been the norm for at least a decade. As Charlotte Priddle has pointed out, the division between special collections and the rest of the university library has historically been the most difficult to bridge.[4] Priddle describes the perceived disconnect between special collections and the academic libraries to which they belong: ". . . special collections remain in many ways separate or 'other' to the larger library system and are often viewed as such by other departments."[5]

And there is no shortage of publications, reports, task forces, and issue briefs from the Association of Research Libraries (ARL) and other professional organizations[6] on this topic. Whether special collections departments are viewed as leaders of the research library, with their distinctive collections, or as small and obscure departments lacking visibility, the recommendation remains that special collections must become part of the larger library ecosystem.

---

4. Charlotte Priddle, "Bridging the Internal Gap: Special Collections and 'In-Reach,'" *RBM: A Journal of Rare Books, Manuscripts, and Cultural Heritage* 16, no. 1 (Spring 2015): 35–47, https://doi.org/10.5860/rbm.16.1.434.

5. Ibid., 40.

6. Examples include: "Special Issue on Mainstreaming Special Collections," *Research Library Issues: A Report from ARL, CNI, and SPARC*, no. 283 (2013). http://publications.arl.org/rli283/; *Special Collections in ARL Libraries: A Discussion Report from the ARL Working Group on Special Collections* (Washington, DC: Association of Research Libraries, 2009), http://www.arl.org/bm~doc/scwg-report.pdf; Philip N. Cronenwett, Kevin Osborn, Samuel Allen Streit, and Nicolas Barker, eds., *Celebrating Research: Rare and Special Collections from the Membership of the Association of Research Libraries* (Washington, DC: Association of Research Libraries, 2007), http://www.celebratingresearch.org/about/index.html.

Amid this discussion, "collaboration" emerges as a key concept. In the foreword to *Collaborating for Impact: Special Collections and Liaison Librarian Partnerships*, Anne Kenney points to several factors that are beginning to break down divisions between special collections and the rest of academic libraries. One factor, she writes, is that libraries "continue to expand their support for teaching information literacy" in light of an increased focus on critical thinking and the concomitant importance of primary source research.[7] This work of breaking down divisions arises from collaborative efforts between special collections and liaison librarians and often revolves around library instruction. In fact, Chela Scott Weber specifically identifies library instruction as an important collaborative space in OCLC's 2017 "Research and Learning Agenda for Archives, Special, and Distinctive Collections in Research Libraries."[8]

While we certainly benefit from greater visibility and integration of special collections, expectations of increased staff time and expertise are often not met with an increase in resources. Eira Tansey describes the current conditions of labor in academic institutions in her 2015 article "Archives Without Archivists," and warns of the vulnerability of the archives and libraries therein, stating: "As American culture has expanded neoliberal business models to institutions such as government and education, invisible labor is often a target for budget cuts and other practices that normalize the experience of 'doing more with less,' a mantra that is all too often accepted as fait accompli in archives."[9]

In the last five years, there has been a profusion of writing focused on undervalued, unrecognized, and precarious labor in libraries. Many of these scholars ground their writing in the history of librarianship as a "feminized" profession, and situate library work within emotional,

---

7. Anne Kenney, foreword to *Collaborating for Impact: Special Collections and Liaison Librarian Partnerships,* eds. Kristen Totleben and Lori Birrell, (Chicago: Association of College and Research Libraries, 2016), v., http://www.ala.org/acrl/sites/ala.org.acrl/files/content/publications/booksanddigitalresources/digital/9780838988848.pdf

8. Chela Scott Weber, *Research and Learning Agenda for Archives, Special, and Distinctive Collections and Research Libraries* (Dublin, OH: OCLC Research, 2017), 10, https://doi.org/10.25333/c3c34f.

9. Eira Tansey, "Archives Without Archivists," *Reconstruction: Studies in Contemporary Culture* 16, no. 1 (2016): 2, http://dx.doi.org/doi:10.7945/C2GW2F

affective, or invisible labor. Lisa Sloniowski, in "Affective Labor, Resistance, and the Academic Librarian,"[10] examines the gendered dimensions of affective labor specific to liaison and reference librarians. Through a Marxist and feminist reading, she identifies areas of our work that are under-recognized or invisible because service work is viewed as caregiving or "pink-collar" rather than the intellectual labor that it is. April Hathcock extends this critique and emphasizes the intersection of gender and race in the devaluation or lack of recognition of work done by nonmale, nonwhite people in libraries and other professional settings, and advocates for this behind-the-scenes labor to "count."[11]

Stacie Williams, in her 2016 keynote address at the Digital Libraries Forum, "All Labor Is Local," traces carework and its subsequent devaluation to the legacies of slavery in the United States and the enslaved people that built and sustained many colleges and universities still in existence today. Williams does more than reframe carework—she asserts that "we can and must acknowledge the need for a radical understanding of labor that points to caregiving as the beating heart that has made it all possible from the very beginning, because everyone ... has benefited directly from that labor."[12]

While the authors above address external views, historical legacies, and oppressive structures that impact library work, Fobazi Ettarh calls out "the set of ideas, values, and assumptions librarians have about themselves and the profession that result in beliefs that libraries as institutions are inherently good and sacred, and therefore beyond critique," what she calls "Vocational Awe"—a term she coined, which has powerfully disrupted the discourse around librarianship and labor. Ettarh describes how this self-conception potentially leads to overcommitment, job creep, and diminished well-being in service of the Library as Sacred Institution.[13]

---

10. Lisa Sloniowski, "Affective Labor, Resistance, and the Academic Librarian," *Library Trends* 64, no. 4 (2016): 645-666, http://hdl.handle.net/10315/31500.

11. April Hathcock, "Let Labor Be Labor," *At The Intersection* (blog), May 12, 2016, https://aprilhathcock.wordpress.com/2016/05/12/let-labor-be-labor/.

12. Stacie Williams, "All Labor Is Local," *Medium* (blog), November 13, 2016, https://medium.com/@Wribrarian/all-labor-is-local-344963e33051

13. Fobazi Ettarh, "Vocational Awe and Librarianship: The Lies We Tell Ourselves,"

The success of a sustainable and scaled-up special collections instruction program necessarily requires that we resist our proclivity towards vocational awe and the potential for overcommitment and erasure of labor contained therein. In other words, we have to put the people before the things. If we cannot control the external factors that ask us to do more with less, we can actively reject the damaging narratives about libraries and archives that we uphold and that render our labor invisible. With this framework in mind, we turn to our local context and the ways in which we attempt to overcome problematic labor practices—self-imposed and otherwise—and use this space to advocate for archivists and librarians as workers.

Sustainability

What began as a co-teaching partnership involving our respective areas of expertise—rare books/archives and artists' books—has expanded into a holistic approach to conceptualizing a sustainable special collections instruction program. For us, sustainability in an instruction program means: the ability to grow and continue to provide meaningful instruction; being in the position to provide a mix of instructional offerings, from one-offs to semester-long partnerships; the freedom to be open to experimentation and new ideas; and the capacity to say "yes" as often as possible—all of which we hope to achieve without overburdening staff or crowding out other goals and responsibilities unrelated to instruction. Moreover, sustainability means tending to the entire ecosystem of primary source instruction and conceptualizes growth as a delicate balance among the needs of librarians/archivists, faculty, and students.

Like many academic special collections in the US, George Washington University's SCRC has experienced significant growth in instruction in the last decade, as trends in higher education have increased focus on critical thinking skills, and librarians and archivists have promoted the

---

in *In the Library With the Lead Pipe* (January 10, 2018), http://www.inthelibrarywiththeleadpipe.org/2018/vocational-awe/.

archives as uniquely situated to support this goal.[14] Between the years 2015 and 2018, SCRC has seen a 40% increase in both the number of instruction sessions and number of students visiting for instruction; in the last ten years there has been a 70% increase in the number of instruction sessions held. This success can be attributed to directed outreach efforts to bring more visibility to the collections as resources for teaching. We are now confronted with how to support the resulting growth and not become victims of our own success.

As of 2019, we have more staff from SCRC and other units actively participating in special collections instruction. Nonetheless, we are a lean organization and everyone is committed to multiple roles and projects beyond instruction. Because of this, Leah approached Shira for support managing the increased demand for special collections instruction and for help building a sustainable instruction program. From the outset, we envisioned a program that engaged colleagues from across the organization to participate in all aspects of special collections instruction, from selection of materials and design of goals to the more routine elements, such as paging materials, room set-up, and calendar management. As experienced instruction librarians, we were aware that much of the work of instruction happens in the preparation phase. Additionally, as regular partners in teaching in special collections, we knew the challenges unique to that environment, such as requesting materials from offsite storage, onsite paging, and the physical and time-consuming work of class set-up and take-down. These aspects of the labor of special collections instruction are part of what makes the work so demanding of our time and energy, and liable to contribute to burnout. Avoiding the overburdening of staff is a primary objective of our collaborative approach.

---

14. Peter Carini, "Information Literacy for Archives and Special Collections: Defining Outcomes," *portal: Libraries and the Academy* 16, no. 1 (2016): 194. https://digitalcommons.dartmouth.edu/dlstaffpubs/17/.

Scaling Up and Scaling Back

A useful paradigm for thinking about sustainability in special collections instruction is: What do we want to scale up, and what do we have to scale back in order to do so? Overall, we want to increase meaningful learning experiences with special collections materials. While detailing specific lesson plans or pedagogical methods is outside the scope of this chapter, we can define meaningful learning experiences as those that engage primary source and information literacy, as well as relate directly to course objectives and assignments. The Guidelines for Primary Source Literacy, developed by a joint task force of the Society of American Archivists and the Rare Books and Manuscripts Section of the Association of College and Research Libraries (SAA-ACRL/RBMS) articulate a broad framework for "the knowledge, skills, and abilities needed by researchers to successfully conceptualize, find, analyze, and use primary sources."[15] In conjunction with ACRL's Framework for Information Literacy for Higher Education, the Guidelines provide a touchstone for creating lessons and instruction sessions that help students develop critical thinking skills.

In creating meaningful learning experiences with special collections materials, we also aim to scale up collaborative teaching while scaling back on gatekeeping and silos. When subject experts come together to, for example, select materials from several collections, the result can be a more enriching experience for students, as well as a decrease in the workload of any one individual. As Kristen Totleben and Lori Birrell point out, collaboration encourages synergistic work that leverages the knowledge and skill sets of its contributors, creates stronger relationships, and ultimately benefits students and researchers.[16]

---

15. ACRL RBMS-SAA Joint Task Force on the Development of Guidelines for Primary Source Literacy. "Guidelines for Primary Source Literacy," revised June 2018, 4, https://www2.archivists.org/standards/guidelines-for-primary-source-literacy.

16. Kristen Totleben and Lori Birrell, introduction to *Collaborating for Impact: Special Collections and Liaison Librarian Partnerships*, eds. Kristen Totleben and Lori Birrell (Chicago: Association of College and Research Libraries, 2016), ix. http://www.ala.org/acrl/sites/ala.org.acrl/files/content/publications/booksanddigitalresources/digital/9780838988848.pdf.

Another aspect of our teaching we wish to scale up is critical librarianship, which is "a movement of library workers dedicated to bringing social justice principles into our work in libraries."[17] We must situate archival objects in the context of authority, power, and absences,[18] as well as thoughtfully contextualize traumatic or objectionable content.[19] In addition, we can practice critical pedagogy by elevating students' voices. Actions which de-center the authority of the librarian by moving away from show-and-tell instruction to activities which, in the words of Patrick Williams, "[cede] control of the session to the observations and interests of the student"[20] allow learners to think critically about the formation of knowledge and the historical record.

As alluded to above, scaling up these meaningful learning experiences means scaling back on instructional models that are not providing value or that take too much time for too little impact. For example, while show-and-tell may be appropriate in some situations,[21] this teaching style can increase labor for librarians while failing to provide meaningful learning experiences for students.[22] The performative nature of presenting each object (sometimes for multiple sessions in a row) creates a burden on the librarian to entertain rather than guide student learning and unwittingly instantiates the librarian/archivist as the

---

17. See "Critlib" about page: http://critlib.org/about/.

18. ACRL RBMS-SAA Joint Task Force on the Development of Guidelines for Primary Source Literacy, "Guidelines for Primary Source Literacy," revised June 2018, 3. https://www2.archivists.org/standards/guidelines-for-primary-source-literacy.

19. Andi Gustavson, Rhae Lynn Barnes, Lae'l Hughes-Watkins, Analú López, Elizabeth Smith-Pryor, "Ethically Teaching Histories of Violence, Racism, and Oppression in Special Collections Classrooms" (panel presentation, Teaching Undergraduates with Archives Symposium, University of Michigan, Ann Arbor, MI, November 5, 2018).

20. Patrick Williams. "What Is Possible: Co-Exploration & Critical Learning in Archives & Special Collections," in *Critical Library Pedagogy Handbook, Volume 1: Essays and Workbook Activities*, eds. Kelly McElroy and Nicole Pagowsky (Chicago: ACRL Press, 2016), 116. https://hcommons.org/deposits/item/mla:927/.

21. Carini, 197.

22. We are not arguing for the wholesale obliteration of the show-and-tell model of special collections instruction. There are many cases in which this model can produce a meaningful learning experience. We are focusing on the labor of the show-and-tell that is exacerbated when there are no learning objectives and seeing "treasure" is the goal.

authority—the precise hierarchy we aim to dismantle through the practice of critical librarianship. Preparation for an instruction session—from coordinating with faculty, to selecting and pulling materials, to lesson planning, set-up, and break-down—is time consuming. It serves us well to use our limited time to have the most impact on student learning. Therefore, we should aim to scale back on visits that are primarily imagined as field trips or, alternately, have too many objectives to realistically address in one session.

Scaling Up and Scaling Back in Practice

The three main areas of practice that we decided to address are communication, documentation, and collaboration. In order to be successful, we need to better communicate our roles and value and set expectations. We need to better document the administrative and intellectual work of instruction and share that documentation to make the work visible and reproducible. And we need to push the boundaries of collaboration with faculty and library colleagues.

Communication in practice
Communication that promotes sustainability begins at the initial point of contact with faculty. At the start of discussions about instruction, it is important to state what you can and cannot do, define roles for each partner, and set actionable and measurable outcomes for the session's participants. In order to avoid confusion and dissatisfaction, clear expectations must be stated and agreed to at the beginning. This conversation about expectations should cover administrative details such as dates, times, and number of participants, and hefty details such as the themes of the course, assignments, and learning goals for the visit and overall course.

Defining roles is another aspect of good communication, but having these conversations with faculty has historically been plagued with barriers to honest talk about the work and value of librarians as educators. Sloniowski, inspired by the work of Cathy Eisenhower and Dolsy

Smith,[23] articulates the emotional labor exerted in conversations about our roles in instruction:

> These negotiations often involve having to educate faculty members as to the intellectual contributions librarians can make to their course or curriculum, and to resist reacting emotionally to the dismissiveness with which our services are sometimes received. As in all service positions, librarians are required, therefore, to disguise fatigue and irritation with library patrons, and our primary affective contributions involve willingness to help, patience, active listening—supplements to the flow of pedagogical power.[24]

We acknowledge that these conversations are tough and often require our emotional labor in order to resist the narratives that situate librarians and archivists as inferior in the academic hierarchy. But the difficulty of this task is precisely why it is important to overcome. When we are operating at our best to make the labor visible, we decide as partners the role of the librarian/archivist and the role of the instructor openly from the start. These roles can range from embedded co-teaching and curriculum design to minimal onsite support. We see the value of any role that creates a meaningful learning experience. Librarians and archivists have a role to play in pedagogical and instructional design but do not necessarily need or want to co-teach every session. A diversity of instructional styles represented across the sessions is a good model for growth and sustainability.

Another challenge to address through improved communication is stereotypes about librarians and archivists. Tropes around librarians in general ("librarians are magic") and around special collections in specific ("crown jewels, treasures, gems" and/or "pack rats, dusty basements, gatekeepers") obscure librarians' labor, intimidate students,

---

23. Cathy Eisenhower and Dolsy Smith, "The Library as 'Stuck Place': Critical Pedagogy in the Corporate University," in *Critical Library Instruction: Theories and Methods*, eds. Maria T. Accardi, Emily Drabinski, and Alana Kumbier (Duluth, MN: Library Juice Press, 2009), 305–318, https://scholarspace.library.gwu.edu/work/qv33rx376.

24. Sloniowski, 660.

create hierarchies within academic libraries, and misrepresent the value we provide to scholarship. We need to push back against the propagation of these ideas whenever they arise.

The instruction session is an ideal arena in which to challenge misconceptions about our work because it is a space dedicated (in theory) to unlearning and questioning historical "facts" and notions of authority. It is productive to frame these challenges to librarian stereotypes not as complaining but as a requisite feature of primary source literacy instruction, as articulated in learning objective 2.D. in the Guidelines for Primary Source Literacy:

> Understand that historical records may never have existed, may not have survived, or may not be collected and/or publicly accessible. Existing records may have been shaped by the selectivity and mediation of individuals such as collectors, archivists, librarians, donors, and/or publishers, potentially limiting the sources available for research.[25]

The learning objective above is rightly interpreted as addressing the problem of archival silences and biases, but we argue that it also lays the groundwork for making archival labor visible. We read this learning objective as a call to acknowledge the intervention of human labor in constructing and making accessible the historical record, for better or for worse, and to connect it for students to their local contexts: These are the archivists, librarians, and curators at your institution, whose salaries you pay with your tuition; these are their names and this is the work that they do. As Stacie Williams writes in her post "Implications of Archival Labor," "we can and should engage those who seek to use our materials: Bring them into our processes in a real and tangible way. Lift up and make visible the employees who do the digital or processing work, allow them to benefit professionally from their labor in the same way that their managers do."[26] Those of us with academic freedom

---

25. Guidelines for Primary Source Literacy, 5.
26. Stacie Williams, "Implications of Archival Labor," *On Archivy* (blog), April 11, 2016, https://medium.com/on-archivy/implications-of-archival-labor-b606d8d02014.

ought to use our voice and privilege to advocate for our colleagues in precarious positions and use every opportunity, especially in front of students and faculty, to educate our users about the value and work of the people who maintain archives and libraries. Talking about this does not detract from the learning experience but rather credits and raises the profile of the people who make access to these resources possible.

Documentation in practice

When we delivered this chapter as a talk at the Teaching Undergraduates with Archives Symposium at the University of Michigan in 2018, we were struck by how many questions and comments we received about our instruction documentation. We initially thought this was a tangential administrative point, but the response we received reinforces how small things like spreadsheets and shared folders can make a big difference in working toward sustainability.

We will outline what has worked for us in our partnership, but we recommend experimentation in this regard. We encourage good records management across any activity, librarian or otherwise, but don't have a one-size-fits-all approach for documenting instruction activities. We are indebted to our colleagues at TeachArchives.org for inspiring us to use tools and create strategies for managing our instruction work and for offering specific ideas to incorporate.[27]

We use our institution's Google Drive to create, manage, and share our instruction-related documents, allowing reuse by our library and faculty colleagues.[28] As an overarching organizational tool we use a Google spreadsheet, divided by academic year and semester, of all instruction sessions and events (see Figure 1). This spreadsheet helps

---

27. Robin Katz and Julia Golia. "Useful Tools," TeachArchives.org, http://www.teacharchives.org/project/useful-tools/.

28. We do not endorse the use of personal accounts to manage these records to avoid personal data expenditures and because these records are meant to live on to support the institution into the future and document the work of archivists and librarians. We are of the opinion that it is important to document and archive the work of librarians and archivists, as the genealogy of library and archival work and workers is often insufficiently represented or altogether absent within the historical record.

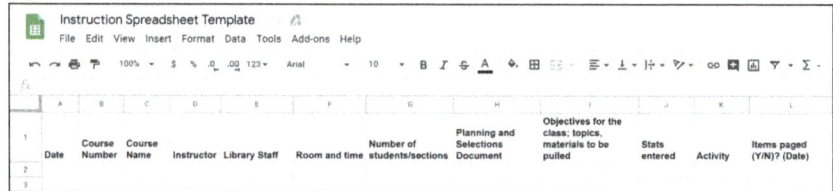

Figure 1. Template of our shared Google spreadsheet for tracking instruction sessions by semester.

us communicate administrative details such as titles of courses and events, contact names, number of participants, and room numbers. It also serves as a communication tool for workflows related to retrieval and reshelving. From within the spreadsheet we connect and link out to the selection lists, syllabuses, and activities for ease of access.[29]

If we are going to create a sustainable special collections instruction program, its success hinges upon transparent and accessible documentation to support growth. Shared documentation makes the work more efficient, thus allowing more time to nurture the intellectual labor of object curation and assignment design. We see documentation in this instance as an opportunity for growing a community of practice around instruction that doesn't involve committees and meetings in order to exist and flourish. A shared document, a shared folder, and the ability to add comments are sufficient conditions for our communities of practice to exist and be more inclusive.

Collaboration in practice

In many ways, working across departments has come as second nature to us, as our library is a highly collaborative organization that encourages work across institutional divisions. The concept of a community

---

29. We have found that having all the selection documents, syllabuses, activities, and lesson plans linked from within the current year's spreadsheet to be the most useful and efficient approach for us. These documents are also saved in folders organized by content type so that someone can locate all of the selection lists in one place. This is what works for us in our environment. A challenge exists in terms of a standardized file naming convention; identification of a specific document by class number /date/faculty name is useful during the teaching phase but is less so when we return to selection lists months or years later when the content is not easily discerned without opening and examining a document. Again, a one-size-fits-all approach doesn't exist.

of practice mentioned above, however, is slightly different from working across divisions. The Association of Research Libraries defines it as "groups of people in a shared field of expertise who seek to deepen their knowledge, skills, and engagement through regular interaction."[30] Expanding on that definition, we imagine a community of practice around special collections instruction that acts as a supportive space in which to make our work visible, cultivate partnerships, and grow through critique.

For us, collaborations that have been successful are not necessarily grand and impressive examples of embedded librarianship, even though we have had great faculty collaborations. Rather, the collaborations that have improved the sustainability of our instruction program have been rather mundane, such as extending room-booking privileges to staff outside of special collections; subject librarians being involved in all aspects of instruction, including room set-up and take-down; and putting out open calls for "all hands on deck" style classes. These small changes have helped us build relationships, find new partners, and achieve more parity around instruction work.

We see the persistence of silos within the profession as being partially self-imposed and upheld in our notions of expertise. We should resist the impulse to guard our own areas of expertise, leading us to view our colleagues as competitors rather than partners. "Turf talk" limits the benefits of collaborative thinking and ultimately creates more work for us. This paradigm for librarianship is toxic to growth and sustainability. This is not to discount knowledge and expertise, but to reframe it as a site of learning and inclusion. Similar to vocational awe, competitiveness is something that we all participate in to a lesser or greater extent. And like overcoming vocational awe, reducing competitiveness does not require a directive from our administrative leaders—rather, it requires us to take note of our behaviors, assumptions, and ideas around the boundaries of our work.

---

30. "Communities of Practice," Association of Research Libraries, https://web.archive.org/web/20190505024732/https://www.arl.org/focus-areas/arl-academy/communities-of-practice.

Conclusion

As special collections instruction continues to take on a more prominent role within academic libraries, it becomes increasingly important to center labor in our discussions around growth. We have argued that by implementing a local approach to special collections instruction in which we communicate effectively with our users, document our processes, and collaborate across areas of expertise, we can move towards achieving sustainability. We cannot stress enough the possibility for cross-departmental and cross-institutional collaboration, and we cannot encourage our colleagues enough to experiment with different models and share those approaches.

Our aim in sharing our approach is to provide a useful template for libraries and archives to expand upon. It is important to state, however, that our program has not yet been fully realized in our own local context. In libraries especially, we know there are changes constantly on the horizon and that sustainability is not a static state: It's not a place at which you arrive and your work is complete, and it's not something that can be addressed by one person, one activity, or even one group. By building communities of practice, we can support one another in adapting to change as it comes and be a collective voice for shaping change.

EXPERIMENTS IN COLLABORATION

DISCOVERING AND VISUALIZING THE INVISIBLE: IDENTIFYING AFRICAN AMERICAN STUDENTS AT THE UNIVERSITY OF MICHIGAN, 1853–1970

Brian A. Williams
University of Michigan

In conjunction with the University of Michigan's bicentennial, celebrated in 2017, the Bentley Historical Library launched an ambitious project to identify every African American student who attended the University of Michigan from its founding in 1817 to the Black Action Movement in 1970.[1] The year 1970 was selected as the cutoff date, since that was when the university began officially tracking students by race. The project was part of a critical examination of the university's past, especially as it related to race on campus.

In many ways, this project marked a new role for archivists. Rather than just collecting and curating archival content, we were uncovering content and creating essential data that would be valuable not just

---

1. Members of the project team have included Chiara Kalogjera-Sackellares, Clint Robert, Emily Swenson, Kyle Whitaker, Margaret Leary, Asia Van Horn-Lee, Greg Kinney, and Caitlin Moriarty. The team is led by Brian Williams.

to archivists, but also to students and faculty. Teaching and learning opportunities arose at many turns, as we gradually brought to light the triumphs and difficulties faced by African American students on campus. As one example, we discovered documentation about a 1921 case where a female African American student was refused service at a cafeteria on campus. This was a highly relatable example for current students, since it had a specific location and extensive details about the people involved. It sparked considerable discussion when brought up in class. As we built up the list of past African American students name by name, we found stories of tremendous perseverance along with oppressive prejudice. In a visualization librarian, we found a partner who could help us see patterns in our data. That partnership helped fuel collaboration with faculty members who could help us teach with the names, stories, and data that we compiled.

Mining Collections

As University of Michigan Professor Angela Dillard noted in her opening remarks at this symposium, it is easy to find and celebrate the firsts. But what about what comes after? Let's start with a first. The first women were allowed to attend the University of Michigan in 1870. We know who those women were. We also know the first African American woman to attend. Mary Henrietta Graham enrolled in 1876: "the first applicant of that persuasion," according to a contemporary newspaper account.[2] But who was the tenth or the one hundredth African American woman to attend? The Bentley Library's team of archivists, researchers, and volunteers set out to find an answer to those and similar questions, with an awareness that these questions have tremendous pedagogical promise.

We anticipated that the number of African Americans would be low, especially before 1900. The first known African American at the university enrolled in the medical school in 1853, and he was likely "passing" as

---

2. *Fenton Independent*, July 11, 1876, p. 3

white.³ During the Civil War, two students from the Caribbean enrolled in the medical school. One of them was summarily driven out of the school.⁴ Gabriel Franklin Hargo, in 1868, is generally seen as the first openly African American student to enroll.⁵ The low number of African Americans, especially women, is made clear in an alumnae survey response by Emily Harper Williams of the class of 1896. Responding to an alumnae survey nearly thirty years after she graduated, Williams recalled the thrill of running into President Angell a week after she came to campus and having the president call her by name. Years later, she realized that "it was probably not too difficult to remember the name of the one brown girl in a group of several hundred new students."⁶

As the project of identifying African American students got under way, we relied on earlier research that focused on Black athletes, Black lawyers, and Black medical students.⁷ We also consulted with others who undertook similar projects. Harvey Long, a graduate student in residence at the Bentley Library for a summer, gave us invaluable advice based on his research on African American students at the University of Wisconsin. Long and others confirmed that a review of photographs

---

3. Samuel Codes Watson attended the University of Michigan Medical School during 1853–1856. Watson was of mixed race. In Civil War draft registration records for Detroit from 1863, Watson is identified as white. Watson's biography in the *Michigan Manual of Freedman's Progress* published in 1915 clearly identifies him as "colored."

4. Cheney Schopieray, "Col[ore]d Men Not Admitted Here," *The Quarto,* William L. Clements Library, no. 46 (Fall-Winter 2016): 6–10, http://clements.umich.edu/Quarto/Quarto%2046_FallWinter,%202016.pdf.

5. Elizabeth Gaspar Brown, "The Initial Admission of Negro Students to the University of Michigan," *Michigan Quarterly Review*, 2. no. 4 (1963): 233–236. http://hdl.handle.net/2027/spo.act2080.0002.004:04.

6. Emily Harper Williams Alumnae Survey, "Hals-Har," Box 109, Alumni Association (University of Michigan) records, Bentley Historical Library. Available digitally at: https://quod.lib.umich.edu/a/alumnae/8730.0109.029/107?rgn=full+text;view=image.

7. These titles include: John Behee, *Hail to the Victors! Black Athletes at the University of Michigan* (Ann Arbor, Michigan: Ulrich's Books, 1974); Edward J. Littlejohn and Donald L. Hobson, *Black Lawyers, Law Practice, and Bar Associations 1844 to 1970: A Michigan History* (Detroit, Michigan: Wolverine Bar Association, 1988); Gloria A. Lewis Johnson, *Black Medical Graduates of the University of Michigan (1872–1960 inclusive) and Selected Black Michigan Physicians* (East Lansing, Michigan: G.A. Johnson Publishing, 1994).

UNIVERSITY OF MICHIGAN
ALUMNAE COUNCIL
ANN ARBOR, MICHIGAN

To the Alumnae:

We are making a special effort at the University of Michigan this fall to complete the record of our women graduates and former students in order to discover the extent of their influence and service. We want to find out the number of teachers, college officials, home makers, authors, artists, business women and women in other pursuits who received all or part of their higher education at the University of Michigan.

Will you, therefore, be good enough to answer and return the following questions, which will take only a few minutes of your time and yet will give us just the information we shall need? When this material has been collected it is to be tabulated and incorporated into a report similar to the reports prepared by other leading universities. A copy of the University of Michigan record, as compiled from this material, will be sent to you as soon as it is printed.

Probably few alumnae have had such a wide personal experience as would enable them to give concrete answers to all of the questions here included; but even should you consider your life lacking in aspects of special interest, rest assured that we are as anxious to have the blank filled out by you as by anyone else.

We enclose a stamped, return envelope and shall greatly appreciate your answering these questions at once. This information will be of particular value to us if you can send it to us by return mail.

Sincerely Yours,

JEAN HAMILTON, Dean.

Name in full _Emily H. Williams_
Maiden name _Emily A. Harper_
Address (Business) _Tuskegee Institute, Alabama_
Address (Home) _Tuskegee Institute Alabama_
Place of birth _Detroit Michigan_
Race _American Negro_
Single or married _Married_
Present occupation _Teaching English and Tuskegee Institute and housekeeping._

Figure 1. 1924 University of Michigan Alumnae Council survey filled out by Emily Harper Williams of the class of 1896. Source: "Hals-Har," Box 109, Alumni Association (University of Michigan) records, Bentley Historical Library. Available digitally at: https://quod.lib.umich.edu/a/alumnae/8730.0109.029/107?rgn=full+text;view=image

and yearbooks was a necessary step. These early explorations felt rather crude: we asked undergraduate students to review yearbooks and class photographs and note anybody who *potentially* looked African American.

We also harvested names from digitized newspapers and secondary sources. The digitized campus newspaper, *The Michigan Daily*, yielded a wealth of information, giving us benchmark data and confirming the low number of African American women on campus. In 1912, there were thirty-nine African Americans on campus: thirty-eight men and just one woman.[8] We mined published sources like early volumes of *Who's Who of the Colored Race* and the 1946 directory of *Holders of Doctorates among American Negroes*, by Harry Washington Greene, searching for mentions of University of Michigan and compiling the returns.

W. E. B. Du Bois and his journal, *The Crisis*, was beneficial to our ongoing research. We searched its annual educational issues in particular, seeking any mention of Michigan among the named graduates. We even found examples of the circular letters sent by Du Bois in the archived records of Michigan's presidents. Regrettably, Michigan did not always respond to the requests for information, at times proudly proclaiming that it did not track students by race. The archives of the Du Bois papers at the Special Collections and University Archives at the University of Massachusetts Amherst was another major asset, yielding names of correspondents and details at Michigan.[9]

By autumn 2018, the research project had identified more than 4,800 individual names and collected information on hometowns, local addresses, years of attendance, membership in campus organizations, and participation in athletics, as well as degrees and fields of study. We also recorded notes on achievements following graduation, while identifying the source of the information.

With thousands of names gathered, we began the process of verifying

---

8. "Michigan Third in Negro Enrollment," *The Michigan Daily*, December 1, 1912, 1, https://digital.bentley.umich.edu/midaily/mdp.39015071755669/226.

9. The W. E. B. Du Bois papers at the Special Collections and University Archives at the University of Massachusetts Amherst have been digitized and are available online at: http://credo.library.umass.edu/view/collection/mums312.

Figure 2. University of Michigan engineering class of 1871, standing on campus with surveying equipment. Source: "University of Michigan Classes, commencement," Box 66, Mortimer E. Cooley papers, Bentley Historical Library. Available digitally at: http://quod.lib.umich.edu/b/bhl/x-hs17197/hs17197

the racial identity. A photograph of engineering students from the class of 1871 in a surveying class on campus is a teaching example we use with students in classes.

How many African Americans are in this image? Three? Four? Certainly two, right? The correct answer is none. This underscores the importance of verifying and confirming our information. We used archived alumni records files on former students and census data as our main sources of verification. Our goal was to have at least two confirming sources. This type of corroboration is equally relevant to our project as it is to courses in primary source literacy.

In this example, as with many others, we looked for clues in the individual alumni files that could help establish identity. The alumni files often held photographs, clippings, and documents related to matriculation and enrollment. Perhaps most important, these files include semester enrollment cards. Students were required to fill out these index-sized cards each term. The cards contain a wealth of information, especially when students using the files learn, through sourcing, how to "read" the cards and what questions to ask. The cards include local campus address, home address, and answers to intermittent questions about religion, membership in fraternities or sororities, other schools attended besides Michigan, occupation of parents, and names of any relatives who attended U-M. The semester cards and other documents in the alumni file often yield important indicators. For example, do the files reveal any connection with historically Black colleges or universities (HBCUs)? Did the students study at or teach at an HBCU before or after they attended U-M? Were they members of one of the historically African American Greek lettered fraternities or sororities, collectively referred to as the "divine nine"[10]? In a few cases, we even found notations indicating "colored" on some documents in the alumni records file.

The local addresses became a key data point for the project. We began to recognize local addresses that repeated year after year. These repetitive addresses were local boarding houses owned or run by African Americans. The identification of clustering in local addresses helped give us insight into local patterns of segregation. Interviews with African American alumni as well as longtime community residents of Ann Arbor helped educate us about the racial divide and provided us with more information on the neighborhoods where African American students could live. We experimented with some preliminary mapping to confirm our understanding of the boundaries and impact of segregation.

Armed with repeating addresses and a knowledge of where African Americans could live, we searched the digitized student directories and collected the individual names that came up for key addresses or streets. The mining of directories resulted in the addition of hundreds

---

10. The oldest African American fraternity, Alpha Phi Alpha, was established at Cornell in 1906. A chapter was established at Michigan in 1909. Delta Sigma Theta, the oldest sorority, was established at Howard University in 1913, and had a chapter at Michigan in 1921. The fraternities Kappa Alpha Psi and Omega Psi Phi founded chapters at Michigan in 1922. Alpha Kappa Alpha established a sorority chapter at Michigan in 1935.

of names that we had not picked up by other means. Students who did not have a photograph taken or were on campus only for a short time emerged through this digital harvesting process.

Partnering with Campus Collaborators

The mass of collected information on local addresses spurred discussions with University of Michigan Visualization Librarian Justin Joque and his team about how we might visualize the collected local address data. A pilot project tested the concept: a 1930 Sanborn insurance map of Ann Arbor was digitally stitched together and used as the basis for mapping local addresses. The insurance map had the extra benefit of showing the physical footprint of the actual houses while providing additional neighborhood context. Mapping where the students lived brought the nature of housing segregation into sharp focus. It also helped us see where our research was heading and how it could be a rich teaching resource with the potential for additional layers of information and context. The visualization experiment gave rise to thoughts about how the compiled data on hometowns could be mapped to show matriculation patterns.

It was at this point that we partnered with Michigan in the World (MITW), a public history program for University of Michigan students to deeply engage with a topic using archival resources.[11] Matt Lassiter and his students provide another chapter in this volume, Give Earth a Chance: History Undergraduates and Environmental Activism in the Archives, describing MITW and their project. For the Department of History and the Bentley Library, it has been a rewarding program, enabling undergraduates to collaborate on history projects under the direction of a professor and a graduate student supervisor. Students conduct historical research, write reports, and curate digital exhibits. The students learn to experience archives, interpret history, and present material online for a public audience.

The 2018 MITW topic was "The Social World of Black Women at the University of Michigan, 1920–1975." It was taught under the direction of

---

11. See the Michigan in the World website at: https://lsa.umich.edu/history/history-at-work/programs/michigan-in-the-world.html.

LaKisha Simmons, Assistant Professor of History and Women's Studies. Simmons previously studied the lives of young Black women in segregated New Orleans and was able to adapt that research to take advantage of the data and history about African Americans at Michigan already compiled and uncovered by the Bentley's research project.

The 2018 MITW program explored the social world of Black women, investigating their lives before, during, and after their time on campus. Students in the course sought to engage several questions:

- How did Black students fit into Ann Arbor—where did they eat, socialize, and live?
- Were they welcome in all spaces of the city?
- Where did they come from?
- Where did they go once they graduated?
- How have they participated in activism on campus and in Ann Arbor?

The fact that the Bentley's research project had already done a lot of the preliminary digging and had amassed a large body of data allowed the students to focus on specific topics and issues that had emerged. It was a unique partnership between archivists, professor, and students. Students worked with archivists and their instructors to discover what life was like on campus for Black women.

The MITW program provided several opportunities for broad contextual education about race in Ann Arbor. A key learning point was that Jim Crow constructs were not limited to the Deep South. We found examples here in Ann Arbor of separate dining rooms for white and "colored" help in drawings of a hospital ward in 1903.[12] Property deeds from the 1920s and later demonstrated the inclusion of restrictive covenants barring African Americans from occupying property in Ann Arbor. Examples like these were eye-opening for the students and helped contextualize segregation.

---

12. Architectural drawing, "Foundation Plan - Rearrangement of South Half of Basement Psychopathic Ward for the University of Michigan, Mason & Kahn Architects – Detroit." Job 137, Drawer 22, Folder 12 Albert Kahn Associates records, Bentley Historical Library, University of Michigan.

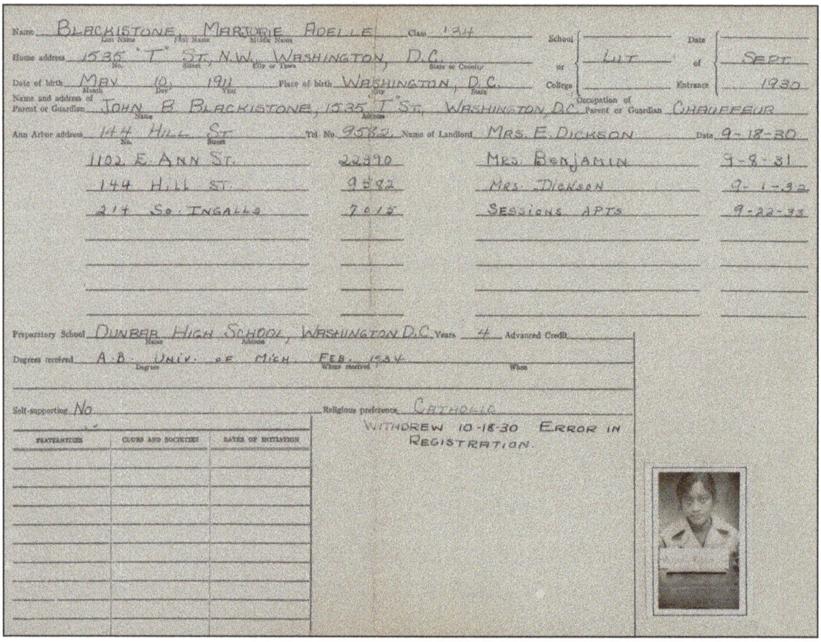

Name BLACKISTONE, MARJORIE ADELLE (Last Name, First Name, Middle Name) Class '34
School or College: LIT — Date of Entrance: SEPT 1930
Home address 1535 "T" ST, N.W., WASHINGTON, D.C. (No., Street, City or Town, State or County)
Date of birth MAY 10, 1911 (Month, Day, Year) Place of birth WASHINGTON, D.C. (City, State)
Name and address of Parent or Guardian JOHN B BLACKISTONE, 1535 "T" ST, WASHINGTON, D.C. (Name, Address)
Occupation of Parent or Guardian CHAUFFEUR

Ann Arbor address	Tel No.	Name of Landlord	Date
144 HILL ST	9582	MRS. E. DICKSON	9-18-30
1102 E. ANN ST.	22390	MRS. BENJAMIN	9-8-31
144 HILL ST.	9582	MRS. DICKSON	9-1-32
214 SO. INGALLS	7015	SESSIONS APTS	9-22-33

Preparatory School DUNBAR HIGH SCHOOL, WASHINGTON D.C. (Name, Address) Years 4 Advanced Credit
Degrees received A.B. UNIV. OF MICH. FEB. 1934 (Degree, Where received, When)
Self-supporting No
Religious preference CATHOLIC

FRATERNITIES	CLUBS AND SOCIETIES	DATES OF INITIATION

WITHDREW 10-18-30 ERROR IN REGISTRATION.

Figure 3. Student record for Marjorie Adelle Blackistone, maintained by the Dean of Women. Source: Marjorie Adell Balckistone File, Alumni Records, 1845-1978, Bentley Historical Library, University of Michigan.

Building from those examples, the instructors and archivists worked together to help the students learn to "read the records" and connect the documents to larger narratives.

The document in Figure 3 shows that the student came from Dunbar High School, a segregated high school, and lived at 144 Hill Street, one of the recurring addresses in student directories where African American students lived. This particular document also gave the name of the landlord, "Mrs. E. Dickson."

Esther Dickson, or "Mother" Dickson to the students, became one of the stories that the MITW students explored and researched in depth. Building on earlier research done by archivists on the project, we could help connect the story of the Dickson house to the contemporary struggle for African American women to integrate the women's dormitories at Michigan.

The fight for African American women to live in the dormitories came to a head when Mosher Jordan, a brand new dormitory with space for more than 400 women, opened in 1930. African American women applied to live in the new dorm but were instead directed to a markedly inferior boarding house, owned by the university, at 1102 East Ann Street. Documents in the archives at Michigan and in the W. E. B. Du Bois archives help tell the story of "University House No. 2." A notice sent to Du Bois for *The Crisis* stated, "University House No. 2, housing colored girls attending the University, has had a very successful year. Thirteen young ladies made their home at the House . . . a large, well arranged house, furnished by the University, and close to campus. Contrary to the general impression, living in the house is not compulsory."[13]

The notice went on to claim, "The University of Michigan is becoming a Mecca for Colored girls." Evidence about the women who lived in the house strongly disputes that claim. Activism and the threat of legal action finally made the university back down and allow African American women into the dormitories. We also learned something about E'Dora Morton, the first woman to live in the dorm, and the sole African American among 400 women. Subsequent women would continue to encounter resistance and would speak of bigotry and double standards.[14]

Beyond just using collections in the archives, the MITW students reached out to alumni and the families of alumni from many different generations to understand what it was like to be a Black woman on campus. Students used the contacts developed through our research to reach many of these women and interview them.

---

13. University of Michigan, University of Michigan notes, ca. July 11, 1932. W. E. B. Du Bois Papers (MS 312), Special Collections and University Archives, University of Massachusetts Amherst Libraries, http://credo.library.umass.edu/view/full/mums312-b191-i368.

14. Jean Blackwell Hutson spoke bitterly of the bigotry of her time at Michigan in the 1930s in "The 'Passing' of Elise Roxborough," Kathleen A. Hauke, *Michigan Quarterly Review* XXIII, no. 2 (Spring 1984): 159. Accessible online at: http://hdl.handle.net/2027/spo.act2080.0023.002:01. Jewel Plummer Cobb wrote negatively of her time at Michigan in the 1940s in "A Life in Science: Research and Service," *SAGE* Vol. VI, no. 2 (Fall 1989): 40.

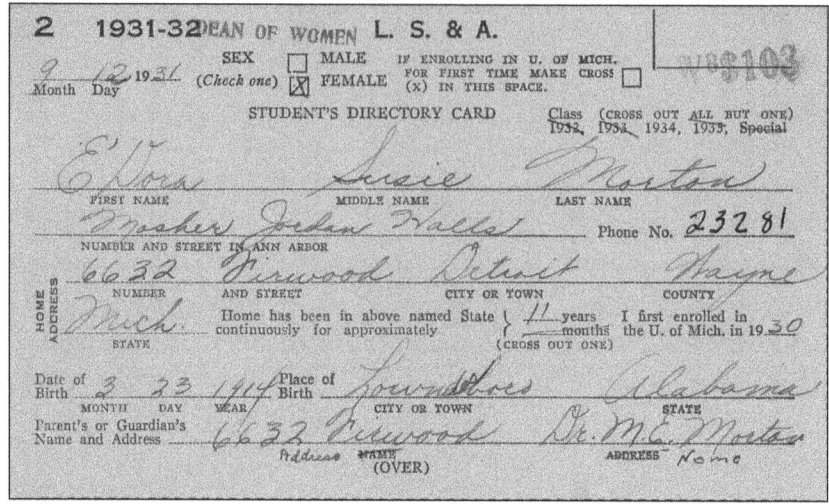

Figure 4. Enrollment card filled out by E'Dora Morton for the fall 1931 semester. Morton was the first African American woman to live in the Mosher-Jordan dormitory at the University of Michigan. Source: E'Dora Morton File, Alumni Records, 1845-1978, Bentley Historical Library, University of Michigan.

One of the outcomes of the MITW project is a website and online exhibit that uses documents and images to help frame stories and build upon the visualization. Another product is a self-guided tour written by the MITW students. Designed to be a walkable forty-minute tour, it features nine stops of importance to Black women. The tour includes the dormitories that Black women had to fight to get into, houses used by Black sororities, the location of a restaurant where a Black woman was refused service in the 1920s, and other sites of importance. The first iteration of the tour is a physical brochure. With support from the University of Michigan Library's visualization team, the coordinates of the sites were mapped as part of an anticipated online exhibit as another layer of visualization. The groundwork laid by the collaboration between Bentley staff and the visualization team allowed the students to expand and make public the results of their research.

Evolving Roles and New Connections

The project to identify African American students has been particularly notable in that it is an expansion of the traditional archival role. Instead of the archivist mediating access or suggesting resources to researchers, we have been actively engaged in creating and interpreting content. This active engagement has greatly assisted the Bentley's academic programming by adding in-depth subject expertise to extensive familiarity with relevant collections and resources in the archives. Beyond being conversant with collections in our archives, we have become fluent in the individuals, their stories, and the institutional context.

The information uncovered by the Bentley's research provided educational opportunities outside of the classroom. As we learned more about the important role played by African American fraternities and sororities, we were able to reach out to members of these organizations and show them archival records pertinent to their organizations. In fact, we uncovered new information previously unknown to even the national organization of one of the fraternities, such as the name and membership of the probationary chapter of Omega Psi Phi, the second-oldest African American fraternity on campus. A group called the "Annex Club" existed on campus as the precursor to the fraternity chapter with most of its members housed in a boarding house at 144 Hill Street—the same boarding house run by Esther Dickson.

From these connections, we were also able to learn of related material held in other archives. Through our work with Omega Psi Phi, we learned that the son of one of the chapter founders had donated his father's papers to the Vivian G. Harsh Research Collection of Afro-American History and Literature at the Chicago Public Library. Jones worked for the prominent African American newspaper the *Chicago Defender*, so it was logical that his papers would reside in a Chicago repository. A visit to the Vivian Harsh Collection revealed a University of Michigan scrapbook kept by Dewey Roscoe Jones, a member of the class of 1922. This is the earliest known scrapbook by an African American student at U-M and offers remarkable insight into the lives of African American students on campus in the early 1920s. It was this scrapbook that contained the only known pictures of "Mother" Dickson.

The out-of-the-classroom interactions included work with members of other organizations. We also worked closely with the Black Student Union as they celebrated their fiftieth anniversary in 2018.

Figure 5. Photograph of Esther "Mother" Dickson ca. 1922 from the scrapbook of Dewey Roscoe Jones, an African American member of the class of 1922 at the University of Michigan. Source: Dewey Roscoe Jones papers, Box 2, Chicago Public Library, Woodson Regional Library, Vivian G. Harsh Research Collection of Afro-American History and Literature.

This in-depth knowledge has also been beneficial in our archival fieldwork. Our familiarity with the issues and organizations enabled us to develop and establish new collections. We accessioned content directly from the Black Student Union for the first time, and we established a collection for the Alpha Kappa Alpha sorority. We also received a scrapbook from Sophia Holley Ellis, an African American woman from the class of 1949. It offered remarkable insight into her life on campus, including details of her first date, and the segregation she encountered during a trip to Washington, DC, with classmates.

The Bentley made a statement when it used the story of the fight to integrate university housing as the cover story for its magazine, *Collections*.[15] During our work with African American groups, they have repeatedly mentioned how important it is to them for archivists to bring stories like this forward, as uncomfortable as these stories may be. Beyond mere archival engagement and outreach, this is an important part of the healing process.

We have learned many lessons in the course of our project, about research and about teaching undergraduates. Experiments with visualization have helped us to see the results of our research in new ways. Once the African American project goes public as a searchable database, we will seek additions and corrections as we continue to add to the story.[16] We intend to use a similar approach as we research and compile names for other minority groups on campus. A Native American student project is slated to be next. We look forward to strengthening existing collaborations and developing new ones with researchers, faculty, librarians, and others as that project progresses. Our hope is that our project and experiences may be relevant to others taking on a similar project on a large or small scale.

---

15. *Collections: A Publication of the Bentley Historical Library at the University of Michigan*, Spring 2017. Accessible online at: https://bentley.umich.edu/magazine-archive/spring-2017/.

16. The database is expected to publicly launch in 2020 on a website linked to the Bentley's website.

TEACHING TOWARDS THE WHOLE: INTEGRATING ARCHIVES AND SECONDARY SOURCES THROUGH COLLABORATIVE INSTRUCTIONAL DESIGN PRACTICES

Elizabeth Call
Kimberly Davies Hoffman
Kristen Totleben
University of Rochester

Introduction

Collaborative teaching across library departments is not a new idea. While there are plenty of case studies on co-taught library sessions, there have been few studies done on how to build successful and sustainable partnerships across departments. Kristen Totleben and Jessica Lacher-Feldman's article, "Creating a Holistic Fabric of Services and Collections from the Inside Out: Exploring Convergences of Liaison and Special Collections Librarianship,"[1] is probably the first one that

---

1. Kristen Totleben and Jessica Lacher-Feldman, "Creating a Holistic Fabric of Services and Collections from the Inside Out: Exploring Convergences of Liaison

defines and lays out a theoretical path to making these relationships successful. To facilitate work between subject liaison and special collections departments, Totleben and Lacher-Feldman describe models for communication, organizational culture, and reporting structures. They argue that liaison and special collections librarians working holistically would be beneficial because, together, the departments would better mirror the research process of integrating primary and secondary sources and perspectives.

Like research, building and sustaining partnerships is not prescriptive; there are no defined stages. It is messy and very much environment-dependent. That said, creating opportunities for library departments to actively participate in professional development learning enables staff to interact and share different pedagogical approaches. In turn, liaison and special collections departments can continue to build professional, collegial relationships where they can combine efforts to provide and model more holistic views of the research process for faculty and students. It is our belief that without this necessary meta work, collaborations in teaching will remain in "parallel play"[2] mode rather than being truly integrative partnerships.

Background

The University of Rochester is an R-1 research institution with approximately 10,000 undergraduate and graduate students. The River Campus Libraries (RCL) is situated on one of three campuses; the others are the Eastman School of Music campus and the medical campus. Since 2013, RCL's outreach (liaison) librarians[3] and staff from Rare Books, Special Collections and Preservation (RBSCP) have been working

---

and Special Collections Librarianship," *Research Library Issues*, no. 291 (2017): 32–49, https://doi.org/10.29242/rli.291.4.

2. Borrowed from Jean Piaget's developmental psychology term, "parallel play," which is a phenomenon where children play separately and not coordinated with other children when in the same spaces. This term is used to articulate how outreach and special collections librarians often work and teach in the same environments and even the same spaces but do not teach together.

3. At the University of Rochester, the River Campus Libraries officially changed their library liaison job titles to "Outreach Librarian" in 2015.

more collaboratively in their instruction. There are seventeen outreach librarians and four special collections librarians with teaching responsibilities. Staff do not all work on the same floor or even in the same building, so there is some physical distance as well as separation in their day-to-day tasks; collaboration is not always front of mind. Typically, the outreach and special collections librarians teach sessions separately and sequentially, where one lesson may inform the following lesson. In other instances, outreach and special collections librarians co-plan the lesson, where the main focus is on primary sources.[4] Neither teaching instance exemplifies an integrative instruction session that combines special and general collections. At RCL, our two departments continue to work toward creating more holistic co-teaching experiences.

With the hire of a new Head of Outreach, Learning, and Research Services in 2015, outreach librarians, in particular, have been training in instructional design principles.[5] With a background in and passion for using interactive teaching techniques, based upon a solid foundation of learning theory, the new instructional leader developed multiple full day and shorter workshops (Appendix A) for librarians. These workshops introduced librarians to learning theory translated into practice; active and constructivist learning (leveraging the power of student-centered projects/challenges, where each group member's strengths and background enhance the overall team learning);[6] and instructional

---

4. For examples, see Helen McManus and Leah Richard, "Teaching Citations as a Multi-functional Approach to Archives Instruction" in *SAA Case Studies on Teaching with Primary Sources,* https://www2.archivists.org/sites/all/files/TWPSCase_2_Teaching_Citations.pdf; and Todd Samuelson and Cait Coker, "Mind the Gap: Integrating Special Collections Teaching," *portal: Libraries and the Academy* 14, no. 1 (2014): 51–66, https://muse.jhu.edu/ (accessed March 26, 2019).

5. Kimberly Davies Hoffman, "Leading Change: Using Instructional Design to Refocus an Information Literacy Program," in *Creative Instructional Design: Practical Applications for Librarians,* eds. Brandon West, Kimberly Davies Hoffman, and Michelle Costello (Chicago: Association of College & Research Libraries, 2017).

6. For further reading: "Social Constructivism," *Berkeley Graduate Division, Teaching & Resource Center,* last modified 2019, https://gsi.berkeley.edu/gsi-guide-contents/learning-theory-research/social-constructivism/.

design principles for engaged classroom experiences. Due to reporting lines, the workshops were mainly intended for outreach librarians, although other library staff with teaching responsibilities were also invited. Follow-up workshops that aligned to strategic projects (e.g., multi-semester surveys of first-year students' experiences connecting in-class and out-of-class librarian support; qualitative coding of what general lessons were taught by librarians and through which delivery method(s)) led librarians to write more effective learning outcomes, group-brainstorm lesson plans for consistent content delivery, employ a backward design process,[7] and, with our Writing Center partners, develop assignments that incorporate the Association of College & Research Libraries Information Literacy Framework.[8]

As new librarians came on board and staffing lines began to blur toward a more collaborative approach to pedagogical training, outreach librarians sought to share what they had been learning and practicing in instructional design with a new crop of special collections librarians.

Building a Collaborative Culture

As mentioned previously, when integrating primary and secondary sources into instruction, we argue that outreach and special collections librarians offer more to students and faculty when they model a more holistic and well-rounded view of the research process. Noticing that this seamless integration is a difficult feat, as not everyone is accustomed to such an approach, a few interested outreach and special collections librarians started meeting in 2015. They met to discuss which classes they might partner with, and which faculty members they should contact in the hope of finding teaching opportunities. Meeting together to discuss potential teaching collaborations was a first step

---

7. G.P. Wiggins and J. McTighe, *Understanding by Design* (Alexandria, Va.: Association for Supervision and Curriculum Development, 1998).

8. Association of College & Research Libraries, "Framework for information literacy for higher education," last modified January 11, 2016, http://www.ala.org/acrl/standards/ilframework.

towards greater transparency in communicating with each other about the teaching that was happening (separately, by department), leading them to work more in tandem rather than in parallel efforts.[9]

As early as 2015, the interdepartmental collaborative work started, with the outreach and special collections librarians co-planning and co-teaching with primary sources. A few librarians within the group took these efforts a step further. They embraced co-lesson planning of more cohesive sessions, which included both primary and secondary sources. Still, this was not yet the comprehensive strategy we envisioned, where all librarians were actively invested. In spring 2018, we designed an active learning workshop for outreach and special collections librarians. We thought the process might resonate more thoroughly if outreach and special collections librarians practiced the lesson planning process for a theoretical co-taught session.

The River Campus Libraries Workshop

The ninety-minute workshop that brought outreach and special collections librarians together followed a pattern of uniting different library staff to brainstorm (Appendix A), learn from each other, and develop something new that each individual entity could not create on their own.

As any professional instructional designer will insist,[10] workshop instructors need to start with learning goals for a training session. We considered who would attend—a mix of long-term, established staff and new hires from different departments and fields of study.[11] Our

---

9. For an example of archivists and librarians working cohesively, see Karen Viars and Amanda Pellerin, "Collaboration in the Midst of Change: Growing Librarian-Archivist Partnerships for Engaging New Students and Faculty," *Collaborative Librarianship* 9, no. 4 (2017): 1–24. Academic OneFile (accessed March 26, 2019).

10. J. Klein, and S. Jun, "Skills for Instructional Design Professionals," *Performance Improvement* 53, no. 2 (2014): 41–46.

11. Librarians who had been at River Campus Libraries for up to twenty years worked alongside librarians who were one to two months on the job and new to the field. Sciences, social sciences, humanities, and special collections librarians worked together in mixed groups during the workshop.

first learning outcome—*with new staff in both departments, participants will get to know each other and what each other does in terms of work and subject specialty*—placed a priority on diversifying groups, listening to each other's ideas for how they would approach a suggested assignment scenario, and emphasizing the strengths that each person brought to the lesson-planning process. The second learning outcome—*participants will become familiar with different sources and strategies each department utilizes in their teaching*—allowed participants to see the primary inclinations of each staff member in how they read the assignment prompt and the first strategies or resources that came to mind. The third learning outcome—*participants will explore and solidify best practices for teaching collaborations and the processes they use to design lessons*—aimed to help everyone (particularly the newest hires and others who had not attended the previous workshops dating back to 2015) learn and practice strategies in the instructional design and lesson-planning process.

An anticipatory set[12] kicked off the workshop, encouraging staff to focus on the learning to follow and sending a broad message of the workshop's major goal: to achieve better results through collaboration. "Saving Sam"[13] is an activity for children, who are given a few objects and a simple set of instructions. The ultimate goal is to take Sam (a gummy worm) out from under a capsized boat (a small cup), place a life jacket (a gummy lifesaver) on Sam, and place Sam on top of the capsized boat using nothing but two paper clips: no hands allowed.

During the workshop, all the materials and instructions were placed at each person's seat with a set of general instructions on the main screen.[14] By encouraging the activity to begin before the official start of the workshop, we were able to save time and have participants engage

---

12. J. Gonzalez, "Know Your Terms: Anticipatory Set," last modified September 6, 2014, https://www.cultofpedagogy.com/anticipatory-set/.

13. (n.d.), "Saving Sam - A Cooperative Activity," https://www.biologycorner.com/worksheets/saving_sam.html.

14. Physical set-up included a large screen TV that was visible at the front of the room as librarians entered the space and six large tables designed for group work of up to five people.

Figure 1. Outreach librarians Adrienne Canino (left) and Sue Cardinal (right) work together using paper clips as tools to save Sam. (Photo courtesy of Eileen Daly-Boas)

right away. The expectation of the activity is that, alone, each person will struggle to accomplish the various tasks using just two paper clips. Together, they will reach their goals more easily and with greater efficiency. Two minutes into the official start of the session, the instructors revealed the point of the activity. The instructors asked the participants how they worked through the various instructions, who was successful, and why. The instructors asked the participants why they thought they engaged in the Saving Sam activity. "Working together" was the obvious response. The instructors connected the Saving Sam activity to the idea of outreach and special collections librarians collaborating more often and systematically to plan library sessions. Ideally, these sessions become more creative, by blending primary with secondary source information literacy; more engaging (for students, librarians, and faculty); and ultimately, more successful.

The workshop was set up in such a way that outreach and special collections librarians worked in like groups (i.e., by similar discipline)

Figure 2. In the spirit of collaboration, Melinda Wallington (right) steadies the cup (i.e., boat) while Autumn Haag (center) attempts to lift Sam to safety. Katie Papas (left) observes the struggles and triumphs of collaborative work. All are staff at the University of Rochester's Rare Books, Special Collections and Preservation. (Photo courtesy of Eileen Daly-Boas)

on Saving Sam and the first official activity. This allowed library staff who typically collaborate (e.g., humanities librarians who frequently work together on joint database purchases) feel comfortable sitting with their closest colleagues.

We also purposely formed these like groups so that participants' first inclinations (or prior knowledge) for approaching the first activity would be authentic and could reveal how each group thinks about designing instruction. Each group was asked to read through the same sample assignment (Appendix B)[15], which the instructors had carefully chosen to appeal to each group in different ways. There was a historical

---

15. John Kirchgessner, "NURS 321: The History of Professional Nursing and Healthcare in America," (course assignment, St. John Fisher College, Rochester, NY, Spring 2016).

aspect (humanities and special collections) related to the nursing field (science) that called upon a critique of social implications (social sciences). We chose a sample assignment that would require primary and secondary source research methods, and we made predictions of how the outreach and special collections librarians would "read" the instructional needs for the assignment. In homogeneous groups, staff were asked to respond to these Poll Everywhere[16] questions: "What's the key concept that you focused on from this scenario? What's one activity that could enhance learning of this concept?" We asked outreach groups to identify their response with an O and special collections librarians with an R (for the department, RBSCP). This allowed the instructors to make comparisons in Poll Everywhere of the differences in teaching approaches based on one standard assignment scenario. Answers attributed to R mentioned ideas like primary source exploration, object analysis, historical contextual inquiry, and provenance. Ideas generated from the outreach librarians included database searches of various types—Google images, historical newspapers, and encyclopedia-type sources—to emphasize the need for simple background research. Outreach ideas also focused on the search process (e.g., brainstorming keywords, making connections between social aspects of gender, economics, and politics, and analyzing source results generated from different databases). Consistent with their past training in constructivist learning techniques, all outreach groups suggested activity design that utilized group work (i.e., social constructivism). We asked each O and R group to share their process for arriving at their chosen concept and activity. Their answers solidified the idea that both outreach and special collections librarians approach assignment prompts differently based on past training and job responsibilities/priorities. When the two parties work in silos, students will only benefit from one research approach and will not see the benefit of working with primary and secondary sources: greater contextual connections and richer analyses of the chosen research question.

---

16. Poll Everywhere (https://www.polleverywhere.com/) encourages live, interactive participation by allowing participants to vote on the spot during a presentation.

The culminating activity was to blend the R and O approaches into a unique and seamless lesson with both primary and secondary research methods. It was important to emphasize to our participants that the goal was not to situate R and O ideas next to each other, as separate entities (i.e., parallel play), but to morph the approaches into one. To do this, we needed to mix up the groups[17] so that there was equal representation between humanities, social sciences, sciences, and special collections librarians as they designed the new, interwoven lesson.

The newly formed groups were asked to put their thoughts together, using any mix of the R and O ideas from Poll Everywhere, to develop a blended activity. Various ideas emerged (Appendix C), where the workshop participants simultaneously worked to document and share thoughts.[18]

Analysis of the River Campus Libraries Workshop[19]

When we facilitated the workshop with outreach and special collections librarians at our institution, we noticed it sparked many conversations about activity planning. Staff participants discussed differences in the ways they approached a lesson based on the materials and ideas they were working with. This led them to explore the others' point of view and imagine together how to combine activities for students so that they would experience both perspectives. Since the workshop, five sessions (all in the fall 2018 semester) have been collaboratively planned and taught. We count this as a success, but we realize the need for more

---

17. Barbara Tewksbury, "Jigsaws," last modified January 30, 2019, https://serc.carleton.edu/sp/library/jigsaws/index.html.

18. Using L.O. Wilson, "Madeline Hunter Lesson Plan Model," last modified 2019, https://thesecondprinciple.com/teaching-essentials/models-of-teaching/madeline-hunter-lesson-plan-model/. Please refer to Appendix D for the details of the specific lesson for "Teaching Towards the Whole." Ideas generated from the workshop activities can be found at http://goo.gl/rm3jZ8.

19. Elizabeth Call, Kimberly Davies Hoffman, and Kristen Totleben, "Teaching Towards the Whole: Integrating Archives and Secondary Sources through Collaborative Instructional Design Practices," Teaching Archives to Undergraduates Conference, University of Michigan, November 8, 2019. https://bit.ly/2SjJDkV.

opportunities to bring the departments together. We also realize the need to include the library's digital scholarship staff in the collaborative workshops and meetings, in order to fully address twenty-first century research that uses multimodal methods to critically engage with and examine questions.

When we agreed to run a very scaled-down version of this workshop at the Teaching Undergraduates with Archives Conference, we decided to give attendees some background information and then jump into the group activity. While the time constraint was challenging, we were able to present the essence of what we achieved: that by bringing different vantage points and approaches to the table, librarian co-teachers achieve a more cohesive, well-rounded approach to research, teaching, and learning.

Although the majority of the Teaching Undergraduates with Archives audience were archivists (i.e., less of a special collections/outreach librarian mix), on a professional development level, they could envision how this type of workshop could facilitate and inspire more integrative teaching at their own institutions. After the workshop, two participants mentioned that they would like to repeat this workshop at their university and asked for our materials. From the discussion at each table, we could tell that the activities expanded the participants' thinking of how co-teaching, with an integration of general and archival collections, could provide students a more realistic view of the research process. With such a collaborative teaching approach, students can move beyond inspiration and discovery and toward the application, integration, and dialogue across sources to form new ideas and knowledge.

Next Steps

We are actively seeking out and creating new opportunities to plan and teach together with faculty using both primary and secondary sources. One initiative, Teaching Towards the Whole, will start soon. As envisioned, Teaching Towards the Whole seeks to create a cohort made up of librarians from across River Campus Libraries departments, the

University of Rochester's Center for Excellence in Teaching & Learning (CETL), and University of Rochester faculty and instructors. All parties will collaborate to build and execute courses that integrate the use of special collections, digital scholarship methodologies, and subject research skills to create authentic learning experiences that promote undergraduate scholarship. We will recruit and work with up to three professors/instructors to build courses that connect library resources and digital tools.

Additionally, we are planning to run another workshop for outreach and special collections librarians where we can continue to combine our strengths in the teaching space. We are modifying a workshop on designing assignments with faculty, which was previously delivered only to outreach librarians, so that it now includes both special collections and outreach librarians. In this case, we will include the digital scholarship staff to leverage the power of primary, secondary, and digital resources to create authentic learning experiences for students.

Conclusion

It is easier to imagine and discuss this collaborative approach than to actually practice it, especially on a library-wide scale. With seventeen outreach librarians and four special collections librarians with teaching responsibilities, we have a small enough number of staff to be nimble. Still, it takes continuous work to turn this type of integrative thinking into everyday practice. Focusing, at first, on early adopters, who can model the approach's success, helps bring validity to the process. It is a model of thinking and working that we believe will persist because, ultimately, it offers a practical counterpoint to the theoretical pathways laid out in Totleben and Lacher-Feldman's article (referenced in the introduction to this article). Teaching one without the other (i.e., separating primary from secondary sources) may be appropriate at times, depending on the overall course and a specific lesson's objectives, but in other circumstances, it undercuts the potential of modeling the research process. It is by encouraging and enabling staff to think differently and outside of current norms—without making too many assumptions on the part of their library colleagues, faculty, and students—that makes for more inspirational, creative, and impactful pedagogical practices. In our case, we are starting with the professional development of our institution's outreach and special collections librarians, with the hope that this thinking will trickle into their work and manifest itself in more thoughtful, communicative, and interdepartmental collaboration.

While not all sessions for students and faculty will require this holistic approach, it is nevertheless important to make opportunities to imagine more for both special collections and subject-based general collections. Once we have this established, multimodal and digital research methodologies can bring the library as well as its students and faculty into twenty-first century instructional practices. Imagining more includes thinking beyond departmental silos, past the materiality of collections to the actual intellectual content and to questions. In combining special and general collections with digital tools that inform and spur faculty and student interests and curiosities, the profession further advances knowledge creation.

Appendix A: History of River Campus Libraries workshops focused on issues of instructional design

Threshold concepts and the Association of College & Research Libraries (ACRL) Information Literacy (IL) Framework (December 2014)/Writing, Speaking, and Argument Program (WSAP) workshop (May 2018) – Outreach, Rare Books, Special Collections, and Preservation (RBSCP)
ACRL IL framework

Effective teaching for the library classroom (March 2015) - Outreach, RBSCP
Learning theories (behaviorism, cognitivism, & constructivism) and tools and terms like anticipatory sets, scaffolding/sequencing, formal lesson plans, and formative and summative assessment.

Active learning (May 2015) - Outreach, RBSCP
Model lesson plans (Madeline Hunter), ADDIE, learning theories, ACRL IL framework, Bloom's taxonomy, multiple intelligences

Backward design for lesson planning (March 2016)
ACRL IL framework, Bloom's taxonomy, backward design framework

Writing effective learning outcomes (June 2016, June 2018)
ACRL IL framework, Bloom's taxonomy, ABCD[Y] model for writing learning objectives

Digital pedagogy, Mini DSI (August 2017, June 2018, August 2018) - Outreach, RBSCP, Digital Scholarship Lab (DSL), Metadata
Negotiating with faculty and familiarity with digital tools (Scalar, Omeka, WordPress, mapping, data visualization)

Applying ADDIE (Analyze, Design, Develop, Implement, Evaluate) to a lesson idea [for new(er) librarians] (October 2018) - Outreach, RBSCP
ADDIE model, learning theories, ABCD[Y]/learning objectives, backward design framework

Course mapping (December 2018) - Outreach, RBSCP, DSL
Alignment of library learning outcomes to academic program learning outcomes (vertical coherence mapping), identifying gaps

Pedagogy specific to Community-Engaged (CE) scholarship (December 2018)
Negotiating with faculty, ACRL IL framework, Bloom's taxonomy, ABCD[Y]/learning objectives, CE specific teaching strategies (e.g. authentic assessment)

Developing/co-creating assignments with faculty (March 2019)
Negotiating with faculty, ACRL IL framework, Bloom's taxonomy, ABCD[Y]/learning objectives, transparent assignment design theory, performance assessments, active learning, multimodal, scaffolding/sequencing

Appendix B: Shared Sample Assignment

NURS 321: The History of Professional Nursing and Health Care in America, course syllabus

DESCRIPTION:

Through historical analysis, this course is designed to provide an understanding of the forces that shaped America's current health care system and the nursing profession. Students will be introduced to the exploration of the historical development of the nursing profession and the major institutions through which nursing care has been provided, including hospitals and community health care agencies. Three major areas are explored: (1) the role that historical inquiry and analysis play in understanding the development of today's health care system, (2) the development of the health professions (nursing and medicine) and institutions (hospitals and public health services), and (3) the interplay among the intellectual, social, economic, technological, and political events that shaped society and the profession. Emphasis is placed on the educational preparation of professional nurses and the clinical care provided by nurses to patients in homes, clinics, and hospitals.

COURSE OUTCOMES:

At the completion of the course, students will be able to:

1. Examine the interplay of national events that shaped America's health professions and the health care system.
2. Discuss the role of professional nurses within a culturally diverse patient population throughout the profession's history.
3. Explore the development of modern hospitals and community health agencies and their impact on the health of citizens and the community.
4. Explore the growth of medical knowledge and technology and its impact on health professionals and nursing care of patients.
5. Compare and contrast the development of the nursing and medical professions.
6. Examine the nursing profession's enduring issues, including workforce shortages, professional image, remuneration for services, education, and advanced nursing practice.
7. Identify the nursing profession's leaders and their contributions to the profession

FINAL ASSIGNMENT NURSING HISTORY PRESENTATION:

Students will choose a historic nursing leader or nursing history topic; all topics must be approved by course faculty. Part 1: Using the social history model, students will review the time/era in which the leader practiced or the topic occurred—including society/culture, politics, economics, gender, class, race, and the state of science and medicine—and develop a detailed outline. Part 2: The state of the nursing profession and an analysis of how the above factors influenced: the chosen leader's actions and his/her influence and contributions to the profession will be discussed or the state of the nursing profession during the chosen nursing history topic. Presentations about nursing leaders should also discuss the individual's leadership attributes.

Presentations will be scheduled during the last three class sessions. Presentations should be fifteen minutes, plus five minutes for questions/answers. Presentations should also include professional quality audio-visual material: PowerPoint, YouTube, etc.

Appendix C: Google Doc worksheet with integrated lesson ideas

Ideas generated from May 2018 River Campus Libraries workshop[20]

Teaching Towards the Whole: Integrating Archives and Secondary Sources through Collaborative Instructional Design Practices

Worksheet

Instructions: Groups of up to 4 are asked to combine both Liz's and Kristen's approaches into a seamless lesson.

Liz would design a session that would have students read and analyze a letter or 1-2 pages of a journal from a nurse (letter or journal sections selected would have details that students would need to infer a little about time period, society, etc.).

Primary Source Literacy Guideline: Interpret, Analyze, and Evaluate—*Critically evaluate the perspective of the creator(s) of a primary source, including tone, subjectivity, and biases, and consider how these relate to the original purpose(s) and audience(s) of the source.*

Kristen would model the process of brainstorming search strategies with a student's topic. Students search through: Google Scholar, Summon, CINAHL, historical abstracts. Compare/contrast, then reflect on change in research topic.

ACRL Framework for Information Literacy: Research as Inquiry

Research is iterative and depends upon asking increasingly complex or new questions whose answers in turn develop additional questions or lines of inquiry in any field.

What will students need to know to prepare for an activity? (direct teaching)	In what way(s) can you engage students to solidify their understanding, perspective, or practice?	What form will your assessment/check for understanding take to be sure they achieved intended outcome?	What makes this a collaboratively designed activity?

---

20. http://goo.gl/rm3jZ8

Appendix D: Workshop lesson plan
Madeline Hunter[21] Lesson Plan Template

Title: RBSCP/Outreach introduction to collaborative teaching

Date/Location: May 24, 2–3:30 pm, Humanities Center, Room D

Objectives	Participants will: • Get to know each other and what each of us does in terms of work and subject specialty (this is especially important because we have new staff in both depts) • Become familiar with different sources and strategies each dept utilizes in their teaching • Explore and solidify best practices for teaching collaborations and the processes we use to design lessons	
Review (What students already know.) For complete course syllabus click here.[22]	**Scenario:** Students will choose a historic nursing leader or nursing history topic; all topics must be approved by course faculty. *Part 1:* Using the social history model, students will review the time/era in which the leader practiced or the topic occurred—including society/culture, politics, economics, gender, class, race and the state of science and medicine—and develop a detailed outline. *Part 2:* The state of the nursing profession and an analysis of how the above factors influenced: the chosen leader's actions and his/her influence and contributions to the profession will be discussed or the state of the nursing profession during the chosen nursing history topic. Presentations about nursing leaders should also discuss the individual's leadership attributes.	
Anticipatory Set	Table arrangements/seat assignments as participants enter the room[23] - Round 1 Saving Sam[24] - assumed to be an individual activity but would necessitate group work	10 min
	Start with a scenario (and prompting questions for consideration) with outreach librarians grouped at similar tables as well as special collections librarians grouped at similar tables	**Time needed:** 5 min to digest
	Small groups would brainstorm how they might approach planning based on the scenario	10 min to discuss and brainstorm

---

21. Wikipedia entry on Madeline Hunter, https://en.wikipedia.org/wiki/Madeline_Cheek_Hunter

22. https://drive.google.com/open?id=10mkcADXCD2XAWtM2azd4nxpxJ6j9BN2s

23. https://docs.google.com/document/d/1cQdGtxda8ZE_NGmxRyPbgOf1cYvlF_9p4RxxmWl5wMk/edit?usp=sharing

24. https://www.biologycorner.com/worksheets/saving_sam.html

		Output: What's the most salient concept that you read from this scenario and what's one activity that could help instruct on this concept? Post to poll everywhere	2 min to type into polleverywhere 20 min
		Share out with the anticipation that each group will have approached the scenario differently. We each heard/read different things in the scenario based on our expertise. **PROMPT: speak to your process of how you arrived at the chosen concept and activity**	(3 min talk per group)
		Label your activity with "R" or "O"	
		Notes are taken by workshop instructors to capture these differences (1) concept per group and corresponding activity and (2) differences noticed between special collections and outreach approaches. Separate conversation than sharing out ideas/activities	
		Cross pollinate groups[25] - Round 2 (diagram of jigsaw puzzle)	3 min
		Each group creates (1) 15–20 min. instructional activity, centered around the scenario.	20 min
		Table A - focus on one activity and see what special collections and outreach each can contribute	
		Table B - take one special collections activity and one outreach activity to combine into a collaborative activity	
		Table C - take one special collections activity and create a collaborative activity	
		Table D - take one outreach activity and create a collaborative activity	
		Google doc[26] with activity ideas Share out	20 min (3 min talk per group)
Closure			
Independent Practice			
Materials, Resources & Physical Space		Gummi worms and life savers Paper clips and plastic cups Name tents Directions for Saving Sam Powerpoint Reserve Humanities Ctr D Polleverywhere	
Reflection		What did you notice? Think of one class in which you could implement this practice in the fall.	

---

25. https://docs.google.com/document/d/1cQdGtxda8ZE_NGmxRyPbgOf1cYvlF_9p4RxxmWl5wMk/edit?usp=sharing

26. https://docs.google.com/document/d/1ejtrUswxNFEeDiaV3MK6dUHPCoAITIXDNTrDb8YjsWM/edit?usp=sharing

HISTORY KEEPERS: COLLABORATION BETWEEN THE YALE AFRO-AMERICAN CULTURAL CENTER AND THE YALE UNIVERSITY LIBRARY

Christine Weideman
Camila Zorrilla Tessler
Shelby Daniels-Young[1]
Yale University

Reflections of Christine Weideman and Camila Zorrilla Tessler, History Keepers Mentors

The History Keepers program at Yale University was originally conceived of by Rise Nelson, Assistant Dean of Yale College and Head of the Yale Afro-American Cultural Center, known as the House. She approached Michael Lotstein, the Yale University Archivist, in 2016, about collaborating on a project to introduce Black undergraduates to research with primary resources by having them explore Black history

---

1. Christine Weideman and Camila Zorrilla Tessler, from the staff of Manuscripts and Archives in the Yale University Library, participated in the program in 2016/17 and 2017/18 as mentors. Shelby Daniels-Young was one of the program participants in its first year.

at Yale. Concomitantly, the students would be introduced to history disciplines and careers as academic scholars or professional staff in libraries, museums, and archives. The specific goals of the program were (and remain):

1. To facilitate purposeful discussions and academic examination of the histories of Black Yale University.
2. To build even more culturally diverse research archives to include a multitude of materials that preserve histories of Africans and African Americans at Yale, in higher education, and in the United States.
3. To increase the number of underrepresented students, who because of their preparation in the History Keepers program, declare a major in African, African American, or ethnic studies.
4. To build a pipeline of Yale students entering postgraduate preparation programs and careers in archival/academic research, library science, and museum administration that relate to the preservation of African Diasporic histories.
5. To increase underrepresented undergraduates' engagement with research, scholars, librarians, archivists, research institutions, and networks on campus, locally and nationally.

The results of the research projects undertaken by the students would be preserved in the House and eventually transferred as additions to the House records in the University Archives. Black history at Yale would be highlighted in new ways, and new sources for that history would be uncovered or created through oral histories.[2]

The program began in January 2017 and was limited to fifteen students, who were hired by the House for ten hours each week to participate. Archivists and librarians from throughout the library were recruited to participate in the program. There were weekly meetings from January through mid-April; Dean Nelson held weekly and

---

2. In the third year, the project also included an oral history program in which students interviewed Black graduates about their Yale experiences.

sometimes biweekly meetings with the students on research strategies and careers in academia, while the library staff met biweekly with the students for ninety minutes (in the early evening, after classes were over for the day) and introduced them to the work of librarians and archivists. They included Skype interviews for the students with three archivists and librarians of color from institutions around the country, who talked about their professional career paths. In addition, each student was assigned a librarian or archivist to be their individual mentor as they developed and carried out their individual research projects.

The students were required to produce a five- to seven-minute oral presentation and a five-page paper on their research. In each they were required to define their research statement; explain the significance of their project; explore the design and methodology of their research process; discuss what they learned from their research; review the challenges and surprises they encountered; and reflect on what they would do to carry on their research if they had more time.

Based on feedback from the students who participated in the first year, Dean Nelson identified revisions to the program in the second year. Ten hours proved to be too much for the students, so students were instead hired for five hours each week. As a result, the number of weekly and biweekly meetings were greatly reduced, both in the House and in the library. The research projects took priority: Dean Nelson wanted weekly meetings between participants and mentors. Two general meetings to introduce participants to the work of librarians and archivists were held, but most of what was accomplished in that regard happened as part of the participant/mentor weekly meetings. Since these one-on-one weekly meetings were generally forty-five to sixty minutes, only four hours per week remained for other meetings and research on the student's projects. The requirements for the students were the same in the second year: a five- to seven-minute presentation and a five-page paper on their research project.

The two years of the program experienced both successes and challenges. The goals of the program were met. Every participant engaged with the research process to some extent; learned what comprises academic scholarship; and developed an understanding of the work of archivists and librarians. Some who were previously uncommitted have decided to major in African American history. Others are beginning to consider careers in archives, libraries, or museums. Participants engaged with the history of Blacks at Yale and understood the importance of the stories they uncovered during their projects. So too did the several hundred Yale and New Haven community members, including members of the Yale president's cabinet, who attended the oral history presentations. Mentors developed strong relationships with their students and learned a good deal about challenges in uncovering the history of underdocumented communities. Librarians who had themselves never worked with primary resources benefitted from their involvement and became much more familiar with how to advise undergraduates in finding and using primary sources. The program generated a good deal of positive publicity for the House and the library.

As with most new programs, however, there were challenges. Students often chose topics that were too current to have adequate representation in the archives, such as incidents that happened as recently as 2015. They had to rely almost exclusively on oral interviews for material and did not learn much about the archival research process. They sometimes chose topics that were far too broad, such as slavery at Yale. Getting students to try to develop more focused research statements was a key responsibility for mentors.

Conducting oral interviews was a challenging aspect of the program. The students were very excited about the interviews, but many of them and the mentors had little experience doing so. As a result, the mentors who knew the most needed to develop and lead a classroom session on conducting an oral interview from start to finish. In the second year, library staff added an assignment in which students listened to an existing oral interview and, with their mentor, summarized it for the finding aid to the collection in University Archives. These efforts made conducting oral histories a bit easier for students.

Students expected to be able to easily contact alumni for interviews. Dean Nelson, however, required that she first contact any Yale graduate the students wanted to interview to explain the program to them and get their permission. This sometimes took quite a bit of time and limited the students to only one or two interviews. If interviews were with current students on campus, her permission was needed before History Keeper participants could conduct the interviews. Students had to obtain releases from interviewees, which at times proved difficult; when they didn't get them, per the Yale General Counsel's office, they could discuss the interviews in their talks and papers, but not reveal any personally identifiable information about the interviewees.

Working with archival material was challenging for the students. Beyond the fact that beginning researchers need extra help in understanding how to do archival research, there was the added challenge of identifying materials that specifically addressed Black history at Yale or helped the students identify the names of Black students who could be pursued for interviews. While the students learned how to search our finding aid database for the few collections available on the Black student experience at Yale, three of our most important sources, the *Yale Daily News* and Yale yearbooks and class books, proved problematic. Search terms were difficult to define—African-American, Black, Afro-American—so multiple searches had to be done using various terms to ensure all information that could be found was uncovered.[3] Yearbooks and class books containing photographs of student groups or athletic teams do not explain how the names are listed, so it is not possible to know what name to attach to the African American in the third row, second from the left.

The students needed help in understanding the limitations of the conclusions they could draw from their research, especially if they relied almost exclusively on oral histories. The mentors were a bit hesitant to do this in the first year, but in discussing amongst themselves things to do differently in year two, the mentors agreed that this was an important responsibility of theirs. They needed to review drafts of the oral presentations and papers, help the students understand what they could conclude from their research, and ensure that the students understood and spent adequate time on the next steps portion of their oral presentation and paper.

---

3. This turned out to be a good learning experience for the students in developing research methodologies.

The greatest challenge for the students in both years was time management. In other jobs on campus, when students encounter time crunches in completing their academic assignments, they call their work supervisors and report that they won't be in. This was a different type of job—they had to prepare an oral presentation and write a paper or explain to Dean Nelson why they couldn't. In the first year, the students committed to ten hours per week, but often two to three hours each week were taken up in meetings. In the second year, the students committed to only five hours per week, but at least one of the hours each week was spent in meetings, mostly with their mentors, and sometimes a second hour was spent at the House with Dean Nelson. Every participant took at least four courses to meet their academic requirements, and this was almost like a fifth course added into their workload. They especially struggled after spring break, when they had only a month of classes before the onset of finals week. This made it especially important for mentors to help the students understand and articulate what it is they learned, even if their research time was limited, and again, to make use of the next steps portions of their talks and papers to demonstrate what they would do if they had the time to continue their research.

The university archivist anticipated the challenge of providing access to records in the university archives that were under restrictions applied to almost all Yale administrative records. He knew that many students would want access to such records to do their research. When a request is made for access to restricted university records, a restriction review is done by the university archivist with access recommendations passed to the Office of the Secretary to be approved or denied. Prior to the start of the History Keepers program, the university archivist made sure the secretary was aware of the program. The secretary became a great supporter of History Keepers and understood the necessity for a quick turnaround on access requests from students. This is exactly what happened.

From the start of the program, both students and mentors proved to be up to the challenges of History Keepers. The excitement of the students was infectious and got them through semesters of full class loads as well as History Keepers' research projects. Even students who chose to pursue difficult topics with little information in our archive not only managed to develop presentations, but often surprised the mentors with their resourcefulness and ability to uncover the beginnings of compelling stories. Programs such as this one can succeed in other academic repositories, even if there is no faculty involvement. It would need to be tailored to the resources of the repository—funding to pay the students, and staff time for mentoring—and would be even more successful if not limited to just twelve weeks. If there is an interest in teaching students how to use primary sources to study the past, especially an underdocumented past of a community on the campus of the academic repository, a program similar to History Keepers could be quite successful.

Reflections of Shelby Daniels-Young, History Keepers Participant

I was in the first cohort of History Keepers and took part in the program in my final semester at Yale. For several years, I had been interested in becoming a professional in the library and archival field, and when I heard about the History Keepers program, I knew I had to participate. Since it was so closely aligned with my career goals, I received permission to take only three classes in my final semester so that I could devote more time to the program. This allowed me room to really embrace and enjoy the project, because it was a sizable time commitment.

There was a large degree of freedom granted to all of us in the program, which was a bit of a double-edged sword. On the one hand, it was nice to be able to do what I wanted with the project and pursue my own interests. On the other hand, this made it easy to get lost, whether trying to refine my project parameters, searching for archival sources, or deciding how to structure my final report. As a result, I would say establishing clear goals for students is important, as well as having mentors who are going to actively provide some guidance. My mentor had a more hands-off approach, and I think I could have benefited from a little more involvement. It seems like emphasizing the mentor-student relationship has been addressed in the second cohort. I also think that since I went through the program as a senior, the meetings that covered basic research practices or different history major programs did not teach me much that I did not already know.

What really made the program special to me was that we were not just researching in a vacuum. We had the Skype sessions with library and archives professionals, and Dean Nelson organized a trip to visit the National Museum of African American History and Culture in Washington, DC. We were connecting with others who worked in the cultural heritage field, often promoting African American history. Most importantly, the work we were doing was needed to provide greater documentation of Black Yale history. In completing my project, I was most pleased by the idea that my efforts would be preserved and potentially reach others in the future.

My Research

The research project I pursued was an investigation into what life at Yale was like for Black undergraduates between the 1900s and the 1940s. I chose this topic because the discussion and knowledge of Black students at Yale is often limited to the very first graduates, such as Edward Bouchet. He received two degrees from Yale—a bachelor's degree in 1874 and a PhD in 1876—and was the first African American in the United States to receive a PhD. There is a picture of Bouchet in the main library on campus, and the Afro-American Cultural Center has an annual event called the Bouchet Ball. Bouchet was also suggested as a potential name for a new building on campus a few years ago. You would be hard-pressed, however, to find anyone with even passing knowledge about Black students who attended Yale between 1874 and the late 1960s, a time that saw an increase in the numbers of Black students attending Yale and the establishment of the Afro-American Cultural Center (1969).

This gap in awareness of Black Yale history seemed to me to echo the general American public's lack of awareness of Black history between the end of the Civil War and the Civil Rights activism of the 1950s and

1960s. Unfortunately, this can make people think that no one was doing anything noteworthy in those decades.

My intentions were to forge a history of Black students at Yale to bridge the gap between the mid-nineteenth century and the mid-twentieth. I wanted Black students to see that they had a past at Yale that is much stronger than is generally known. By making people aware of overlooked Black student pioneers, I could expand and diversify the list of Yale heroes.

I began my research by examining Yale College class books, which describe each class's years at Yale and served the same general purpose as yearbooks. The biographies section of each class history contains a photograph of each undergraduate as well as a few paragraphs about his life and Yale career. I tried to identify Black members of each class mainly by their photographs and corroborating evidence in the biography text itself. It gradually became clear to me that one semester would not be enough time for me to compile a complete list of Black students for the almost one hundred-year span between Bouchet and the 1960s. My mentor informed me that pre-1900 class books were not guaranteed to have photographs. As I wished to find the earliest possible instances of Black students, but also wished to ensure early success, I began my search with the 1915 class book, operating under the assumption that I would be more likely to find Black students a few years into the twentieth century as opposed to at its very beginning. As I worked forward and backward from 1915, hoping to reach 1900 and 1960, I realized that the lengthiness of my search method—which required me to look at the photographs of several hundred students for each year—would prevent me from reaching that goal. In the end, I only managed to cover twenty-seven classes, those from 1908 to 1936, in the time I allotted for that phase of my project. It is possible that I overlooked some Black students due to their race not being obvious to me by their image, but barring that potential error, I determined that there were fifteen Black students who attended Yale College from 1908 to 1936—and of those, thirteen graduated. No more than three Black students were enrolled in Yale College at any given time in those years.

Results

In working on my project, I found a 1931 letter in the archives from W. E. B. Du Bois to James Angell, the president of Yale, asking for a statement about the "presence of the Negro in the institution."[4] "As far as I am aware," read Angell's reply, "there has been no discrimination shown in dealing with members of the colored race, and I do not recall ever hearing any complaint with reference to the matter. I think colored boys, when they come here, are accepted on their merits and so dealt with, just as are other students."[5]

While Angell's statement might have been true on an administrative level, my discoveries about the fifteen students indicate that Black undergraduates had a more isolated experience compared to their white counterparts. Almost all the students who were not natives of New Haven either lived alone or with other Black students—in some cases, Black undergraduates even lived with Black students enrolled in the divinity or law schools. And while other students had lists of extracurriculars in their class biography profiles, ranging from the performing arts to secret societies to campus publications, Black students had few to no activities listed. There were a few instances of Black undergraduates who inserted themselves into mainstream life at Yale. For example, Edward Morrow, class of 1931, published four literary reviews on works by Black authors in the *Yale Daily News*. He was also the only Black student who participated in a Model League of Nations conference hosted by Yale that included more than thirty other universities.

To supplement research on my subjects, I chose a select number of students I found intriguing and traced the trajectory of their lives after college to learn more about them on a personal level. I settled on three men and investigated their careers through class books in the archives and historical newspapers online. Jefferson Ish, class of 1909, worked as

---

4. Du Bois to Angell, May 15, 1931, James Rowland Angell, President of Yale University, Records (RU 24), Manuscripts and Archives, Yale University Library, Box 143, Folder 1510.

5. Angell to Du Bois, May 21, 1931, James Rowland Angell, President of Yale University, Records (RU 24), Manuscripts and Archives, Yale University Library, Box 143, Folder 1510.

an administrator and professor at several colleges and later became an executive in an insurance company. Edward Gaylord Howell, class of 1920, became a doctor who was concerned with addressing alcoholism. Edward Morrow worked as a journalist who also served in the military and later conducted research into Black history.

For my project report, I wrote an in-depth narrative profile of each of these three men, as well as a discussion of the broader trends of Black undergraduate life at Yale College.

Looking Forward

There are many more avenues to explore that I did not have time to pursue. My main recommendations for future researchers who wish to continue with my topic were:

1. Search for Black students in the Sheffield Scientific School. In the first half of the twentieth century, the undergraduate population at Yale was divided into Yale College and the Sheffield Scientific School, and in working on my project I only examined students in the former. There is an entire other student population to investigate.
2. Find Black students who were in Yale College before the class of 1908 and after the class of 1936, as that would continue my goal of bridging the gap between the 1870s and the 1960s.
3. Look into Alpha Phi Alpha's presence at Yale before the 1940s, as a few of the students I found were members of this historically Black fraternity. I did not have time to research the chapter's activities during my own project, but learning about its influence might further illuminate details about Black life on campus.

Looking Back

One of the takeaways I had from my project was learning to live with gaps when conducting archival research. Sometimes what you need or wish you had does not exist. I learned to treasure what I found, and I was careful not to overlook information hidden in the sources I was able to secure.

While doing my research, I was often struck by how much today's Black students at Yale have in common with those of the past. Black students still make up a relatively small population at the university, and with that comes a feeling of responsibility to "make a good showing" (as one of the fifteen students once put it) while one is at Yale, and afterward to do one's best to succeed. This is just as true now as it was a hundred years ago.

ARCHIVISTS AND LIBRARIANS: CO-TEACHING CONNECTIONS WITH PRIMARY SOURCES

Chloe Morse-Harding
Laura Hibbler
Brandeis University

Introduction

As librarians and archivists, one of our shared goals is for students to gain a better awareness of the breadth of resources available to them during their college careers. Most students enter college with some degree of experience using secondary sources, but many have had only limited interactions with primary sources. Often, college students, and many high school students, have encountered primary sources in a highly mediated setting, such as in a curated collection of materials with background information provided for each source. While exploring and interpreting primary sources in a less mediated setting may be intimidating at first, it can also set the stage for an engaging learning experience.[1]

---

1. Barbara Rockenbach discusses how different learning theories can be applied in

Although we—a Reference and Instruction Archivist and a Research and Instructional Services Librarian—work in different units within the Brandeis University Library, we have developed ways to use our shared interest in active learning and primary sources to reduce the intimidation factor and instill a sense of engagement among students. We have found that when we give students time to examine and explore primary sources in a less mediated setting, they take a more active role in learning: they interpret sources, ask critical questions, and connect ideas presented in those sources. With that in mind, we began designing learning experiences that incorporate interactive elements, discussion, and reflection instead of a lecture and database demonstrations. This chapter presents a case study from one of the classes we have team-taught.

Narrative: Collaborating to Develop an Engaging Learning Experience

Our example comes from a session we taught for an undergraduate African & African American Studies class in the fall semester of 2017. For the final research paper, the professor wanted each student to identify an individual represented in the archives who self-identified as Black or belonging to the African diaspora. Students would select individuals who interested them and research these individuals, learning more about their identities and their roles in historically significant events. As a way to introduce students to both physical and digital archival material before they selected their research subjects, we designed an interactive session in which students worked in small groups, analyzing a physical photograph from the Robert D. Farber University Archives & Special Collections at Brandeis University and exploring one of the library's databases. This class was an eighty-minute session, divided into four sections: a brief introduction and overview of the rules and guidelines for working with and handling physical archival collections;

---

teaching students with unmediated primary sources in "Archives, Undergraduates, and Inquiry-Based Learning: Case Studies from Yale University Library," *The American Archivist* 74, no. 1 (2011): 297–311. http://www.jstor.org/stable/23079010.

an interactive component, during which students analyzed primary sources; short presentations from each small group; and a wrap-up and reflection period.

After we had gone over the guidelines, students were divided up into small groups (two to three students per group), and each group was given a photograph of an individual to examine, from either the Brandeis University photography collection or the Carl Van Vechten photograph collection. If the students were unfamiliar with the individual pictured, they were encouraged to look for biographical information online.

The images selected from the Brandeis University photography collection depict prominent African Americans who have spent time on the Brandeis campus:

- Maya Angelou, lectured on campus spring 1989
- James Baldwin, lectured on campus fall 1962
- Angela Davis, alumna, class of 1965; lectured on campus spring 1987 and spring 1995
- Lorraine Hansberry, lectured on campus spring 1961
- Langston Hughes, lectured on campus spring 1967
- Coretta Scott King, lectured on campus fall 1986
- Martin Luther King Jr., lectured on campus fall 1957 and spring 1963
- Pauli Murray, professor of American Civilization, 1968–1973

We selected photographs of individuals who had taught or spoken at Brandeis in the hopes that students would feel a greater sense of connection to the people and historical periods they were researching.

The Carl Van Vechten collection includes photographs taken between 1932 and 1964 of authors, artists, and other prominent African Americans. Van Vechten (1880–1964), an art critic and novelist, began his photography career in the early 1930s. His role as an art critic for the *New York Times* led to the formation of many friendships and connections with a variety of prominent individuals, including many key figures from the Harlem Renaissance.² From this collection, we selected images of Mary McLeod Bethune, Eldzier Cortor, Countee Cullen, Ruby Dee, W. E. B. Du Bois, Zora Neale Hurston, and James Weldon Johnson for the class to review. These images were selected based on the level of information readily available online about each individual.

After students had examined their photographs for about ten minutes, we called the class together and directed them toward an online library research guide that we had created for their class. The research guide included a list of suggested databases and online collections containing digitized primary source materials—including the online resource that each group was assigned to use as a counterpart to the photograph they were given—as well as research tips and suggested strategies for identifying relevant sources. We then asked students to search their assigned database or collection for sources related to their individual. The assigned online resources included:

- Ethnic NewsWatch database (Ruby Dee and Eldzier Cortor)
- HistoryMakers database (Maya Angelou and Mary McLeod Bethune)
- NAACP Papers, part of the ProQuest History Vault database (Pauli Murray and James Weldon Johnson)
- Black Freedom Struggle, part of the ProQuest History Vault database (Langston Hughes)
- The Sixties: Primary Documents and Personal Narratives, an Alexander Street Press database (Martin Luther King Jr.)
- Digital Public Library of America (Coretta Scott King)
- Historical Black Newspapers, part of the ProQuest Historical Newspapers database (Lorraine Hansberry and Countee Cullen)
- Women in Social Movements in the United States, an Alexander Street Press database (Angela Davis)

---

2. "Carl Van Vechten Photographs," Robert D. Farber University Archives & Special Collections Department, Brandeis University, accessed January 28, 2019. http://findingaids.brandeis.edu/repositories/2/resources/207.

- *The Crisis* magazine, available through Google Books (W. E. B. Du Bois)
- Federal Surveillance of African Americans, part of the Gale Archives Unbound database (James Baldwin).

We selected this group of databases and collections with the goal of introducing students to a wide range of types of primary sources, including organizational records, video oral histories, newspaper articles, diaries, correspondence, and memoirs.

As students conducted their searches, we circulated throughout the room, answering questions, suggesting strategies, and offering praise and encouragement. One group was confused by the sections of blacked-out text on a document they had found. This "teachable moment" allowed us to describe the act of redacting and the possible effects that redaction can have on their research, particularly when using declassified government documents. Other groups asked about ways to refine their results, and this provided us with an opportunity to discuss different keywords that they might use in their searching, as well as how to refine their results by historical period or type of document. We encouraged students to develop a sense of historical empathy as they explored the materials.[3] This shift in thinking allows students to think strategically about how people and events might have been defined and categorized during a time period other than their own. Thus, when confronted with difficulty finding information, a student can explore strategies, such as brainstorming additional keywords, by considering, "how would I have described this if I was living in 1960?" or "what words would I have used to define this person if it was 1800?"

As students searched these databases, they were directed to think about and discuss what they had learned from analyzing both physical

---

3. For an introduction to the concept of historical empathy in the classroom, we recommend the following overview: Lina Mai, "Use Historical Empathy to Help Students Process the World Today," Facing History and Ourselves, last modified March 27, 2018, http://facingtoday.facinghistory.org/use-historical-empathy-to-help-students-process-the-world-today.

primary sources and the digitized ones. Additionally, students were asked to consider how they might use these sources when writing a research paper. We asked students to include these ideas in the short presentations they shared with the rest of the class.

Results

During the last portion of the class, after examining and exploring the resources, each group gave a short presentation (approximately two minutes long) to the class about the individual depicted in their photograph and the additional digitized primary sources they used to find information. These short presentations also provided students with the opportunity to share research tips and recommendations with their classmates based on discoveries they had made during their searching. For example, the group that had encountered redacted FBI files defined redaction for the rest of the class. One of the groups that had explored the idea of historical empathy shared the challenges they had faced when looking for primary sources about a historical figure's gender identity and sexuality. They had found that the terminology we use now to describe certain topics was not always present in the historical primary sources. The students who had searched historical newspapers emphasized the importance of looking beyond the national newspapers and toward publications that included underrepresented voices, including African American newspapers such as the *Chicago Defender* and *New York Amsterdam News*. Students who had searched in the historical newspapers also emphasized the importance of limiting their article searches by publication date so that they could focus on articles published during their individual's lifetime. Several groups talked about their experiences searching databases that contain organizational records from civil rights groups. While organizational records may have initially sounded dry, students demonstrated that they made exciting and surprising discoveries while searching within the papers of the National Association for the Advancement of Colored People (NAACP), the Southern Christian Leadership Conference, and the Congress of Racial Equality, such as different relationship dynamics between historical figures.

After presenting their sources, students reflected on what they had learned and shared their thoughts with the class. Setting aside time for a reflection period allows students to internalize and synthesize the information they have taken in during the class session. Then they can begin to articulate what they have learned. This discussion and reflection period also reinforces the concepts covered during the session, which helps students to retain what they have learned. Both the group presentations and class discussion served as an informal assessment, demonstrating to us that students had learned about the range of sources available to them and strategies for working with these materials. They also showed that they felt confident about applying these collections in their own work.

Lessons Learned

Through the process of working with images from the Brandeis University photography collection, searching a database, and sharing their findings with their classmates, students learned about the variety of resources available to them in their library's physical and digital collections. Even more importantly, this session helped students build transferable skills, as they were asked to explore, examine, and select. This new understanding of the library's resources and these transferable skills were crucial for students as they each took the next step: selecting an individual to research for their term paper. Following the session, many students scheduled research consultations and contacted us with research questions; their curiosity had been sparked during the instruction session and they felt comfortable and motivated about reaching out to us for research assistance.

While it can be tempting as librarians and archivists to cover as much archival theory and content as possible or demonstrate multiple online databases in a library instruction session, we did not do that. Instead, we asked each group to analyze one image and search one database and then teach their classmates about their findings. This active learning structure takes up a significant amount of class time, and it is possible that some faculty members may feel wary about giving up class time that could be spent covering content. Some instructors may feel uneasy about starting off a class without any sort of script, but we have found that students are much more engaged when they are empowered to conduct their own searches, troubleshoot search results, and synthesize their findings for their classmates. We also recognize that with this type of student-centered instruction session, we give up some level of control over the topics covered. Because we wanted the students to do their own research and have a less mediated experience, we devised a student-centered session that gave students the opportunity to take ownership of their work and rely on themselves to find information. As students take a more active role in their learning process by interpreting sources and connecting ideas presented in the sources, they gain confidence about their ability to conduct meaningful historical research.

In our experience, although students are usually interested in primary sources, they may not feel confident about their ability to apply primary sources in their work. The active learning experience allows students to develop a greater degree of confidence, while also deepening their understanding of primary sources and how they could use these sources in their own research.

We have also found that the time spent engaging with a physical primary source prepares students to work with the digital collections. Students are accustomed to databases of PDFs, but their level of interest rises when that PDF is a letter authored by the individual in their group's photograph. Students make a deeper connection with the digitized primary sources than they might have if they had used the database without the physical counterpart.

By collaborating with one another, we were able to facilitate an instruction session that would have been much more difficult to complete individually. As a research and instruction librarian, Laura would not have known about the range of individuals depicted in the photograph collections of University Archives & Special Collections. As an archivist, Chloe does not frequently work with library databases and would not have known about the contents of many of the resources. We each brought our own expertise and experience to planning the session and to our discussions with students throughout the session. Chloe shared information with students who were interested in exploring other archival materials beyond the selection of photographs we used in the class. Laura discussed research tips and strategies with students as they conducted database searches. While an instruction session like this could certainly be planned independently, we highly encourage our librarian and archivist colleagues to explore collaborations with one another, as this will lead to a rewarding experience for both you and your students.

Although we have presented only a single class as a case study, we have taken a similar approach with a variety of classes, including a First Year Experience class, a course on the history of childhood in America, and a class on student and youth revolutions in 1968. We work together before the start of each semester to identify courses that cover content related to materials available in the University Archives & Special Collections. We then contact the faculty members teaching those courses and offer to provide an active learning session using both physical and digital primary sources. For future semesters, we would like to develop an online research guide with a list of suggested "pairings" between physical archival materials and databases of primary sources. An example pairing might match our physical Victorian ephemera collection with Victorian Popular Culture, an Adam Matthew Digital database. This online guide would be an asset when we discuss with faculty members the range of ways we can partner with them when teaching students how to conduct research with primary sources.

In our outreach to faculty, we emphasize that, even if the course does not have a research assignment, students can still apply the concepts covered in a session to their understanding of other course themes. With the First Year Experience class, for example, students viewed a diary and photographs donated by an alumna who participated in voter registration efforts in 1965 as part of the Summer Community Organization and Political Education (SCOPE) Project of the Southern Christian Leadership Conference (SCLC). Students were asked to look for additional materials about SCOPE in a ProQuest database containing digitized primary sources related to the Civil Rights Movement. While students did not have to do any further research after this session, this approach successfully engaged students with a variety of library materials and empowered them to think about the contributions they might make toward social justice causes.

This model of active learning sessions pairing physical and digitized materials could be repurposed in a range of instructional scenarios. In situations where subscription databases and archival collections may not be accessible, one could use freely available online collections, such as those searchable through the Digital Public Library of America, paired with more readily accessible physical primary sources, such as a school's yearbooks. When given the opportunity to explore these primary source materials, students develop transferable research skills that can be used during their college careers and a greater degree of confidence regarding their use of primary sources—both of which can contribute to excitement about research with primary sources.

Bibliography

Mai, Lina. "Use Historical Empathy to Help Students Process the World Today," Facing History and Ourselves. Last modified March 27, 2018. http://facingtoday.facinghistory.org/use-historical-empathy-to-help-students-process-the-world-today.

Robert D. Farber University Archives & Special Collections Department. "Carl Van Vechten Photographs." Accessed January 28, 2019. http://findingaids.brandeis.edu/repositories/2/resources/207.

Rockenbach, Barbara. "Archives, Undergraduates, and Inquiry-Based Learning: Case Studies from Yale University Library." *The American Archivist* 74, no. 1 (2011): 297–311. http://www.jstor.org/stable/23079010.

THE ARCHIVES AS HISTORY LAB: THE PRINCETON & SLAVERY PROJECT

Martha A. Sandweiss
Daniel J. Linke
Princeton University

Martha A. Sandweiss

I spent the first part of my career as a museum curator, a practice that made me comfortable with visual culture, and with the small artifacts and documents that find their ways into museums, libraries, and archives. From single images and documents, large stories can unfold.

Over the course of my teaching career at Amherst College and Princeton University, I have often tried to bring my own enthusiasm for the archives into my classrooms. I have taught classes in special collections classrooms, museum study rooms, and university archives, focusing on photographs, illustrated books, travel journals. But no teaching experience I've had in the archives over the past thirty years comes close to matching my experience of working with Dan Linke, Princeton University archivist, on the Princeton & Slavery Project.

Our one-off class evolved into an enormous team project. What we found, in the end, is easily summarized: The history of Princeton

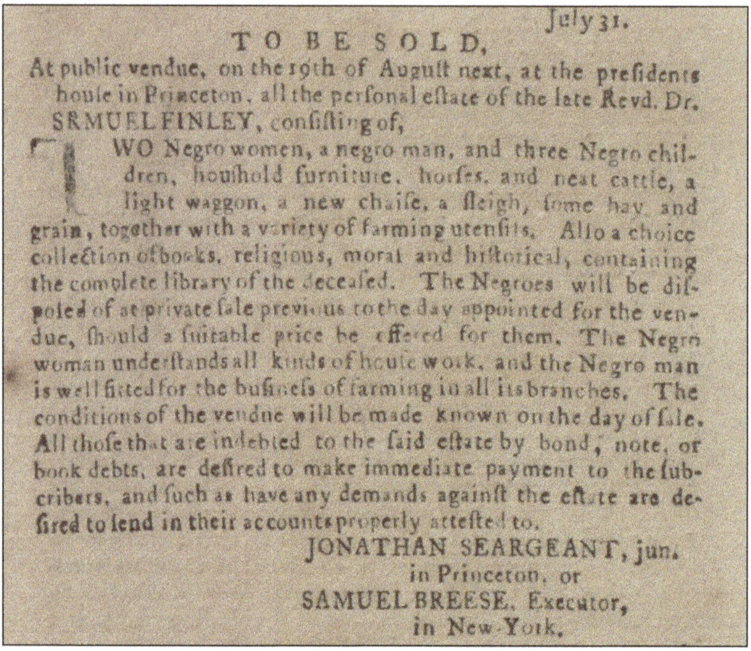
July 31.

TO BE SOLD,

At public vendue, on the 19th of Auguſt next, at the preſidents houſe in Princeton, all the perſonal eſtate of the late Revd. Dr. SAMUEL FINLEY, conſiſting of,

TWO Negro women, a negro man, and three Negro children, houſhold furniture, horſes, and neat cattle, a light waggon, a new chaiſe, a ſleigh, ſome hay and grain, together with a variety of farming utenſils. Alſo a choice collection of books, religious, moral and hiſtorical, containing the complete library of the deceaſed. The Negroes will be diſpoſed of at private ſale previous to the day appointed for the vendue, ſhould a ſuitable price be offered for them. The Negro woman underſtands all kinds of houſe work, and the Negro man is well fitted for the buſineſs of farming in all its branches. The conditions of the vendue will be made known on the day of ſale. All thoſe that are indebted to the ſaid eſtate by bond, note, or book debts, are deſired to make immediate payment to the ſubſcribers, and ſuch as have any demands againſt the eſtate are deſired to ſend in their accounts properly atteſted to.

JONATHAN SEARGEANT, jun.
in Princeton, or
SAMUEL BREESE, Executor,
in New-York.

Figure 1. Advertisement from the *Pennsylvania Journal* (July 31, 1766) announcing the estate sale of Princeton president Samuel Finley, held at the President's House on campus in August 1766. (Courtesy of the Library of Congress)

University is the history of America writ small. Our university (founded in 1746) is, like our nation, a place where liberty and slavery were intertwined from the very start. Princeton hosted a meeting of the Continental Congress on the campus in 1783, but the university also hosted a slave sale.[1]

Princeton educated many men who became leaders of our fledgling democratic republic. But it was also a place where most of the founding trustees, all nine of the first presidents, and many of the early faculty members were, at some point in their lives, slaveholders.[2] That does not make us special. It makes us like other early American universities. It makes us deeply American.

1. https://slavery.princeton.edu/sources/two-women-a-man-and-three-children.
2. https://slavery.princeton.edu/stories/founding-trustees.
https://slavery.princeton.edu/stories/slaveholding-presidents.
https://slavery.princeton.edu/stories/princetons-slaveholding-professors.

What evolved into the Princeton & Slavery Project now centers around a website with some nine hundred pages of text (written by forty contributors, mostly students), more than three hundred digitized documents, dynamic maps and graphs, and a documentary film. The project also involved newly written theater pieces, a specially commissioned work of public art, and many community-based programs.[3] Every piece of this project is informed by materials from the Princeton University archives.

This was not a project mandated by or funded by the central administration. In every regard, it was a bottom-up project rooted in—though not confined to—an undergraduate class, and it is, I like to think, a model for how faculty members and archivists can work together to do what neither could do alone.

The origins of this project lay in my ignorance and curiosity. I was familiar with the university and slavery studies being done elsewhere. After I moved to Princeton in 2009, I wanted to learn more about my new institution. I'd heard that Princeton was a conservative school, and that it was the "southernmost Ivy" (a baffling designation, given our geographical location to the north of the University of Pennsylvania). I made some inquiries and learned that no one was investigating Princeton's historical engagement with the institution of slavery. I was curious to see what I could figure out.

In the spring of 2013, Dan agreed to be my partner in what I think both of us would characterize as an experiment. What could we and a small group of undergraduates figure out in a semester-long history seminar on the topic of Princeton and slavery, taught in the classroom of the university archives? The supporting evidence for our inquiry was likely to be widely scattered. But surely, a lot of it would be at the university itself.

---

3. https://slavery.princeton.edu.
https://slavery.princeton.edu/sources.
https://slavery.princeton.edu/multimedia/visualizations.
https://slavery.princeton.edu/multimedia/videos/Videos/facing-slavery.
https://slavery.princeton.edu/multimedia/symposium-videos.
https://artmuseum.princeton.edu/campus-art/objects/132361?lat=40.349209&lon=-74.660278.

There are two ways to describe that first iteration of the class. First, we were clueless. But to put it more positively, we accepted the open-ended nature of our project. We had not pre-selected documents or written structured research assignments. This was a labor-intensive class. And I acknowledge our open-endedness was a luxury afforded by the small size of our class and our ability to both be present for every session. A student would ask a question in the middle of class and fifteen minutes later there would be a box in front of her containing documents that might address her query. Those students have no idea how lucky they were! Despite the fluid and open-ended nature of our work, I think there are some general take-away points from our project that might be useful to a broader range of teaching collaborations between faculty and archivists.

As the project developed and grew, our questions expanded. We built "history lab" sessions into the syllabus, creating in-class time for students to work on their selected research topics. After the second iteration of the course, students understood that these research papers would—if they passed muster—end up on a public website (which thus far has been visited by more than 30,000 unique users from 148 countries). That got their attention. These sessions worked best when students requested material in advance, and then worked with Dan and me, one on one, as we walked around the classroom helping them learn how to decipher a record, interpret eighteenth-century script, or locate related analog and digital sources.

The class often grew noisy, as students shared discoveries from one box of papers with classmates working on related topics.

In relationship to the archives, our intellectual queries about Princeton and slavery fell into three categories:

1. Obvious questions whose sources would lie elsewhere. Examples of these sources include the colonial wills and court records kept in the state archives, and documents about Princeton's local African American community, which are stored at the local historical society.
2. Obvious questions that would meet with limited results in the archives. We were able to answer some of our questions about

Figure 2. Faculty advisors and student researchers for the Princeton & Slavery Project seminar in fall 2017, at Princeton University's Mudd Manuscript Library. (Princeton University, Office of Communications, Denise Applewhite)

the university's financing and the impact of money[4] derived from wealth in human property and from slave labor. But sloppy record keeping and disastrous fires in 1802 and 1855 mean we don't have the detailed records we'd wish to have. That said, an enormous number of questions for which we could find only limited answers in the archives *could* be answered with the *digital sources* that have transformed the study of American history. So, for example, if we could reconstruct lists of all of Princeton's early professors and tutors from archival sources, our ability to understand whether they owned human chattel depended on our ability to access digitized newspapers and census records.

3. Finally, questions that *could* be answered from Princeton's archives. And here's the example I'd like to focus on: the origins of our student body. Most university archives allow you to reconstruct where the school's students come from. We launched into this,

---

4. https://slavery.princeton.edu/stories/moses-taylor-pyne.

working with Dan's staff at the archives to compile a database of all seven thousand students who attended Princeton between its founding in 1746 and the Civil War. To understand our core questions about slavery we needed to understand just who attended what was then known as The College of New Jersey. I did not anticipate how important this project would prove.

Undergraduates in our seminar worked with the student files to find the place of origin for a great many of the students. But then we brought in a SWAT team of graduate students, and while the soundtrack of *Hamilton* blasted away, and stacks of pizza sat in the archives' ante room, some fifteen graduate students tackled the more challenging names on a snowy February night and knocked off another two thousand names or so.

What did our hard-won database of student origins[5] teach us? We really were, as the old saying goes, the southernmost Ivy, at least in terms of our student body. During the early Republic and antebellum eras, some 40% of our students came from the South (comparable numbers from Harvard and Yale are on the order of 10%). At some moments, more than 60% of students in a given class hailed from the South. This had multiple consequences. First, the violence that erupted in the 1830s and 1840s, as students from slaveholding families encountered free people of color in the town of Princeton.[6] And second, the evolution of a conservative political ethos on campus during the antebellum period, as the university administration struggled to make the school a place that remained accommodating to northern and southern students alike, as sectional tensions threatened to rip the country asunder. The financial well-being of the school depended on the tuition money flowing in from southern states.

We graphed the data from our student origins database in multiple ways. In this graph, one sees just how high the percentage of southern

---

5. https://slavery.princeton.edu/sources/database-of-princeton-student-origins.
6. https://slavery.princeton.edu/stories/riot-of-1846.
https://slavery.princeton.edu/stories/african-americans-on-campus-1746-1876.

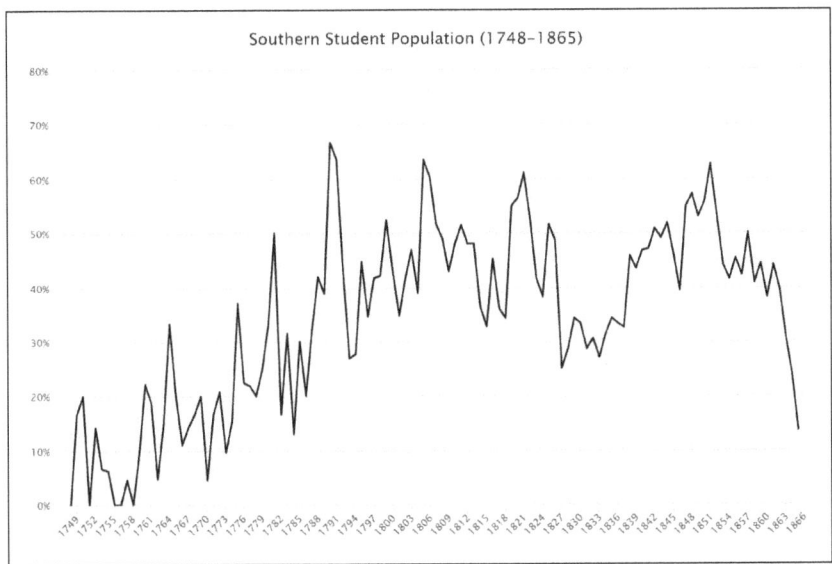

Figure 3. Percentage of southern students in the Princeton student body from the Class of 1748 to the Class of 1865.

students at Princeton was at any given moment. In the class of 1851, for example, nearly 63% of students hailed from the South.

We also created a dynamic heat map[7] that visualizes where Princeton students came from between 1746 and 1865. Here, one can see that New England students rarely came to Princeton. One can observe that southern and southwestern students flowed to Princeton in greater numbers after the Revolution. One can watch those students disappear at the outbreak of the Civil War, as southern students left Princeton to return home and take up arms against their northern classmates. Most importantly, one can see this: the southern origins of Princeton's student body track the spread of the southern plantation economy. Slavery and capitalism explain the geographical diversity of the school's student body.

The student origins data, and the multiple ways in which it was visualized, led to a number of interesting student projects. It allowed one

---

7. https://slavery.princeton.edu/multimedia/visualizations/student-origins-heat-map.

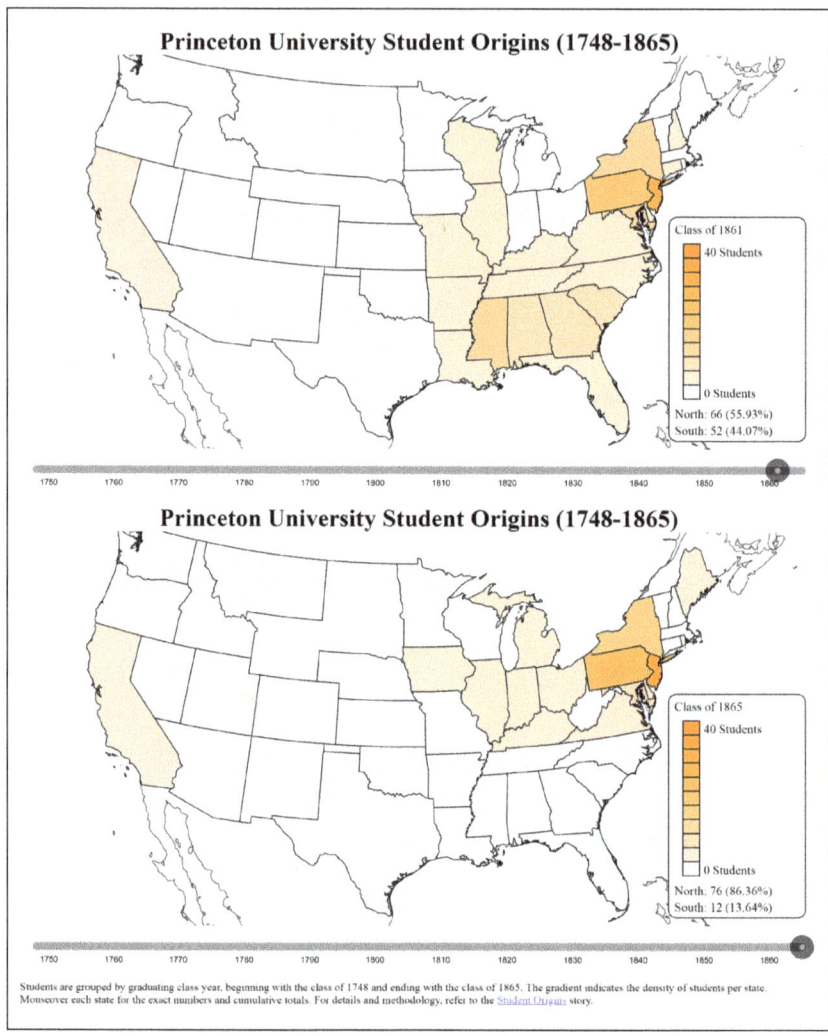

Figure 4. Origins of Princeton students in the Class of 1861 and Class of 1865.

student to investigate why Princeton attracted so many students from territorial Mississippi. It encouraged another to explore why we had so many students from Charleston.[8] These stories would not have emerged without the student origins data.

---

8. https://slavery.princeton.edu/stories/princeton-and-mississippi. https://slavery.princeton.edu/stories/princeton-and-south-carolina.

I don't want to overstate the case here. The Scottish moral philosophy students learned at Princeton pushed many to reconsider the moral basis of slavery. But if I were to characterize the general tone on campus in the antebellum era, it would be one of conservative caution, a reluctance to rock the boat. The student origins data—data we really didn't focus on in the beginning, as we searched for the more direct evidence of slaveholding by Princeton affiliates—helps us understand how that came about.

The student data helps us understand why, in 1835, the trustees turned down an offer of $1,000—a tremendous sum at the time—if the college would admit students "irrespective of color."[9] That was not the Princeton way.

Indeed, abolitionism seemed a more threatening and incendiary topic than slavery did. In 1835, the year the trustees rejected that gift, sixty students nearly lynched an abolitionist speaking at a house in town.[10]

Large numbers of southern students (as well as the conservative position of the Presbyterian Church) also help explain why Princeton became ground zero for the American Colonization Society, a movement begun around 1816 that called for free Blacks to be sent to Africa. The founders were largely Princeton men. Princeton professor John Maclean, Jr., who would become the college president in 1854, became the steward of the New Jersey branch of the society.[11] Maclean saw the colonization movement as a safe middle way that would pacify Princeton's southern slaveholding families (after all, he wasn't advocating for abolition) and keep her northern families happy too (after all, he was concerned for the welfare of free Blacks).

Traces of all three of these stories—about donations, abolitionism, the American Colonization Society—lay in the archives, but the student

---

9. https://slavery.princeton.edu/sources/1000-subscription-from-david-leavitt.

10. https://slavery.princeton.edu/stories/attempted-lynching.

11. https://slavery.princeton.edu/stories/princeton-and-the-colonization-movement.
https://slavery.princeton.edu/stories/john-maclean-jr.
https://slavery.princeton.edu/stories/princeton-and-the-new-jersey-colonization-society.

origins data unexpectedly helped us pull those stories together into a single narrative.

The legacy of Princeton's conservative middle way lingered for a very long time.

Consider the Civil War Monument[12] in Nassau Hall, our oldest campus building. This memorial was not erected until *after* the university erected a monument to honor the fallen of World War I. Prior to that, the school didn't know quite what to do.

Princeton saw approximately six hundred of her sons enlist for military duty during the Civil War; some eighty-six—the majority fighting for the Confederacy—died.[13] The original plans for the memorial, carved in 1921–1922, called for the students to be grouped by their Union or Confederate affiliation. But the university president rejected this plan: "No, the names shall be placed alphabetically, and no one shall know on which side these young men fought."[14] The resulting memorial may be the only one in the nation to list the dead from both sides, without indicating the cause for which they died. Well into the twentieth century, Princeton University sought to remain a congenial home for northerners and southerners alike, steering clear of controversy and emphasizing the sacrifice that drew its students together rather than the politics that pushed them apart. This is what we call reconciliationist memory. There is a politics to it; it minimizes the importance of slavery as a cause of the war.

Princeton's very southern orientation, so carefully documented by students as a part of this project, helps explain why Woodrow Wilson and his own conservative racial views should find Princeton a congenial home in the early twentieth century.[15] And it helps explain one of the most shameful facts in the history of a great institution: the first African American undergraduates did not enroll at the school until after World War II.[16]

---

12. https://slavery.princeton.edu/stories/civil-war-memorial.

13. https://slavery.princeton.edu/stories/counting-princetonians-in-the-civil-war.

14. W. Barksdale Maynard, "Princeton in the Confederacy's Service," *Princeton Alumni Weekly*, 111, no. 9 (March 23, 2011).

15. https://slavery.princeton.edu/stories/erased-pasts-and-altered-legacies-princetons-first-african-american-students.

16. https://slavery.princeton.edu/stories/integrating-princeton-university-robert-joseph-rivers.

Figure 5. Princeton University's Civil War Memorial (Princeton University, Office of Communications, Denise Applewhite)

If a committed archivist and the availability of digital resources enabled our work, we also benefitted from other intellectual and professional turns: a new interest in slavery in the North; our graduate students' eagerness to get experience in public history; and the support of a new university librarian who saw our independently created website as one that showcased university resources and agreed to host and maintain our project on the library servers.

Our project started small, but by the time we launched our website[17] in November 2017, we had bigger ambitions. We wanted to change Princeton's historical DNA, to make our story something people thought of at the same time they thought about the defeat of the British forces on our campus during the Revolutionary War. And that is happening. Across campus, new plaques are going up, new names are being attached to campus sites, and new walking tours are being designed. Classes across the university—ranging from astronomy to dance—are engaging our work in ways we could not have foreseen. Colleagues have approached us about how to do companion projects on Asians and Asian Americans at Princeton, and on Princeton's historical engagements with Native American history.[18]

It is all immensely gratifying, and I like to think one end result has been to make the Princeton archives an unexpectedly relevant and useful resource for colleagues across campus. The broader campus community now understands, in an immediate way, that the past has something useful to say to the present. Certainly, the project has been transformative for both the undergraduates who took the classes or participated in other ways, as well as for the graduate students who volunteered to research and write stories for the website. They get it. History matters. And after some pushback on this project, I think Princeton University understands that, too.

---

17. https://slavery.princeton.edu/.
18. https://slavery.princeton.edu/stories/indians-slavery-and-princeton.

The Archives as History Lab

Daniel J. Linke

I was very fortunate to have been able to work with Professor Sandweiss on this project, and while I am proud of the university archives' contributions to this amazing project, none of it would have happened without her. I say that because at the time of Brown University's report on slavery around 2006, I was asked about Princeton's connections and I couldn't answer that question in any fashion typical of an archivist.

Then, in 2007, I bought a collection of papers related to John Maclean Jr., a long-serving member of the faculty, who finished his Princeton career as the college president. Within the papers was the estate inventory of his father, the college's first chemistry professor, who died in 1814. Listed last, after his furniture, books, clothes, silverware, and other worldly goods, were two striking entries: Negro Girl Sal, $175; and Negro Boy Charles, $75.

As an archivist, like many of you, I handle historic documents all the time. We become inured to them. Presidential signature? Dime a dozen! Right?

But that moment, handling the Maclean inventory was electric for me. I knew this estate inventory provided a sliver of insight into the question of Princeton and slavery, because here was evidence that one typical member of the Princeton faculty owned human beings. So it raised the question: how many others on the faculty owned slaves? It was a tantalizing question, because the answer would surely link to broader themes historians were beginning to investigate on the issue of higher education's connections to human servitude.

So when Professor Sandweiss proposed teaching a course in the Mudd Library to explore this question and to use the archives collections right there in our classroom, I was all in.

Here are a few things I want my fellow archivists to know that helped me and the archives be a good partner for this project:

1. Make your collections accessible.
First, get your collections in order. Greene-Meissner's "More Product, Less Product" article[19] is nearly fifteen years old. I hope it is no longer controversial, but I do worry that people only pay lip service to it. If you have a longstanding backlog, please find a way to whittle it down to next to nothing. In the archival literature, there have been a growing number of articles focusing on archives and social justice, but we cannot address those important issues if we don't have a basic handle on our holdings. No access? No social justice!

That said, in the course of this project, we certainly found collections that were under-described or inaccurately described, but the fact that a student was using the material meant that it was at least minimally described, and that's what you should aim for, as per Greene and Meissner. If possible, use this need for access to make an argument for more or temporary staff to get it done.

2. Be open to failure and be ready to be wrong.
I had no idea how successful the students would be, but I was, to be honest, pessimistic. I thought in a class of seven or eight, only one or two would come up with much, but it was the opposite. The great majority of the students were successful in their research and made contributions to the project. By asking new questions of old sources, they were able to find and do a lot. This is not to say that every avenue of inquiry met with complete success, but sometimes incomplete information would open up new questions that could be answered. A mentor of mine was fond of saying that "there is no such thing as useless knowledge, just knowledge that hasn't yet been used."

3. Ride the wave!
As the project expands, keep going, and find ways to do the things needed to support the next step. If Professor Sandweiss had said to me

---

19. Mark Greene and Dennis Meissner, "More Product, Less Process: Revamping Traditional Archival Processing," *The American Archivist*: 68, no. 2 (Fall/Winter 2005): 208–263. https://doi.org/10.17723/aarc.68.2.c741823776k65863.

at the outset that she wanted to host a class in the building—multiple times—and that the work would lead to a massive website, a history hackathon, an art exhibition with a commissioned work by a major artist, a film documentary, original plays by leading African American playwrights, and a symposium that drew a national all-star faculty line-up that included Toni Morrison and Ruth Simmons, I would have gotten a headache or had an aneurysm thinking about how to accommodate all that. But as the project unfolded and we were asked to support many of these activities, we accommodated the demands within our normal course of business as best we could.

Frankly, the University archives' profile has never been higher. Yes, it's great to be mentioned in the *New York Times* and other national publications, and then have Facebook friends give you shout-outs when they see them, but from my viewpoint, it's even better when you're known on campus.[20] Despite what one might think, Princeton is like a small town where people know each other, and while I benefited from and built upon the work that my predecessor, Ben Primer, had done to raise the profile of the university archives, nothing has come close to the dividends of the Princeton and slavery project.

Because of my involvement in the project, I have subsequently been part of a number of campus initiatives and committees that make decisions about university historically-related projects, including the funding of university history research projects, adding alumni portraits to campus spaces, and the hiring of a project specialist to undertake the work to highlight neglected aspects of Princeton's history. I also was invited to the President's annual holiday party last year for the very first time, something that I don't think will happen again, unless Professor Sandweiss has planned some other project she hasn't told me about yet.

More importantly, I have had conversations with faculty about doing parallel work tracing Princeton's connections to Asia and the opium

---

20. "Princeton Digs Deep Into Its Fraught Racial History," *New York Times*, https://www.nytimes.com/2017/11/06/arts/princeton-digs-deep-into-its-fraught-racial-history.html and "Slaves in the Ivy League: Princeton Discovers Its Racial Past," *Chronicle of Higher Education*, https://www.chronicle.com/article/Slaves-in-the-Ivy-League-/241692, both accessed April 2, 2019.

trade, and fielded all sorts of inquiries spurred by people who came to the archives after learning about its involvement with the Princeton and slavery project. Involvement with the project was its own reward, but it's also valuable that people have come to see that history matters, and that the archives matter. And that, I think, should help us with the future work of the archives, whatever it may be.

Q and A:

MAS: How did the demands of this project impact your staff? Collecting? Cataloguing?

DJL: I mentioned that we were lucky to have our house in order, in the sense of having collections described and virtually no backlog, but because of the importance of this work, I received requests for the project on a "yes until no" basis. I don't think we ever said no!

"I did not anticipate how important this project would prove," you said. Nor did I, but I knew it had substantial value and that we could accommodate requests with various resources, i.e. work-study student labor, which was how the student origins database was started.

When I hire people, I tell them I am paying them for their judgment, and the same is true for me. While some of the things we did for Princeton & Slavery were "extra," in my judgment, they were worth it. And what were those extra things? We digitized some material at the request of you and the first post-doc and didn't charge our usual fees; for history lab days, because the students often weren't good about putting in their box requests in advance, we would have three to four people do a group retrieval to get materials pulled in time. There were other things that staff would come and ask me about, but after a while, they knew if it was for Princeton & Slavery, and it wasn't a big ask, we'd make an exception. A university archives must ultimately serve its university, and this project has served Princeton University very well.

MAS: Did this project reshape how you think about your collection?

DJL: Yes and no. I always knew that the student perspective was an important part of our collection: the scrapbooks, the autograph books, the student memoir. In thinking about how we would capture that today, when I had the chance recently, I hired a student life project archivist who is processing student collections we already hold and also collecting the records that current student groups are creating. Almost all of that is electronic. So I don't know specifically what future research we will be supporting, but I know that for this part of Princeton's history, there will be something to study.

MAS: Is the intensity of this sort of project and the attendant demands on your time replicable or sustainable?

DJL: Replicable? I don't know if there is a question out there even remotely equivalent to the question of slavery, but I am talking with faculty about the Princeton and Asian American history that you mentioned, which has many similarities to the Princeton & Slavery project, but I don't think it will have the same depth, at least in terms of the archives. Sustainable? There are good problems and bad problems. A bad problem is a leaky roof. A good problem is having so many people who want to use your resources that you are stretched thin. It allows you to ask for more resources.

PEDAGOGICAL APPROACHES

HISTORICAL THINKING THROUGH THE ARCHIVES

Caroline S. Boswell

University of Wisconsin–Green Bay

Jonathan C. Hagel

University of Kansas

Introduction: Teaching Historical Thinking Through the Archives

History pedagogy has undergone a number of seismic shifts over the past decade. This new pedagogical landscape is marked by its diversity, but nearly all its features direct teachers of history to move away from educational models that privilege delivering content about the past. Rather, history instructors are encouraged to help students develop the cognitive skills that characterize the discipline—to think like historians.[1] Likewise, these new modes of teaching promote a range of active

---

1. For a sampling of this growing literature, see: Sam Wineberg, *Historical Thinking and Other Unnatural Acts: Charting the Future of Teaching the Past* (Philadelphia: Temple University Press, 2001) and *Why Learn History (When It's Already on Your Phone)* (Chicago: University of Chicago Press, 2018); Lendol Calder, "Uncoverage: Toward a Signature Pedagogy for the History Survey," *Journal of American History*

or experiential learning techniques that take students out of the classroom and out of the role of passive learner.

Despite the fact we are history faculty at two rather different institutions—the University of Wisconsin–Green Bay (UW–Green Bay), a regional comprehensive public institution, and the University of Kansas (KU), a R1 flagship public university—we have both welcomed these transformations of the history classroom. Our paths first crossed in the graduate program in history at Brown University, but we hardly viewed ourselves as future collaborators, given the very different fields we research (early modern British history and modern United States history). Years later, following a series of critically reflective discussions of pedagogy, we continue to support each other as instructors of the gateway-to-the-major history methods courses at our respective institutions. Our shared view—that engaging students in archival research promotes an authentic, learner-centered approach to teaching disciplinary habits of mind—brought us together at the Teaching Undergraduates with Archives Conference. This essay outlines two approaches that we have developed, in partnership with the archival staff at our respective institutions, to use archival materials to promote historical thinking through active learning in the history methods course.

The first approach, developed at UW–Green Bay, asks students to think about the contingency of the historical record by delving into an unprocessed and uncatalogued collection. Students justify what they wish to include or exclude from their collection, and, in doing so, learn to see how the primary materials that are available shape the kinds of historical stories they can tell. The second approach, developed at the University of Kansas (KU), uses rephotography—the act of retaking

92, no. 4 (March 2009): 1358-1370; David Pace, "Decoding the Reading of History: An Example of the Process," in *Decoding the Disciplines: Helping Students Learn Disciplinary Ways of Thinking. New Directions for Teaching and Learning*, eds. David Pace and Joan Middendorf 98 (Summer 2004): 13-22, accessed February 3, 2016, http://www.indiana.edu/~tchsotl/part3/decoding%20pace.pdf; Joel M. Sipress and David J. Voelker, "The End of the History Survey Course: The Rise and Fall of the Coverage Model," *Journal of American History* 97, no. 4 (March 1, 2011): 1050-1066, https://doi.org/10.1093/jahist/jaq035.

historical photographs—to enable students to "see" change over time. Students select historic images of the KU campus and the surrounding town of Lawrence, Kansas, from archival collections, attempt to reshoot those photographs, and then use additional collections to explore what has changed between the two photos. Taken together, these exercises use the archive to challenge students' sense of history as a set of inherited narratives, and help them engage with the techniques by which historians make sense of the past.

Archiving the Past: Using Unprocessed Collections to Complicate Historical Narratives at the University of Wisconsin–Green Bay[2]

Caroline Boswell, Associate Professor of
History, Humanities and Director of the Center
for the Advancement of Teaching and Learning

As many history professors and advisors know, students who major in history often gravitate toward the program because of their love of fascinating stories about the past. While students who conflate history with stories may provoke consternation among some historians, such language provides instructors an opportunity to complicate historical narratives for students early in the program. We all know students love engaging with tales about the past, but how often do instructors ask undergraduates to question not just those narratives, but also the systems through which they were constructed?

Recent scholarly conversation around learning outcomes for undergraduate history majors has offered guidance on how to approach teaching the discipline's habits of mind. The American Historical Association helped provoke this discussion through its 2016 publication of six core competencies and learning outcomes for undergraduate history majors. The second competency relates explicitly to historical methods, and it

---

2. I would like to thank Debra Anderson, the archivist at UW–Green Bay Archives and Area Research Center, for her help designing the history methods course and this assignment.

includes four learning outcomes: 1) recognize history as an interpretive account of the human past—one that historians create in the present from surviving evidence; 2) collect, sift, organize, question, synthesize, and interpret complex material; 3) practice ethical historical inquiry that makes use of and acknowledges sources from the past as well as the scholars who have interpreted that past; and 4) develop empathy toward people in the context of their distinctive historical moments.[3] This nuanced articulation of historical methods challenges instructors to create assessments that move well beyond primary and secondary source analysis and synthesis and the much-lauded but often ambiguous goal of fostering "critical thinking."

Engaging students in authentic disciplinary inquiry
The first unit of "The Craft of History," the gateway history methods course at UW–Green Bay, uses the UW–Green Bay Archives and Area Research Center as a lab to introduce the concepts and tensions underlying each of these four objectives. As archivists know best, history instructors often view archives as a fun place to teach students primary source literacy. The thrill of discovery and authenticity that students describe following such visits fosters motivation and deep learning of the materials placed before them. Yet, working closely with archivists, instructors can draw on students' enchantment with archives to engage them in conversations around the production, dissemination, and consumption of historical narratives. Done well, this necessarily informs students' ability to practice ethical inquiry and develop historical empathy.

Working in close collaboration with the Cofrin Library's sole archivist, Debra Anderson, I plotted a series of assignments in the first unit of this course—"History, Identity, and the Ideal of Objectivity"—to engage students with Michel Rolph Trouillot's complex theory about the production of historical narratives.[4] We began the unit by asking

---

3. "AHA History Tuning Project: 2016 History Discipline Core | AHA," accessed February 1, 2019, https://www.historians.org/teaching-and-learning/tuning-the-history-discipline/2016-history-discipline-core.

4. Michel Rolph Trouillot, *Silencing the Past: The Power and Production of History*

students a simple question—do they perceive history to be more of a science or an art? The wide variety of answers immediately revealed that people approach the study of the past from multiple perspectives, and, more importantly, that thinking about the past in terms of these distinct domains of knowledge promotes Western-centric conceptions of history. Those who described the craft of writing history as an art spurred a conversation about history as narrative. These elementary conversations provided the perfect segue to the class's engagement with Trouillot's *Silencing the Past: The Power and Production of History*. As they read the first two chapters of this dense text, students learned of the tensions between constructivist and positivist approaches to the past. The class grappled with reconciling the view that history is a construct—"another form of fiction" —with the positivist view that, through a rigorous examination of historical artifacts, a historian is able to uncover the past.[5] Students practiced close reading of a specific part of the text to unpack Trouillot's distinction between what he terms "historicity 1" and "historicity 2":

> What happened leaves traces, some of which are quite concrete—buildings, dead bodies, censuses, monuments, diaries, political boundaries—that limit the range and significance of any historical narrative. This is one of many reasons why not any fiction can pass for history: the materiality of the sociohistorical process (historicity 1) sets the stage for future historical narratives (historicity 2).[6]

Understandably, many students wrestled with their first exposure to theory, yet they also sensed that they had to reckon with Trouillot's distinction between historicity 1 and historicity 2. To help support them, we took to the archives.

(Boston: Beacon Press, 1995). Catherine Denial's "The Subjective Self: Teaching Student Historians to Ask 'Who Am I?,'" *Syllabus* 5, no. 2 (2016), http://www.syllabusjournal.org/syllabus/article/view/186, influenced the design of this unit.

5. *Ibid.*, 5–6.
6. *Ibid.*, 29.

Bringing theory to practice: using unprocessed collections to complicate historical narratives

Early in the course design process, the archivist, Debra Anderson, boldly proposed that we introduce students to boxed, unprocessed collections that she was willing to share under her supervision. With the outcomes for the first unit of the course in mind, I eagerly agreed, as such an experience had the potential to engage students more tangibly with Trouillot's concepts. Having first provided students with a taste of the richness of archival sources through sessions that immersed them in the analysis of challenging primary sources, we had students wade into the unprocessed collections.

Our multiday activity asked groups of three to five students to explore one of these collections in the archives and answer a series of questions about how they might make decisions about the collection. Student groups considered why the archives would agree to take the collection, whose materials were in it, how they ended up at the archives. Finally, students provided a brief summary of the collection that described its materials. At the end of two class sessions, students also had to contemplate why the collection *matters*. What questions might historians, or anyone with a stake in studying the past, ask of it? Finally, our worksheet asked groups to isolate one item type within the collection that they would keep—such as pictures, personal letters, cards, or newspaper clippings—and why. Groups also had to grapple with exclusion by choosing one item type they would not retain and offering a similar justification. After completing the lab activity, students wrote a reflection that unpacked their approach to the assignment and discussed how preconceptions of what they believed to be of historical value influenced their decisions. Further, they had to contemplate the power that conceptions and decisions have on future historical narratives, including a discussion about the silences that may exist in "official" archives.

During our evaluation of the success of the activity, our archivist and I quickly assessed that one of the collections had particular pedagogical value: papers from a Green Bay family in the 1950s, left at the archives' door, which are of unknown provenance.

Figure 1. Unprocessed collection of family papers from 1950s Green Bay, Wisconsin. Located in the University of Wisconsin–Green Bay Archives, Green Bay, Wisconsin.

The collection included items familiar to archivists: newspaper clippings, greeting cards, a daily record of family accounts, a series of letters and personal notes, and the notorious lock of hair so often found in family collections. Initially the student group viewed the collection as a relatively mundane window into the life of an average Green Bay family. Not all members engaged deeply with the various sources in the collection, and they were a little too quick to appraise the potential value of the various items within it. One student remarked, for example, that the greeting cards, while interesting, did not have much historical value. Though there was some disagreement, the group choose to keep the account book. Generally, the students noted that the accounts could help people piece together the financial realities of everyday life for an "ordinary" family in 1950s Green Bay.

Upon deeper examination, however, other students in the group realized that the collection documented the experience of a family with two parents who suffered from serious illnesses, including mental illness. Outside of the newspaper clippings and hair (which everyone agreed to leave out), each of the other items provided some insight into that experience from a variety of family perspectives. The account book noted when the father was admitted to Winnebago State Hospital, which a quick reference check would reveal as a mental health institute. A series of get-well cards to the mother addressed to a hospital in Madison uncovered her struggles with health. When read along with the letters, it became clear that the children often lived with relatives as a result of their parents' illnesses. Further, letters and personal notes also suggest that the father abused his wife and children. By limiting their engagement to a quick perusal of the letters, cards, account book, and notes within the collection, some students entirely missed this theme. Their preconceptions of the value of such "mundane" documents informed their willingness to engage closely with each.

Reflecting on artifacts, collection, and the production of narratives
Student reflections provide suggestive evidence that delving into unprocessed collections pushed many to think about the construction of historical narratives in relation to how people collect, read, and analyze artifacts from the past. Reflecting on the 1950s family papers, one student claimed, "The simple writings back and forth could give us new insight into mental health and the stigma surrounding it in 1950s Wisconsin." The student further noted that the "ignoring of subsets in our society such as mental health patients is a shame that could, and should be corrected." Other students wrote with concerns about how the availability of evidence controls narratives, and how the decisions that individuals, families, and archivists make "can affect future availability of narratives." A few wrote with concern about how strategic collections decisions may silence voices, and, in a particularly telling example, one student wrote:

> I value the belongings and objects that have relation to people with status, over people who do not have any prominence. Many people will know these people of prominence and care about their belongings, whereas most people will not know who [X] was. So, I value [this] history over the history that is largely overlooked (ordinary people of no prominence).

After writing the previous sentence, I had to pause and think about what I had just wrote. I do not like that is the way I value some history over other types of history. I hope that over the course of the semester and my college career that this will change.

Asking students direct questions about how we curate the past drove them to consider how dominant cultures and identities influence what remains of the socio-historical processes that Trouillot described, as well as the narratives created from them.

For those considering a similar assignment in a course, first and foremost you either need to find or be a Debra Anderson—an archivist whose love of student learning and engagement outweighs valid concerns of having students' hands in unprocessed collections. Instructors will also need to see the archivist as a true partner and collaborator on the assignment. Though we did not design the assignment to teach students about best archival practices, they did ask several questions of the archivist that provided small insights into that scholarly world. In the end, we found that our discussions of the way an archivist approaches a collection compared to a historian prompted indispensable conversations about how these processes intersect in the creation of historical narratives.

Seeing Change: Rephotography as a Tool to Promote Historical Thinking

Jonathan C. Hagel, Assistant Teaching Professor of History, University of Kansas

Archives are essential to the work historians do as scholars. Curiously, though, the archives play little or no role in most of the work historians do as educators. Most renditions of undergraduate historical methods courses take their students for an introductory visit, and it is not uncommon for professors to schedule a "show and tell," as archivists call it, to expose students to documents that pertain directly to course content. But historians rarely connect the processes of archival research, as they experience it, to the way they teach history.

Of course, the reason for this is that such work is hard, complex...

and slow. Even in courses that are not built around specific content, like the history methods course, time is precious. It is hard to justify spending more than a class session or two exploring the archives when our courses have to tackle other problems—like basic literacy in the different forms of historical knowledge (encyclopedias, journals, books, and the like), the relationship between primary sources and historical truth, and the mechanics of proper citations.

That said, what we historians love most about our work is the thrill of discovery in the archives. In my experience, when history students get to experience the archives the way that historians do, they too feel that excitement. Moreover, promoting such authentic experiences can advance larger pedagogical goals, especially those connected to the model of "historical thinking" articulated by Sam Wineberg, among others.[7]

I adopted the technique of rephotography (or repeat photography), as sketched out below, in my rendition of "The Historian's Craft," the introduction to historical methods for undergraduate majors at the University of Kansas. Rephotography, I hoped, could both engage undergraduates in a more authentic archival research experience as well as teach basic concepts of historical thinking: namely *change* and *continuity* through active learning.

Rephotography

Rephotography as a technique may be as old as photography itself. Put simply, rephotography is the act of retaking a given photograph at a later time. The practice is predicated on a simple effect—namely, that the juxtaposition of two images of the same place at different historical

---

7. See Sam Wineberg, *Historical Thinking*, and also the work of his Stanford History Education Project, particularly their schema for "historical reading" and "historical thinking." There are a number of brief and useful introductions to the concepts of historical thinking. See Thomas Andrews and Flannery Burke, "What Does It Mean to Think Historically," *Perspectives on History*, January 1, 2007, which mentions Mark Klett's rephotography work as an example of historical thinking. Also, "The Historical Thinking Project" website put together by a team of Canadian educators under the direction of Peter Seixas and Jill Coyler. See "The Historical Thinking Project," accessed 08 February 2019 at http://historicalthinking.ca/.

Figure 2. Matthew Conaghan used his rappelling skills and basic photo-editing tools to create this image. Note the church steeples for points of reference. Matthew Conaghan, *Bird's Eye View of Downtown Lawrence*, 190x/2017 (2017). Reproduced with permission.

moments confronts the viewer with historical change. That effect can vary widely, from intriguing to striking or even sublime. There are a range of practices that fit into this space. For instance, environmental scientists have taken up rephotography in recent years as a means of documenting climate change.[8] Moving from the utilitarian to the artistic, the work of photographer Mark Klett, the widely acknowledged

---

8. For examples and a comprehensive bibliography of environmental scientists' use of rephotography, see The Forest Society, "The Repeat Photography Project," accessed 08 February 2019 at http://repeatphotography.org/intro/.

master of the technique, has graced the galleries of the finest museums in the world. As Klett describes it, rephotography allows people to look back through "overlapping layers in time, much like the layered strata in rock."[9] And yet, while a few historians have made use of repeat photography in their work, its value as a pedagogical tool has remained largely unexplored.[10]

In broad outline, the rephotography assignment I implemented in my history methods course was fairly straightforward. My version of "The Historian's Craft" is capped at fifteen students, but the only real limit to the assignment is the size of the archival reading room or teaching space. From the outset, my objectives for the assignment were quite modest: expose students to the handling of historical materials, namely old photographs; introduce students to the kind of purposeful browsing through collections that historians do; and create a structured-yet-fun assignment that promoted team work. Underneath these specific objectives, the assumption of the assignment was that students would need to engage a number of historical thinking skills if they were going to successfully reproduce their historical image. Close observation of their efforts strongly suggests that this assumption proved correct.

Step 1: Browsing, selection, and mapping
After learning about United States mobilization for World War I in previous sessions, the class met at KU's archive, the Kenneth Spencer Research Library, to browse through boxes of historic photographs from the late 1910s and early 1920s. Here, the work of the Curator of

---

9. Aaron Rothman, "Views Across Time: The Art of Rephotography," *Places* July 2011, accessed on 08 February 2019 at https://placesjournal.org/article/views-across-time/?cn-reloaded=1. See Mark Klett's professional website for list of books and examples: https://www.markklettphotography.com. Mark Klett, with Ellen Manchester and JoAnn Verberg, *Second View: The Rephoto-graphic Survey Project* (Albuquerque: University of New Mexico Press, 1984) and Mark Klett, *After the Ruins: Rephotographing the 1906 San Francisco Earthquake and Fire* (Berkeley, Ca.: University of California Press, 2005), among others.

10. For example, see James Sherow and John R. Charlton, *Railroad Empire Across the Heartland: Rephotographing Alexander Gardner's Westward Journey* (Albuquerque: University of New Mexico Press, 2014).

Collections, Sheryl Williams; the University Archivist, Letha Johnson; and the Head of Public Services, Caitlin Donnelly Klepper, was crucial. Knowing the task I had put before the students, Sheryl and Letha pulled from KU's photography archive a range of items with an eye toward pictures of the campus and the town of Lawrence, Kansas—in other words, photos that the students might be able to reproduce. In all, they pulled approximately twenty boxes of photographs. Caitlin and other archive staff were on hand during the class session to help the students handle material, identify what they were looking at, record necessary citation information, and direct them to other photograph collections based on their interests. Working in teams of two, each student selected one or two photos to be scanned and printed by the archive staff.

During this session, the students also used both historical and contemporary campus maps to try to figure out the approximate location from which their photo was taken. The process of browsing, selecting, and mapping their photos involved a number of historical thinking skills: they had to read their images closely for clues; use other photos and maps to corroborate their idea of where the photo was taken; and empathize with the person who took that photo, asking themselves where that person was when they took this photo, why they took it, and what was interesting about the photo for them.

Step 2: Scouting and shooting
In the subsequent class session, students headed out onto campus to retake their historical photos. Armed with their phones and a paper copy of their photo, they had to identify where the photographer was when they took that shot. This simple task demanded that they gauge their image of the campus against the physical reality and look closely at the campus itself as a historical artifact, as David Halliwell is doing in Figure 3. In doing so, the photo became a window onto the past.

Step 3: Presentation and explanation
In the third session, the students presented to their peers both their original photo as well as their effort to reshoot. This led naturally to a discussion of what had changed and what had stayed the same. Some

Figure 3. David Halliwell lines up his shot. Or, at least, he tries to. Sometimes whole buildings just disappear, like the one on the right of his photo, which was demolished in the 1960s.

Figure 4. Kathryn Ammon, *Cadets in front of Marvin Hall*, 1917/2016 (2016). Reproduced with permission.

continuities and changes were clear, as when buildings were built or knocked down, or the number of trees expanded (a lot!). Other changes were more subtle, like changes to the elevation of the landscape or even camera technology. Still others, particularly those that showed students working, playing, or posing for the camera, as the World War I-era cadets are doing in Kathyrn Ammon's composition (see Figure 4), opened up surprising conversations about changes to the nature of student life at KU.

Through these conversations, students demonstrated two key insights about the nature of history. First, by tapping into their curiosity and intimate knowledge of *their* campus, rephotography motivated them to try to figure out how that campus had changed. Using their old photos as windows onto the past, they started to see historical change. Second, and perhaps more interesting, because of the challenges of recomposing their historical photos—many of which are impossible to retake for myriad reasons—they began to confront the limits of what they can know about the past at all. Historic photos are windows onto the past, but those windows are never completely clear, and they rarely give historians the kind of view they really want.

Alterations, next steps, and deploying rephotography as a teaching technique

As a technique for teaching about historical change, rephotography offers a host of powerful features. It gets undergraduates into the archives and engages them in the kind of purposeful browsing that is essential to what historians do. Then it enables them to take the archives out into the world.

Through speaking with colleagues, getting input from students, and my own experimentation, I have developed a range of alterations and next steps that can make rephotography useful in a number of contexts, depending on the resources available at your campus.

For step 1, browsing and selection, students can capture historic photos using a photo scanning app on their phones, like Google Photoscan. Simplifying matters further, students can go directly to digitized archival collections.[11] Such options cut out the need for archival staff to scan the photos at all, and they streamline the process of presentation of student work (see below).

For step 2, scouting and shooting, technology is making new options available all the time. Phone applications like Photobond and other photography overlay apps make lining up and retaking digitized photographs much easier. Websites like Historypin, Timepatch, re.photos, and Clio, which integrates user-uploaded photographs with Google Maps and Google Street View, promise to allow students to conduct virtual rephotography—a boon for students with disabilities or those who face other restrictions.[12] It is worth noting that the speed and direction of technological change in this space has been uneven in the past few years, but remains quite promising. That said, when it comes to composition, nothing can substitute for imagination, as Jared Schultz reminds us in his striking interpretation of romance on campus (Figure 5).

Step 3, explanation and presentation, offers the greatest space for striking out in new directions. At the most basic level, oral presentation with images projected on a screen provides a very effective way for student to show their work and demonstrate their understanding of change. The websites listed above, or even a course blog hosted by a learning management system (e.g. Blackboard or Canvas), can provide places for students to upload and link to their rephotographic efforts. Using free, open-source tools like JuxtaposeJS or Adobe Spark, students can embed their work in websites, making it publicly accessible to a wider audience.

For those teachers seeking a deeper engagement with the archives, a rephotography element can provide a starting point for a bigger project. For instance, after completing the stages outlined above, students can devise research questions that aim to explain why or how the changes they observed came to fruition. These questions, in turn, can lead them

---

11. These can be local or state collections, or the vast holdings of the Library of Congress and National Archives, which include famous collections like the Depression Era FSA photos and the EPA's Documerica collection from the 1970s.

12. See Historypin at https://www.historypin.org/en/, accessed 10 September 2019, Timepatch at http://ajapaik.ee, accessed 08 February 2019, and Clio at http://www.theclio.com, accessed 08 February 2019.

Figure 5. Jared Schultz, perhaps feeling lonely. Or liberated. Jared Schultz, *Strolling in front of Wescoe Hall*, 198x/2017 (2017). Reproduced with permission.

back into the archives. After all, as historians know, the archives are where the real joys of history are found.[13]

Conclusions

Our experience as two historians using the archives to teach disciplinary habits of mind presents us with several key takeaways for readers to consider. First, we believe history instructors should engage archivists early and often as partners in course and assignment design. While there is clear value in visiting the archives to spark students' interest through "show and tell" sessions, instructors should also consider how archives and archival staff may support history learning outcomes beyond primary source literacy or engagement with original content—exciting as those experiences may be. Indeed, we believe more research on the use of archives as labs, and how such history labs may work as high-impact undergraduate research experiences within the larger

---

13. For additional examples and resources, please check out https://tinyurl.com/kurephotography.

history curriculum, would promote the development of closer relationships between archivists and instructors, to the benefit of learners.[14]

Second, we wish to advocate for institutional environments that support thoughtful experimentation with assignments—and even overall course designs—that make greater use of archival resources. Of course, changes require trade-offs: Authentic research assignments that take full advantage of archives and archivists require significant class time that might otherwise go toward standard content or skill-building lessons like primary source analysis, historiography, book reviews, and term papers. Further, real experimentation always carries with it real risk. Rephotography asks students to use technology to explore and articulate their understanding of the past; even if instructors and archivists are prepared to support the use of new media, technology can be capricious. And, beyond those challenges, rephotography inherently carries the risk of failure—some photographs simply cannot be retaken. Similarly, while the unprocessed collections assignment empowered students to examine artifacts not yet explored in detail by archivists or instructors, it also required both instructor and archivist to be prepared to respond to a variety of possible scenarios. Not all collections offered the same complexity as the family papers described above, and within that very collection students encountered offensive, troubling, and traumatic materials. Other groups in this lower-level course struggled to find meaning in a given collection that we did not curate particularly for the assignment.

On top of these challenges of execution, experiments like these overturn prevailing expectations of what history education should look like. Overwhelmingly, our students have responded to these

---

14. Perhaps the most successful example of such a history lab is The Princeton and Slavery Project, which grew out of a research seminar taught in the Seeley G. Mudd Manuscripts Library by Professor Martha A. Sandweiss. For more on the Project see https://slavery.princeton.edu/. The History Department at the University of Michigan also runs a regular seminar series predicated on undergraduate students exploring archival materials, which they group under the title "Michigan in the World: Local and Global Stories." For more, see https://lsa.umich.edu/history/history-at-work/programs/michigan-in-the-world.html.

assignments with gameness, enthusiasm, and a spirit of play. That said, upsetting expectations can also cause the kind of anxiety or dissatisfaction that ends up reflected in traditional student evaluations and broader complaints.

Such concerns notwithstanding, we find that the upsides far outweigh the downsides. Our unconventional assignments at UW–Green Bay and KU enabled us to tackle certain learning outcomes—understanding history as the interpretation of surviving evidence or the significance of change and continuity—by immersing students in processes that required them to confront these realities as historians. We view such issues to be teachable moments for students; for us, the instructors; and for our partners, the archivists. Our assessment of student work suggests that such unconventional assignments may promote deeper learning of some of the most challenging elements of the historical discipline.

ETHICALLY TEACHING HISTORIES OF VIOLENCE, RACISM, AND OPPRESSION

Andi Gustavson
The University of Texas at Austin

Analú María López
Newberry Library

Lae'l Hughes Watkins
University of Maryland

Elizabeth Smith-Pryor
Kent State University

Introduction

How can educators prepare students to grapple with archival materials that reflect histories of violence, racism, and oppression? This chapter considers strategies for facilitating discussions that feel safe for learning while recognizing that not all undergraduates will experience an encounter with a primary source from the same perspective. Each author of this chapter has reflected on how best to ethically teach these histories despite the varied institutions where we work and teach. Andi Gustavson is the Head of Instructional Services at the Harry Ransom Center, a humanities research library and museum at The University of

Texas at Austin; Analú María López is the Ayer Librarian at Chicago's Newberry Library; Lae'l Hughes-Watkins was the university archivist at Kent State University and is now university archivist at the University of Maryland; and Elizabeth Smith-Pryor is an associate professor of African American history at Kent State. Based on our teaching experiences at our institutions, this chapter lays out three case studies where we offer other educators our pedagogical strategies for ethically teaching histories of violence, racism, and oppression, especially strategies to help students interpret, contextualize, and interrogate relevant primary sources. We also discuss our planning and framing techniques to prepare students for content that reflects a violent, racist, and oppressive past, and we discuss methods to help students self-select materials they feel equipped to interpret. We share how to support students as they identify and interrogate absences in the historical record and examine evidence of power relationships in the primary sources.

This chapter grew out of a participatory conference session in which the authors presented papers describing their experiences teaching the histories of violence, racism, and oppression with archival materials. The presentations were followed by facilitated group discussions with the audience about possible best practices, ethical considerations, students' required prior knowledge, and desired learning outcomes.[1] Therefore, we'd like to thank the audience from our conference session for those suggestions for best practices that emerged from the group discussions. In our discussions with the conference attendees it became clear that we, and many of the attendees, approach our teaching from a social-justice perspective and believe that there are many pedagogical possibilities for supporting our students when we ask them to engage with the histories of violence, racism, and oppression. At the same time, as educators we also recognize our ethical responsibility to remain attentive to the risks of reproducing injustice when teaching with materials that document violent, racist, or oppressive acts.[2]

---

1. http://wayback.archive-it.org/5476/20181205132607/https://www.teachingwitharchives.com/.

2. Kristie Dotson, "Tracking Epistemic Violence, Tracking Practices of Silencing," *Hypatia* 26 (spring 2011): 236–257.

Case Study #1: Towards Reconciliation within Indigenous Histories

Analú María López

Photographs of Native American boarding school students have often been used to illustrate the federal forced assimilation practices of the 1870s–1930s. At the Newberry Library, I teach instruction sessions on material from the American Indian and Indigenous Studies Collection, also known as the Edward E. Ayer Collection. Within this collection, the photographs are referred to as the Ayer Photograph Collection, containing a wide variety of photographic media (e.g. postcards, cabinet cards, and stereographs). In terms of content, it consists of approximately six thousand images of Native Americans, including portraits taken at Carlisle Indian Industrial School, landscapes, and Western views. Within a special collection classroom, photography as a medium, combined with other manuscript material, lends itself well to teaching with primary resources to help students begin a dialogue regarding violence, racism, and oppression. As Cass Fey mentions in "Exploring Racism through Photography," "Representations such as photographs shape how we view people and the world and can also be used to enable students to think about race and race relations."[3]

Photographs created in the nineteenth and twentieth centuries of Indigenous peoples, such as ones from the boarding school era, can be used to begin discussions investigating societal, institutional racism, class dynamics (e.g. who had access to photography and who didn't), and commercialization and commodification of Native peoples and culture in the United States. As Antonia Valdes-Dapena quotes Frank Goodyear in "Marketing the Exotic: Creating the Image of the "Real" Indian," "Commercialization and commodification of a race emerges after there has been a power struggle and one culture has been clearly marked as dominant."[4] Photography quickly became popular as a way

---

3. Cass Fey, Ryan Shin, et al. "Exploring Racism through Photography," *Art Education*, 63, no. 5, Art Education and Social Justice (September 2010): 44–51.

4. Antonia Valdes-Dapena, "Marketing the Exotic: Creating the Image of the "Real" Indian," *Visualizing a Mission: Artifacts and Imagery of the Carlisle Indian School,*

to document westward expansion and Native peoples. "Much of the success of photography in the nineteenth century is due to the public's obsession with seeing the previously unseen. Celebrities, exotic lands, and peoples."[5]

Founded in 1879 by Captain Richard Henry Pratt, under the authority of the United States federal government, Carlisle Indian Industrial School was the first federally funded off-reservation Native American boarding school. It had enrolled more than 10,500 students by the time of its closing in 1918. Pratt believed Native Americans could be the equals of European-Americans, and that Native American children immersed in mainstream Euro-American culture would become assimilated. His slogan at Carlisle was "kill the Indian, save the man."[6] While at the school, students were forbidden to speak their own languages. Their hair was cut; they were dressed in suits and ties and corseted dresses. They did not go home for years at a time. The students were taught trades, like baking and blacksmithing, which were meant to give them a foothold in the white world after graduation. To document his experiment, and what scholar David Wallace Adams referred to as "Education for Extinction," Pratt commissioned John N. Choate to take before and after "contrast" photos to document the progress they were making in "civilizing" the Native American children (Figures 1-4).[7] Since Pratt's mission was to show that Native Americans still had a place in a world that was destroying their homes and cultures, he was eager to hold up

---

1879-1918, The Trout Gallery, Dickinson College, Carlisle, Pennsylvania, January 30-February 28, 2004, 35.

5. Laura Turner, "John Choate and the Production of Photography at the Carlisle Indian School," *Visualizing a Mission: Artifacts and Imagery of the Carlisle Indian School, 1879-1918*, The Trout Gallery, Dickinson College, Carlisle, Pennsylvania, January 30-February 28, 2004, 14.

6. "Kill the Indian, and Save the Man": Capt. Richard H. Pratt on the Education of Native Americans. Source: *Official Report of the Nineteenth Annual Conference of Charities and Correction* (1892), 46-59. Reprinted in Richard H. Pratt, "The Advantages of Mingling Indians with Whites," *Americanizing the American Indians: Writings by the "Friends of the Indian," 1880-1900* (Cambridge: Harvard University Press, 1973), 260-271.

7. David Wallace Adams, *Education for Extinction: American Indians and the Boarding School Experience, 1875-1928* (Lawrence: University Press of Kansas, 1997).

examples of students succeeding on his terms. These photographs were then sent to officials in Washington, to potential charitable donors, and to other reservations to recruit new students. In some instances, these same photographs were sold at John Choate's studio for profit.

So, how do we teach about histories of violence, racism, and oppression? First, let us begin speaking about, confronting, and centering these histories. We give voice to Indigenous perspectives that have been omitted from the narratives of history. These histories are difficult to read and talk about. There are traumas we carry from the past. Historical and intergenerational trauma is a very real thing. I have used restorative justice on a grassroots level as an approach while speaking about histories of violence, racism, and oppression. I have slowly been integrating this practice into instruction at the Newberry. Restorative justice views a crime as more than breaking the law—it also causes harm to people, relationships, and the community. A just response must address those harms as well as the wrongdoing.[8]

In terms of using the restorative justice approach within a special collections' environment, this can be done through respectful dialogue, where harms can be healed and relationships restored. An important thing to keep in mind is building trust. This can be challenging in a special collection classroom, where it may be a class of students one is meeting for the first time. One can begin by asking questions in order to get acquainted and build a trusting environment. I do this at the Newberry with a brief introduction to the collection, a description of what we are going to focus on that day, and a little about myself. Each class is different, but the majority of the time the dialogue begins fluidly. Some questions can be very simple: "What is a special collections library? What does it mean to do research at a special collections library? Who has been here before?" As we get into the activity, I have a list of "high quality prompts" related to the material (see handout in appendix). High quality prompts are open-ended; they are about discovery and

---

8. *Teaching Restorative Practices with Classroom Circles,* developed for San Francisco Unified School District, online resource: https://studentsatthecenterhub.org/resource/teaching-restorative-practices-with-class-circles/.

Ethically Teaching Histories of Violence, Racism, and Oppression 247

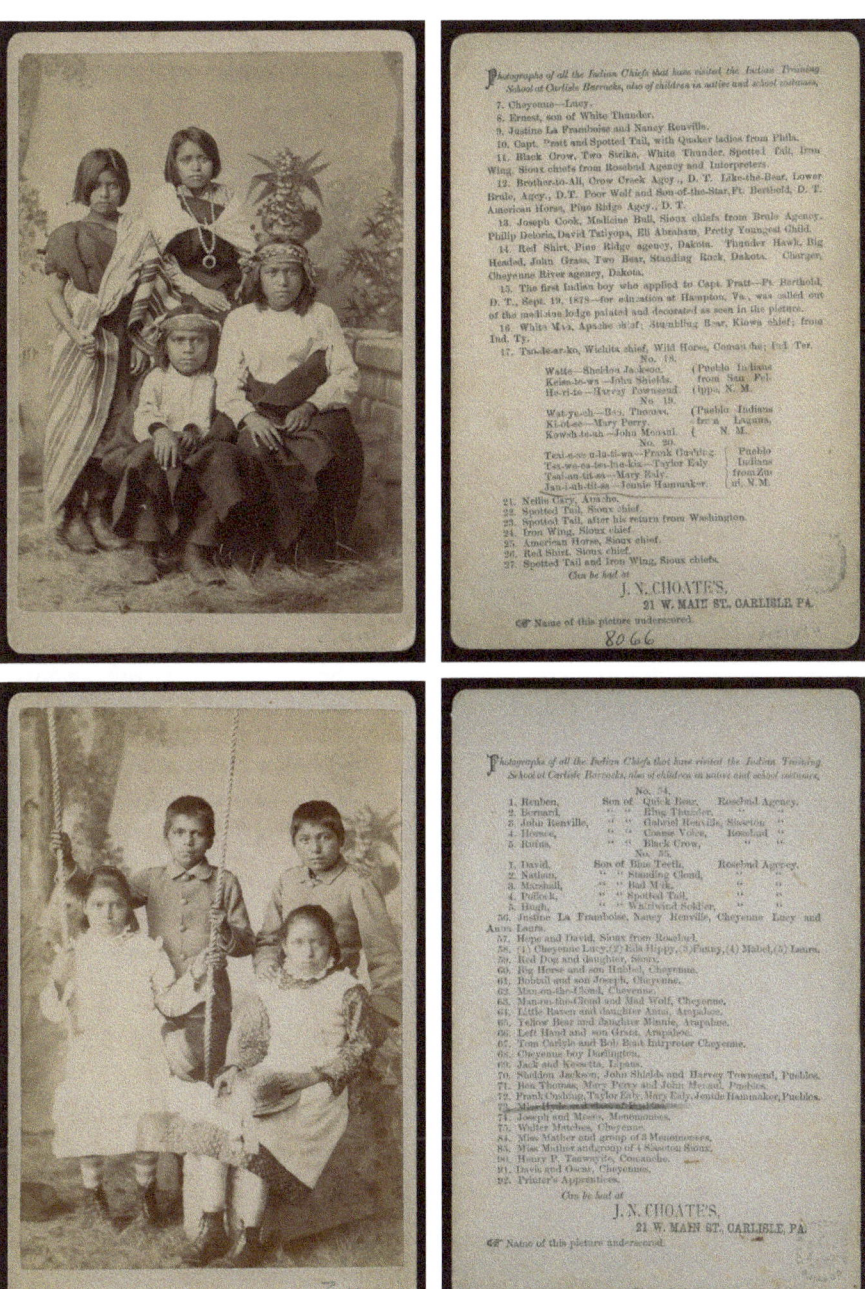

Figure 1-4. Before and after photographs of four Pueblo children from Zuni, New Mexico, c. 1880. Photographer: John N. Choate, Carlisle, Pennsylvania. Edward E. Ayer Photograph collection, AP 1689 and AP 1690, box 50. The Newberry, Chicago.

These photographs show four Pueblo (Zuni) children. This is one of the few studio portraits combining girls and boys. It depicts the before and after assimilation practices at Carlisle Indian Industrial School. It was taken in 1880, just a year after the school opened.

The first image was taken upon arriving to Carlisle Indian Industrial School and the second shortly after. The names of the children are on the reverse side of the photograph but only their assigned Christian names are written: Teai-e-se-u-lu-ti-wa (Frank Cushing), Tra-wa-ea-tsa-lun-kia (Saylor Ealy), Tsai au-tit-sa (Mary Ealy), and Jan-i-uh-tit sa (Jennie Hammaker). The student Taylor Ealy is incorrectly identified as Saylor Ealy.

Two of the four children died while at Carlisle Indian Industrial School. Teai-e-se-u-lu-ti-wa (Frank Cushing), a member of the Pueblo (Zuni) Nation, entered the school on July 31, 1880, and died on July 22, 1881. He was buried in the cemetery on the school grounds. Tra-wa-ea-tsa-lun-kia (Taylor Ealy), also a member of the Pueblo (Zuni) Nation, entered the school on July 31, 1880, and died on July 10, 1883, while on an outing in Schellsburg, Pennsylvania.

Tsai au-tit-sa (Mary Ealy), left the school on July 10, 1883. Reports indicated she was living in Zuni, New Mexico in 1910. Jan-i-uh-tit sa (Jennie Hammaker), left Carlisle on February 6, 1882.

not about teaching facts. They can also be related to current events. Prompts for restorative dialogue can include the following: "What do you think the intention was behind the creation of this image? And why? Who has been affected by what happened and how?"[9] The first time I did this activity, it took some encouragement to get the students talking, but after a couple of guided questions, the conversations went well.

Prior to the activity, we begin with introductions, as mentioned above. Then I break them out into groups and give them copies of the questions I have prepared in the curriculum (see handout in appendix). At this time, I have already laid out the photographic and manuscript materials on the table for students to interact with. Within this activity, I discuss how photography played a role in representation and documentation of Native peoples. Depending on the class, I collaborate with the instructor and suggest short readings prior to the class visit.

---

9. *Teaching Restorative Practices with Classroom Circles*, developed for San Francisco Unified School District, online resource: https://studentsatthecenterhub.org/resource/teaching-restorative-practices-with-class-circles/, 12.

After students analyze and describe the material, they report back to the group and we begin a dialogue. This is also an opportunity for them to raise any other questions they may have.

When teaching histories of this nature, we should also keep in mind we do not know what will trigger any one person. Holding space to speak on these topics is just the first step towards reconciliation. I have encountered instances where an item triggers someone to tears; that same item may not have triggered another person. In this situation, I let them express their pain and anger. If someone is in pain, I listen and allow simple listening to be a comfort; I do not try to take their pain away. Restorative practices cultivate a culture in which everyone feels like they belong. They build a particular sense of community in which all members—students, teachers, parents, volunteers, aides—feel they are seen, heard, and respected.

Activities such as the one I describe in the handout can be used for students from high school to graduate school to get them thinking critically about these difficult topics. This also touches on the core ideas of the Guidelines for Primary Source Literacy: Analytical concepts (users need to understand how sources were produced and delivered); ethical concepts (taking the cultural context into consideration and how users should responsibly consider how their scholarship can affect creators); theoretical concepts (users must seek to understand resulting silences and absences of certain histories); and practical considerations (how is this material accessible; how is it described?).[10]

This case study provides just one example of how one can approach teaching histories of violence, racism, and oppression within special collection classrooms by integrating restorative justice techniques at the entry level. I feel there is still room for this activity to grow and be integrated into teaching histories of violence, racism, and oppression.

---

10. Guidelines for Primary Sources Literacy, SAA-ACRL/RBMS Joint Task Force on the Development of Guidelines for Primary Source Literacy, 2018: 5, https://www2.archivists.org/sites/all/files/Guidelines%20for%20Primary%20Souce%20Literacy_AsApproved062018_1.pdf, accessed 3/30/2019.

Case Study #2: Pedagogies and Power Relationships when Queering the Archives

Andi Gustavson

Over the past year, I have supported classes that focused on queering the archives. The goal of these classes is to encourage students to engage with the archives in ways that consider both the primary sources and the practices of describing, accessing, and interpreting those sources through the lens of queer theory and recovering and creating new LGBTQIA+ histories.[11] One box of photographs that I frequently teach from for these classes comes from the Magnum Photos Collection. Magnum, a group of twentieth-century photojournalists, filed their prints so that they could be sent and resent to different photography publications. The collection of 200,000 prints retains Magnum's organizational structure from the 1940s to the 1990s—a system that was constantly evolving and reflects the moments in which it was created and revised. The photographs in Box 455, labeled "Psychology," were organized by Magnum into folders titled "Sex," "Divorce Clinic," and "Monkey Research," but also "Homosexuality," "Sex Film," and "Transexuals" (Figure 5 and 6).[12] When I teach this content, I facilitate a discussion on oppressive or outdated metadata and help students analyze the box label before ever looking at the prints inside. Together, we discuss the ways in which institutions—both photography collectives and the archives in which their collections are held—are implicated in histories of oppression.

When teaching these photographs, I put in place several practices to prepare students to grapple with the content they will encounter. Faculty and I check in about prior class discussions and students' abilities to contend with these images. When there is material present

---

11. For more on this, see Erin Baucom, "An Exploration into Archival Descriptions of LGBTQ Materials," *The American Archivist* 81, no. 1 (2018): 65–83. https://doi.org/10.17723/0360-9081-81.1.65; Ramzi Fawaz, "How to Make a Queer Scene, or Notes toward a Practice of Affective Curation," *Feminist Studies* 42, no. 3 (2016): 757–768. https://doi.org/10.15767/feministstudies.42.3.0757.

12. Box 455, Magnum Photos Collections, Harry Ransom Center, The University of Texas at Austin.

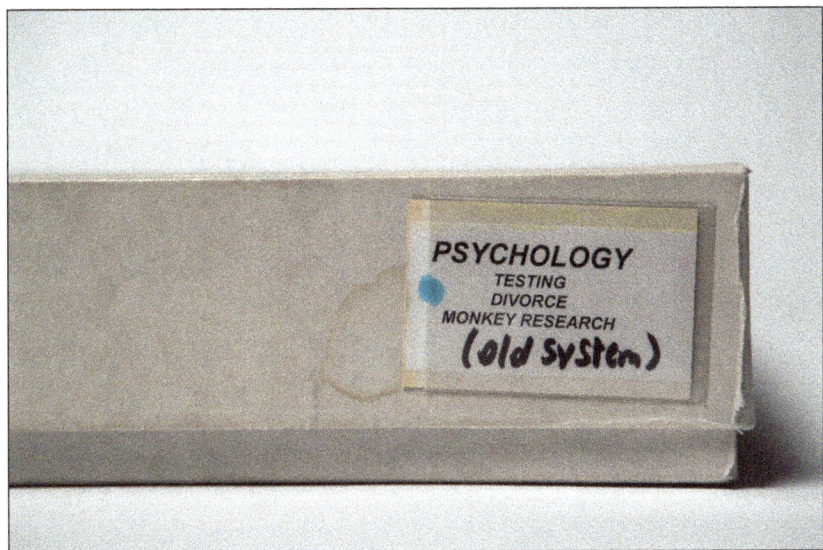

Figure 5. Photograph of exterior of Box 455 of Magnum Photos, Inc. Collection. Derek Rankins. Harry Ransom Center, The University of Texas at Austin. Label was created by members of Magnum Photos collective and reflects their original organization for the collection.

Figure 6. Photograph of contents of Box 455 of Magnum Photos, Inc. Collection. Derek Rankins. Harry Ransom Center, The University of Texas at Austin. Writing on the folders was created by members of Magnum Photos collective and reflects their original organization for the collection.

that the faculty member and I determine reflects overt violence or oppression, or has the potential to overwhelm students, I employ a trauma-informed pedagogy. In these instances, I always offer content warnings; provide students the opportunity to self-select to work on these sources; intentionally stage materials of varying intensity in the room; and let students know that they can tune out or step away if they need to take care of themselves.[13] I help students consider the medicalized histories of the descriptive terms and the risk of pathologizing identities. For example, we discuss how queer studies has indicated the problems inherent in phrases like "homosexuality" and then consider how Magnum's folder labeled "Psychology: Homosexuality" reflects those problems. We then consider how Magnum's systems of organization and the archive's retention of original order reflect and uphold those oppressive structures. We explicitly discuss outdated metadata and changing description practices.[14] Finally, before we move into any group discussion, I model for students how to avoid adopting the language of documents from the past that no longer align with how communities describe themselves today.

When I move from teaching single sessions to multi-visits or semester-long engagements, the students have the opportunity to engage more deeply with learning objectives centered on social justice and power structures at play in the archives. Another class I've supported, "Queering the Archives," met all semester at the Harry Ransom Center, and the students, faculty member, and I worked collaboratively

---

13. Lauren White and Sarah Le Pinchon, "Trauma-Informed Teaching" handout from training, "Trauma-Informed Practices in the Higher-Education Classroom" presented at the Inclusive Teaching and Learning Symposium, The University of Texas at Austin, November 5, 2018. See also Janice Carrello and Lisa D. Butler, "Potentially Perilous Pedagogies: Teaching Trauma Is Not the Same as Trauma-Informed Teaching," *Journal of Trauma & Dissociation* 15, no. 2 (March 15, 2014): 153–168, https://doi.org/10.1080/15299732.2014.867571 and "Practicing What We Teach: Trauma-Informed Educational Practice," *Journal of Teaching in Social Work* 35, no. 3 (May 27, 2015): 262–278, https://doi.org/10.1080/08841233.2015.1030059.

14. Stacy Wood, Kathy Carbone, Marika Cifor, Anne Gilliland, and Ricardo Punzalan, "Mobilizing Records: Re-Framing Archival Description to Support Human Rights," *Archival Science* 14, no. 3 (October 1, 2014): 397–419, https://doi.org/10.1007/s10502-014-9233-1.

to curate an exhibition as their final project.[15] While working on the final drafts of the label texts, the students discussed the lack of diversity within the display and the predominantly white creators within the collections overall. Though there are queer artists of color in the holdings, they were not a part of the social networks or same historical periods the students were studying, and the class wrestled with their desire to create a cohesive narrative documenting queer networks and their commitment to curating inclusively. Much of the teaching at the Ransom Center is centered on Guidelines for Primary Source Literacy from the SAA-ACRL/RBMS (Society for American Archivists, Association of College and Research Libraries, Rare Books and Manuscripts Section), and a key concept for the professor for this class was emphasizing the "silences, gaps, contradictions" within archives.[16] Having discussed all semester the silences within archives, the class grappled with the recognition that they were selectively shaping and mediating their audiences' experiences of the collections.

The struggles faced by this class are indicative of some of the larger questions I want all students to consider when their course visits the Ransom Center. In order to help students consider how past collecting practices and the present-day decisions of archivists and others contribute to the historical record and reflect "evidence of power relationships,"

---

15. This semester-long class was taught by Professor Ann Cvetkovich, who developed the content and designed this final assignment. I am indebted to her for her theoretical expertise and her thoughtful pedagogical approach to this material. For more on this see Anjali Arondekar, Ann Cvetkovich, Christina B. Hanhardt, Regina Kunzel, Tavia Nyong'o, Juana María Rodríguez, Susan Stryker, Daniel Marshall, Kevin P. Murphy, and Zeb Tortorici, "Queering Archives: A Roundtable Discussion," *Radical History Review* 2015, no. 122 (May 1, 2015): 211–231, https://doi.org/10.1215/01636545-2849630; Ramzi. Fawaz, "How to Make a Queer Scene, or Notes toward a Practice of Affective Curation" *Feminist Studies* 42, no. 3 (2016): 757–768, https://doi.org/10.15767/feministstudies.42.3.0757; Alana Kumbier, *Ephemeral Material: Queering the Archive*, Gender and Sexuality in Information Studies, number 5. Sacramento, CA: Litwin Books, LLC, 2014.

16. ACRL RBMS-SAA Joint Task Force on the Development of Guidelines for Primary Source Literacy. "Guidelines for Primary Source Literacy," revised June 2018: 5, accessed December 12, 2018. https://www2.archivists.org/sites/all/files/Guidelines%20for%20Primary%20Source%20Literacy_AsApproved062018_1.pdf.

I employ a variety of pedagogical strategies.[17] These strategies include openly discussing the acquisitions process and the role of curators; highlighting the decisions I made when staging the materials in the room; discussing the labor—and the decision to fund that labor—that goes into preservation and description; discussing how students feel in the space and possible barriers to access for some; asking students which items they think should remain if I teach the class again next semester; and asking which voices are not reflected in my selection of primary sources and why that might be. While this curation final project was not a seamless process, and there were several tense moments of discussion in class, all of these practices allowed us to remain attentive to the small and daily ways that violence takes shape, both in the lived experiences of the people the students studied and within the archival records of those experiences. These students both explored methods for queering the archive and—even when they knew they were struggling—still actively worked to create new queer histories based on their research with primary sources.

Case Study #3: Archives, Student Activism, and the Historian's Classroom

Lae'l Hughes-Watkins and Elizabeth Smith-Pryor

At Kent State University in 2016 and again in 2018 we (a faculty member in history and the University archivist) collaborated to redesign and teach a course on the history of the Civil Rights and Black Power movements, with a special focus on the untold history of both social movements at Kent State. In this course, students would be exposed to both national and local stories about how historically oppressed groups responded to racism, violence, and oppression. This collaboration between history faculty and the University archives would do something that previously taught iterations of the course could not do—give students access to the type of archival collection that they and professional scholars could use to disrupt the "master narrative" of the history of a traditionally white institution of higher education.

---

17. Guidelines for Primary Sources Literacy, 5.

Kent State's place in American history centers on the events of May 4, 1970, and it is frequently associated with images of white student antiwar activism. Students in this class, however, would encounter a "counter" narrative focused not on predominantly white student activism but instead depicting a history of racism and oppression on campus and Black students' responses.

In the fall of 2014, the University archivist launched the Black Campus Movement project to establish a reparative archive via acquisition, advocacy, and utilization. This archive was meant to assist in decolonizing traditional archives and bring historically oppressed voices in from the margins.[18] The University archivist pulled materials from presidential papers, faculty records, University police records, and newly acquired items from Black alumni from the Black Campus Movement project, such as the Lafayette Tolliver collection.[19] The 2016 and 2018 redesign of the course would allow students to use these new collections regarding marginalized identities and student activism. The final project for the class—a digital history project—would place students in the role of meaning-makers, as they used the Black Campus Movement project to produce their own histories of Civil Rights and Black Power on their campus. Preparing students to encounter these materials and engage in historical analysis and narrative creation required a great deal of planning before the students even walked into the classroom.

In planning for the course, we anticipated student engagement with the class would be high, given the focus on campus history. We also anticipated that such a course offered us the opportunity to meet key pedagogical goals for undergraduates in the history and archival classroom. Too often students arrive in college with a misleading understanding of history. The role of historical interpretation plays little part

---

18. Lae'l Hughes-Watkins, "Moving Toward a Reparative Archive: A Roadmap for a Holistic Approach to Disrupting Homogenous Histories in Academic Repositories and Creating Inclusive Spaces for Marginalized Voices," *Journal of Contemporary Archival Studies* 5 no. 6 (2018), https://elischolar.library.yale.edu/jcas/vol5/iss1/6.

19. Lafayette Tolliver collection. Lafayette Tolliver is a Kent State University alumnus who attended the university from 1967 to 1971, graduating with a bachelor of science degree in photojournalism. Due to his extensive campus involvement, Tolliver produced thousands of photographs, many of which were never published or otherwise made accessible until the Black Campus Movement project, https://omeka.library.kent.edu/special-collections/exhibits/show/tolliver.

in most undergraduates' knowledge of the discipline of history. Students often encounter history only through the unified narrative of a textbook that reduces the history of complex events to one-dimensional accounts. Many students never realize that historians reconstruct the past from primary sources, and most students have no idea how historical sources end up or don't end up in the archive. Students are rarely introduced to the problem of archival silences, the missing voices from marginalized communities that deprive students of a more complete understanding of key events in American history.

To move beyond a one-dimensional approach to the past, we designed the course schedule to ensure students would spend a significant amount of time in the archives—essentially the last third of the semester (about four to five weeks). But before students could begin to work with and make sense of evidence related to a history of violence, racism, and oppression on their own campus, especially antiblackness in the University's archives, we recognized that students needed a larger context within which to understand what they might find, as well as the context of how such materials ended up in the archives. Consequently, we designed the first two-thirds of the course as an intensive introduction to the history of racism and the Civil Rights and Black Power movements. The historian selected and assigned scholarly texts on racism and the Civil Rights and Black Power movements. Students blogged about their assigned reading. During class time, students engaged further with the assigned readings and began to develop a deeper knowledge of the Civil Rights and Black Power movements, as well as a sense of the different methods historians use to study the past. Class time was also used to analyze and interpret primary sources related to the assigned texts and develop the skills necessary for work in the archives. Exposure to these primary sources also helped prepare students to encounter archival materials (such as, for example, information about the surveillance of Black campus activists) depicting the history of violence, racism, and oppression at Kent State, particularly from the 1960s and 1970s.

Right before students began the archival portion of the semester, we decided the University archivist would attend two class sessions and introduce the students to archival practices. In particular, given the focus of this course on a "counter" archive related to marginalized students on campus, students needed to understand how collections are developed, the selection process for determining what is kept or not, and the impact of those decisions on the history that can be developed by the researcher based on the collected sources. This proved to be a critical part of the course, since students had little knowledge of collection development, the impact of gaps in an institutional record, the centering of administration voices, or how white supremacist views can impact collections. These discussions helped students understand the limits of many of the records housed in academic repositories. This portion of the course also detailed the efforts behind the Black Campus Movement project, which had been established by the University archivist in an effort to create a robust collection highlighting Black student life at Kent State. Students learned about how this initiative sought to acquire and record the evolution of Kent State University's Black Campus Movement by collecting correspondence, diaries, photographs, newsletters, oral histories, and a variety of personal and organizational materials documenting the Black Campus Movement from 1965 to 1970. Students also learned about the purpose of this initiative—to serve as a counter narrative to the white homogenous narratives that proliferate in much of the university record.

Once in the archival classroom, we worked together to facilitate students' work with archival materials. We helped students consider the kinds of questions they could answer with the existing archival materials. When students encountered racist narratives or records underscoring periods of campus unrest, we helped them draw on the larger contextual knowledge gained earlier in the semester to better understand what they found. The weeks spent in the archival classroom also provided the instructor and archivist with useful feedback on course design.

Despite the usual difficulties working in archival collections (such as being unable to find exactly what one would like to find), students engaged with the archival collections and developed new narratives of the history of their own campus. In our view, student success highlights both the significance of giving students the tools to ask new questions of previously collected content and the importance of the Black Campus Movement initiative—a counter narrative that allows for a reparative approach to collections housed in an academic repository and advocates for identities that have been traditionally oppressed. Preparing students to work effectively with a counter-archive that reveals previously unexamined acts of violence, racism, and oppression can give students the ability to create new narratives that are more inclusive or representative of the varied voices of the past and that perhaps better help academic institutions deal with their present.

Conclusion and Recommendations for Best Practices

These three case studies offer the reader examples of how archivists and historians can ethically teach the histories of violence, racism, and oppression using archival materials. Although each case study approaches these histories in different ways and reflects teaching experiences in different institutions, together they offer pedagogical strategies to help instructors prepare students to interpret, contextualize, and interrogate these important primary sources. In particular, these case studies point out the importance of spending time well before any instructional activities planning techniques and framing strategies to prepare students to encounter violent, racist, and oppressive content in the archives. Educators can help students develop greater knowledge about the context within which these histories of violence, racism, and oppression existed. Once in the archives, educators can draw on trauma-informed pedagogy or aspects of restorative justice practice, such as restorative dialogue prompts, when students work with primary sources. Perhaps most importantly, educators who aspire to ethically teach the histories of violence, racism, and oppression in an archival setting need to share with students how these sources came to be located in an archive and help students understand how the historical record is created. Only then can students begin to identify and interrogate absences and understand the role of power relationships in the sources and thereby develop a better understanding of how histories of violence, racism, and oppression come to be.

APPENDIX

Newberry Library Chicago, Edward E. Ayer photograph collection
Analyzing 19th – 20th century photographs & exploring racism through photography

Overview: At its invention in the 1820s, the making of photographic images involved a complex and laborious process with limited application. However, with the creation of the wet-glass negative in the 1840s, one could produce a limitless number of prints by exposing the negative image onto paper that was made light sensitive through a coating, or emulsion, of sodium chloride. This dramatically invented a new format for disseminating an image on a social and cultural level. Much of the success of photography in the nineteenth century is due to the public's obsession with seeing the previously unseen. Celebrities, "exotic lands and peoples," and international events that used to be out of reach for the middle classes could now be purchased for a few cents. The celebrity and souvenir photograph market was extremely successful and accelerated the photography craze of the nineteenth century, setting the stage for the manufacturing and marketing of portraits of American Indians and of scenes from places such as the Carlisle Indian School.

Race, Representation, Social Justice, and the classroom
As Cass Fey mentions in *Exploring Racism through Photography*, "Representations such as photographs shape how we view people and the world and can also be used to enable students to think about race and race relations." Photographs created in the 19th and 20th centuries of Indigenous peoples, such as ones that came out of the boarding school era, can be used to begin discussions investigating societal and institutional racism and class dynamics (e.g. who had access to photographs and who didn't?) in the US. Photographs of American Indian boarding school students have often been used to illustrate the federal forced assimilation practices of the 1870s–1930s.

American Indian boarding schools were important centers for photography at the turn of the century. John Leslie (Puyallup) learned photography at Carlisle Indian School. In 1895, Leslie published a book of his photography and exhibited his photographs at the 1895 Atlanta International Exposition. By 1906 Carlisle Indian School built a state-of-the-art photography studio and taught photography classes to its Native students. Photographs of American Indian students were taken by official school photographers, and these propagandistic images were produced to emphasize the "civilizing" benefits of the boarding school system. Although some Native students obtained cameras and recorded their own boarding school experiences, the visual history still relies primarily on the institutionally-produced images.

Assigned readings: *The School News*, United States Indian Industrial School (Carlisle, Pa.), October, 1880 issue, and "Exploring Racism through Photography," Art Education, Vol. 63, No. 5, Art Education and Social Justice (September 2010), pp. 44-51.

Learning objectives
- Understand photography as a subjective medium that can encourage discussion about racism, social justice, and inequality
- Discuss and investigate institutional racism through the lens of photography and photographs within the American Indian and Indigenous Studies material and photographs at the Newberry
- Develop an awareness of social justice by discussing issues within specific photographs such as discrimination, stereotyping, and oppression of racial and ethnic groups

Definitions & terms:
<u>Carte-de-visite</u> - the carte de visite, abbreviated **CdV**, was a type of small photograph patented in Paris by photographer André Adolphe Eugène Disdéri in 1854, although first used by Louis Dodero. It was usually made of an albumen print, which was a thin paper photograph mounted on a thicker paper card.

Real photo postcard (RPPC) - is a continuous-tone photographic image printed on postcard stock. The term recognizes a distinction between the real photo process and the lithographic or offset printing processes employed in the manufacture of most postcard images. These real photo postcards had a limited distribution in comparison to lithographic postcards.

Stereoview - Stereoscopy (also called **stereoscopics**, or **stereo imaging**) is a technique for creating or enhancing the illusion of depth in an image by means of stereopsis for binocular vision. Any stereoscopic image is called a stereogram. Most stereoscopic methods present two offset images separately to the left and right eye of the viewer. These two-dimensional images are then combined in the brain to give the perception of 3D depth.

Questions
- What type of photograph is this? (i.e. a postcard, stereoview, carte-de-visite, other?)
- What do you see in the image?
- What do you think the intention was behind the creation of this image? And why?
- What role does the text (if any) play with the photo?
- If American Indians were actively learning photography and producing work, then why do we rarely see this work?
- How would you feel if you were being photographed in this way?
- Even though the U.S. Constitution declares that no person can be discriminated against because of his or her race, why were Native American children forced to attend residential schools?
- What other aspects of the history of Native Americans and their resistance to oppression do these photographs make you think of?

Further readings
- Fey, Cass, Shin, Ryan and et al. "Exploring Racism through Photography," Art Education, Vol. 63, No. 5, Art Education and Social Justice (September 2010), pp. 44-51. Published by: National Art Education Association

- *Teaching Restorative Practices with Classroom Circles*, developed for San Francisco Unified School District, online resource: https://studentsatthecenterhub.org/resource/teaching-restorative-practices-with-classroom-circles/
- Turner, Laura. "John Nicholas Choate and the Production of Photography at the Carlisle Indian School."[20] Visualizing a Mission: Artifacts and Imagery of the Carlisle Indian School, 1879-1918. Retrieved 1 Feb 2012.

Resources
- Carlisle Indian School Digital Resource Center[21]
- Teaching Resources page,[22] Dickinson College, Carlisle, PA
- Edward E. Ayer Digital Collection,[23] Newberry Library
- Souvenir of the Carlisle Indian School[24] / by J.N. Choate, Call number: Ayer 389 .C2 S72 1902
- United States Indian Industrial School,[25] Carlisle Pennsylvania, Call number: Ayer E97.6.C2 C45
- Culturally Sensitive Indigenous Materials (available as a pdf file) in The Newberry's collections.

---

20. https://scholar.dickinson.edu/cgi/viewcontent.cgi?article=1006&context=student_work

21. http://carlisleindian.dickinson.edu/

22. http://carlisleindian.dickinson.edu/teaching

23. https://publications.newberry.org/ayer/#/

24. https://archive.org/details/Ayer_389_C2_S72_1902

25. https://archive.org/details/Ayer_E97_6_C2_C45

Bibliography

Arondekar, Anjali, Ann Cvetkovich, Christina B. Hanhardt, Regina Kunzel, Tavia Nyong'o, Juana María Rodríguez, Susan Stryker, Daniel Marshall, Kevin P. Murphy, and Zeb Tortorici. "Queering Archives: A Roundtable Discussion." *Radical History Review* 2015, no. 122 (May 1, 2015): 211–231. https://doi.org/10.1215/01636545-2849630.

Baucom, Erin. "An Exploration into Archival Descriptions of LGBTQ Materials." *The American Archivist* 81, no. 1 (2018): 65–83. https://doi.org/10.17723/0360-9081-81.1.65.

Carello, Janice, and Lisa D. Butler. "Potentially Perilous Pedagogies: Teaching Trauma Is Not the Same as Trauma-Informed Teaching." *Journal of Trauma & Dissociation* 15, no. 2 (March 15, 2014): 153–168. https://doi.org/10.1080/15299732.2014.867571.

Caswell, Michelle. "Teaching to Dismantle White Supremacy in Archives." *The Library Quarterly* 87, no.3 (2017): 222–235.

Dotson, Kristie. "Tracking Epistemic Violence, Tracking Practices of Silence." *Hypatia* 26 (spring 2011): 236–257.

Fawaz, Ramzi. "How to Make a Queer Scene, or Notes toward a Practice of Affective Curation." *Feminist Studies* 42, no. 3 (2016): 757–768. https://doi.org/10.15767/feministstudies.42.3.07.

Fey, Cass, Ryan Shin, et al. "Exploring Racism through Photography," *Art Education*, 63, no. 5, Art Education and Social Justice (September 2010): 44–51.

Guidelines for Primary Sources Literacy, SAA-ACRL/RBMS Joint Task Force on the Development of Guidelines for Primary Source Literacy, 2018: 5, https://www2.archivists.org/sites/all/files/Guidelines%20for%20Primary%20Souce%20Literacy_AsApproved062018_1.pdf. Accessed 12/12/2018.

Hughes-Watkins, Lae'l. "Moving Toward a Reparative Archive: A Roadmap for a Holistic Approach to Disrupting Homogenous Histories in Academic Repositories and Creating Inclusive Spaces for Marginalized Voices." *Journal of Contemporary Archival Studies* 5 no. 6 (2018) https://elischolar.library.yale.edu/jcas/vol5/iss1/6.

"Kill the Indian, and Save the Man": Capt. Richard H. Pratt on the Education of Native Americans. Source: *Official Report of the Nineteenth Annual Conference of Charities and Correction* (1892): 46–59. Reprinted in Richard H. Pratt, "The Advantages of Mingling Indians with Whites," *Americanizing the American Indians: Writings by the "Friends of the Indian," 1880–1900* (Cambridge: Harvard University Press, 1973): 260–271.

Kumbier, Alana. *Ephemeral Material: Queering the Archive*. Gender and

Sexuality in Information Studies, number 5. Sacramento, CA: Litwin Books, LLC, 2014.

———. "Practicing What We Teach: Trauma-Informed Educational Practice." *Journal of Teaching in Social Work* 35, no. 3 (May 27, 2015): 262–278. https://doi.org/10.1080/08841233.2015.1030059.

Rokenbach, Barbara. "Archives, Undergraduates, and Inquiry-Based Learning: Case Studies from Yale University Library," *The American Archivist* 74 (Spring/Summer 2011): 306.

Teaching Restorative Practices with Classroom Circles, developed for San Francisco Unified School District, https://studentsatthecenterhub.org/resource/teaching-restorative-practices-with-class-circles/.

Visualizing a Mission: Artifacts and Imagery of the Carlisle Indian School, 1879–1918, The Trout Gallery, Dickinson College, Carlisle, Pennsylvania, January 30–February 28, 2004.

White, Lauren and Sarah Le Pinchon, "Trauma-Informed Teaching" handout from training, "Trauma-Informed Practices in the Higher-Education Classroom" presented at the Inclusive Teaching and Learning Symposium, The University of Texas at Austin, November 5, 2018.

Wood, Stacy, Kathy Carbone, Marika Cifor, Anne Gilliland, and Ricardo Punzalan. "Mobilizing Records: Re-Framing Archival Description to Support Human Rights." *Archival Science* 14, no. 3 (October 1, 2014): 397–419. https://doi.org/10.1007/s10502-014-9233-1.

ACTIVE LEARNING WITH PRIMARY SOURCES

Peter Carini
Morgan Swan
Dartmouth College

Introduction

Whether teaching at the reference desk or forming instructional partnerships with faculty across the disciplines, librarians are becoming increasingly responsible for research instruction. While this instruction can be a gratifying aspect of librarians' professional lives, meeting the teaching and learning expectations of various constituencies can prove challenging. Most current library school curricula include pedagogical methodology courses for future K-12 librarians, but hardly any provide instruction for teaching students who want to work in academic libraries at the college level. In part to address this lack of educational programming, Dartmouth College Library established the Librarians' Active Learning Institute (LALI) in 2011. Four years later, LALI introduced a new program designed specifically for educators in archives and special collections (LALI-ASC).

LALI and LALI-ASC are designed to develop librarians and archivists as teachers by introducing them to the practice of active learning pedagogy—that is, pedagogy in which students are made active collaborators in the common endeavor of research instruction. Students engaged in active learning are transformed from novices attempting to absorb information to developing experts strategically constructing their information literacy. LALI and LALI-ASC are designed so that participants will experience what it is like to be students in an active learning environment, in that the institute facilitators not only "talk the talk" but "walk the walk" of active learning. Both programs are designed around an intensive multiday workshop experience on the Dartmouth College campus for a very small cohort of participants, no more than twelve per program.

Active Learning

The initial ideas related to active learning were put forward by Friedrich Froebel in relation to very young children.[1] Froebel's ideas eventually translated into the creation of the kindergarten in Germany and the United States. Over time, others have expanded on Froebel's work and applied it to higher levels of learning. John Dewey was a significant influence in bringing the concepts of active learning to primary education in this country, but higher education has been slower to adopt these ideas. More recently, the concepts of active learning, also referred to as experiential learning and problem-based learning, have been applied to science, technology, engineering, and math (STEM) classes. The humanities have been slow to recognize the effectiveness of active learning, but archivists and librarians, working across the curriculum, have adopted these concepts into their teaching in recent years.[2]

---

1. Friedrich Froebel, *Pedagogics of the Kindergarten: Or, His Ideas Concerning the Play and Playthings of the Child*, trans. Josephine Jarvis (New York and London: D. Appleton and co., 1912), 244–246.

2. While evidence of this trend is anecdotal, articles outlining active learning concepts applied in archives and special collections teaching have been appearing in the literature with more frequency in this time period. The rise of programs like LALI and online resources such as TeachArchives.org, which are focused on active learning with primary sources, also bears this out.

Recently, researchers in the field of brain science have tried to gain a better understanding of how people learn. These studies and studies by those teaching in the sciences— such as Scott Freeman and his colleagues, who are trying to better understand the effectiveness of active learning—have led to a better understanding of the learning process and have shown that active learning is more effective than traditional lecturing. In fact, one study showed that students in a traditional lecture course are 1.5 times more likely to fail than students in an active learning environment. The same study found that in active learning environments, the overall letter grade medians rose from a B- to a B or B to B+, an increase in examination performance of 0.47 by a standardized mean difference.[3]

While there is no one definition of active learning that everyone agrees on, the basic concept is having students engage actively in the learning process. Engagement can be through reading, discussion, problem solving, role playing, analysis, or reflection.

The Librarians Active Learning Institute (LALI) at Dartmouth has identified three core principles for active learning. The ideas behind these three core principles are commonly recognized as aspects associated with active learning and are supported by the science behind learning, but they are not unique to Dartmouth. By breaking these ideas down into three core principles, the LALI program creates a simple set of the primary steps to accomplish active learning. There are a number of methods or concepts associated with these principles that are particularly effective in facilitating active learning. One pedagogical strategy in particular, a method called backward design, lends itself to implementing the principles of active learning in the classroom.[4]

---

3. Scott Freeman, et al., "Active learning increases student performance in science, engineering, and mathematics," *Proceedings of the National Academy of Sciences*, 111, no. 23 (June 2014): 8413.

4. Backward design asks the instructor to identify the desired outcomes or results for the session, determine what will constitute acceptable evidence that those results have been met, and finally, plan the learning experience. In other words, the instructor determines what the students should know about primary sources by the time they leave the classroom, selects ways to measure what they've learned, and structures a lesson plan that will provide the necessary measurements for success. This sounds straightforward,

LALI's three principles are meet, engage, and reflect. *Meet* refers to meeting students where they are, or student-centered learning. *Engage* is the process of engaging the students in the learning process in the classroom. *Reflect* refers to the process of consolidating the knowledge acquired during the engagement process.

Meet

An important part of active learning is student-centered learning. This means that the student is the most important component in the classroom, more important than the teacher and even more important than any information the teacher wants to impart. In fact, imparting information to the student is the opposite of student-centered teaching. Paulo Freire outlines a problem-posing model of education, where the teacher joins the students in a dialogue that explores a problem or set of problems. In this model, the teacher takes on the role of a guide who works and learns alongside the students.[5] For example, instead of presenting students with an eighteenth-century letter and telling them all about it, the teacher allows the students to explore the document, its physicality and its content, and encourages them to come up with questions or suppositions that the whole class discusses and explores. In this scenario, teachers may find themselves alternately providing guidance and discovering aspects of the document they had not noticed before.

In the student-centered classroom, the teacher becomes the designer of experiences.[6] In this role, the instructor provides meaningful, relevant experiences that lead to the growth of the student. We know from science that meaningful experiences cause increased brain activity, and that this activity, particularly when it is emotionally driven, literally

---

but often it's not as nice and linear in real life. Often, a lesson designer may need to go back and reexamine the desired results once they start work on outcomes.

5. Paulo Freire, *Pedagogy of the Oppressed*, trans. Myra Bergman Ramos (New York: Continuum, 1970), 72–73.

6. G. Christian Jernstedt, "How the Brain Learns," Dartmouth, College Library, Librarians Active Learning Institute, July 18–19, 2016, and Librarians Active Learning Institute-Archives and Special Collections, July 21–23, 2016.

results in the creation of stronger synapses in the brain.[7] Thus it is up to the teacher to create emotionally involved classroom experiences that lead to critical explorations of concepts and ideas, which in turn result in the opening up of new pathways and new knowledge on the part of the students.

Before we can design experiences for students, we need to gain some idea of what they already know. This means understanding their past experiences, particularly their past experiences with the kinds of material they will engage with in the classroom. Those same physical structures in the brain that we are hoping to influence with our carefully designed experience already have existing, well-ingrained connections created by their past experiences, some of which may create barriers to learning.[8] To determine students' existing knowledge, we need to create some kind of pre-assessment before designing for the classroom. This type of pre-assessment can be simple (a conversation with the faculty member to determine the students' level of knowledge) or complex (a carefully designed exercise that the students perform prior to a class session that helps gauge their level of knowledge and experience in the topic or issues to be covered in the session).

An example of such an exercise is to ask the students to look at a document related to the classroom experience and answer three simple questions, such as, "What is it? What does it tell you? What surprises you?" The level of detail you receive back from this mini assignment can give you a sense of the level of sophistication of the students' experience with primary sources and what barriers may exist to their ability to interpret the materials in the classroom.

Negative and positive emotions affect a student's ability to learn. Negative emotions, such as fear, may block students from fully participating in the classroom or clearly understanding the experiences designed for them. Teachers have little control over students' fears, but they can provide a welcoming environment that is not overly structured

---

7. James E. Zull, *The Art of Changing the Brain: Enriching Teaching by Exploring the Biology of Learning* (Sterling, Va.: Stylus Publishing, 2002), 223–225.

8. Zull, *The Art of Changing the Brain*, 92.

or filled with rules and arcane jargon. This can go a long way toward alleviating the problem. On the other hand, positive emotions can make experiences more important to the learner and increase the uptake of ideas and concepts. Emotion is a biochemical reaction, and as such it may take time to solidify and for the learner to fully integrate the experience. Ultimately, emotions create meaning, which creates a learning experience that matters to students.[9]

Engage

Engagement, the activity that occurs in the classroom, can take many forms. It can include reading, writing, discussion, problem solving, presentation and acting, or some combination of these activities. The form chosen as part of the overall design of the class session, or sessions, should be based on the goals that have been worked out ahead of time with the faculty member. Learning is, and should be, a social activity. While this often translates to students working in groups, this is not a necessity. However, the advantages of group work are that students form a cohort or community of learning in their groups as they labor to solve a problem, and this leads to discussion and verbalization. Verbalization has been shown to deeply engage the brain, and this engagement, likewise, results in deeper learning.[10] In addition, it can alleviate some negative emotions, since it distributes the responsibility for learning among the participants. Group work also allows students to test out their ideas with their peers, and this testing results in stronger learning.[11]

Stories, another social construct, are also an important component of engagement. Stories are all around us. They are part of our daily lives, whether in the form of video games, gossip, books, or movies. A recent remapping of the brain rediscovered an area known as 55b, which had

---

9. Zull, *The Art of Changing the Brain*, 226.
10. Zull, *The Art of Changing the Brain*, 207–208.
11. Charles E. Galyon et. al., "Comparison of group cohesion, class participation and exam performance in live and online classes," *Social Psychology of Education: An International Journal* 19, Issue 6 (2016): 64–65.

previously been ignored and then forgotten by scientists. In the new mapping of the Brocas region (the area of the brain associated with language), scientists discovered that 55b became highly active when people were listening to stories. While researchers have not yet drawn any conclusions related to 55b, it appears that it is primarily devoted to stories. This may, in part, explain why stories are so much a part of the human experience.[12] Stories are also strong emotional learning tools that engage multiple parts of the brain, and the more parts of the brain that are engaged, the deeper the learning.[13] Thus, the integration of stories, or story elements, as part of the learning experience will engage students' minds in a way that is more likely to result in their learning and recalling the lessons associated with that story.

In addition to stories, activities that involve discovery or problem solving are also particularly effective. In high school science curriculums, faster and better learning is the result when students are asked to improve mechanical devices by first following instructions from the teacher and then working hands-on with the same devices.[14] While this particular type of activity may be hard to replicate in the archives or special collections setting, integrating discovery into a narrative-based session, where students create a story out of a group of primary sources, can provide a similar sense of discovery and problem solving.

For instance, students are divided into groups of four or five and each group is provided with one or two primary source documents. The documents, when considered together, form a narrative about an historical incident or social issue. The students are asked to spend some time assessing and interpreting the documents. After they have completed this step, each group reports on their document(s). As the groups report, the narrative unfolds, and questions that one group may

---

12. Carl Zimmer, "Updated Brain Map Identifies Nearly 100 New Regions," *New York Times*, July 20, 2016, accessed March 31, 2019, https://www.nytimes.com/2016/07/21/science/human-connectome-brain-map.html.

13. Zull, *The Art of Changing the Brain,* 228.

14. Philip M. Sadler, Harold P. Coyle, and Marc Schwartz, "Engineering Competitions in the Middle School Classroom: Key Elements in Developing Effective Design Challenges," *The Journal of the Learning Sciences* 9, no. 3 (2000): 310–312.

have had about their documents are answered by information provided by the other groups, resulting in the discovery of the whole story.

There are many ways to structure engagement in the classroom, from jigsaws to think-pair-share, to narrative-building[15], but all of these can incorporate student-centered learning, emotional engagement, narratives and stories, group work, and discovery and problem solving.

Reflect

Reflection allows students time to consolidate the knowledge they have gained in a class session. Reflection is necessary because the sensory brain takes in information very quickly as a survival mechanism. The sense organs in the brain are highly coated with myelin, the fatty substance that insulates neurons in the brain, which allows signals to move quickly across the sensory cortex of the brain. In addition, it takes very few neurons for signals to reach the sensory cortex. In contrast, the integrative regions of the brain are distributed widely throughout the brain, and the neurons are less myelinated. This means that signals move more slowly, and it takes information longer to be consolidated.[16] In fact, it can take hours or even months for some knowledge to be consolidated. This means that students in the classroom, trying to take in and make sense of complex ideas, can be left swimming in data that makes little sense to them.

To attempt to counteract this problem of inadequate time to consolidate knowledge, it is important to build in time for students to reflect on what they've learned. Reflecting at the end of the session is a good way for students to consolidate the knowledge they've begun to process,

---

15. There are too many examples of books and articles that provide session structures for active learning to list here, but three examples are: Elizabeth F. Barkley, K. P. Cross, and Claire H. Major, *Collaborative Learning Techniques: A Handbook for College Faculty* (San Francisco, CA: Jossey-Bass, 2005); Anne Bahde, Heather Smedberg, and Mattie Taormina, eds., *Using Primary Sources: Hands-On Instructional Exercises* (Santa Barbara: Libraries Unlimited, 2014); and Teacharchives.org, http://www.teacharchives.org/exercises/.

16. Zull, *The Art of Changing the Brain*, 163.

but it is better if reflection can occur at multiple points during and after the session.

Reflection can take many forms—it can be anything from a simple strategically placed break during a class session to a reflective assignment that is completed several days after the session. During the session, it can work well to have students discuss what they've learned or discovered in small groups, and then again as an entire class at the end of the session. This type of discussion forces student to reach back into the knowledge they just acquired, which results in better consolidation in the integrative regions of the brain.[17]

Teaching LALI Principles Outside of Dartmouth

The original LALI-ASC program at Dartmouth College Library fills four full days of activity. The program opens mid-afternoon with a keynote address about the brain science of learning and the physiological underpinnings of active learning. This is followed by a reception and dinner with the instructors. On the second day, participants explore and consider various diagnostic methods for assessing students' existing research competencies and habits. As the day goes on, participants gain hands-on experience with a variety of active learning strategies that encourage students to take authority and responsibility for their learning. They also utilize a number of assessment techniques, together exploring their application for library instruction, and practice backward design methods. The third day opens with two model sessions taught by Dartmouth special collections librarians. Participants, working in groups of two, then spend time in the Rauner Special Collections Library researching and designing a class session of their own, utilizing Dartmouth's special collections materials. In the afternoon, the first groups co-teach their sessions to their peers and members of the faculty. During the fourth and final day, the remaining groups co-teach their sessions to their peers and members of the faculty. The teaching practicum sessions are followed by feedback and reflection.

---

17. Zull, *The Art of Changing the Brain*, 77, 164–166.

It is difficult to determine qualitatively the impact that LALI and LALI-ASC have had on their alumni, given that most of the participants had applied for the program because of their pre-existing interest in and commitment to teaching. However, if application numbers over the past several years are any indicator, LALI-ASC programs have been extremely successful. In any given year, there are typically twice as many applicants as the program can accommodate. Clearly, there is a demand for this sort of instruction that the traditional LALI-ASC program can't satisfy. This challenge is why the Teaching Undergraduates with Archives symposium at the University of Michigan, hosted by the Bentley Historical Library on November 7–9, 2018, provided an exciting opportunity to adapt the LALI-ASC program to an extremely stripped-down and truncated version of the traditional onsite, multiday experience.

This opportunity immediately presented several challenges, however. The most obvious hurdle was how to condense four days of a complicated and immersive learning experience into four hours. Ultimately, the decision was made to approach the Michigan workshop as a brief introduction to the LALI-ASC experience rather than to attempt to recreate the entire program. This allowed instructors to focus on immediately practical and straightforward intended outcomes—namely, that participants would be able to identify how LALI's active learning principles foster student learning; experience and reflect on active learning pedagogy; and utilize the backward design strategy in their own teaching. Another challenge was how to recreate an actual classroom experience when archival materials weren't available for in-classroom use at the Michigan workshop. An acceptable compromise was the creation of high-resolution color facsimiles of materials from the Dartmouth College Archives. We also reduced the quantity of material in the model session, from four tables of artifacts to two letters of correspondence.

In the workshop at Michigan, each participant group was given a unique scenario and was charged with answering the question, "What do I want the students to know, do, and think?" They were also encouraged to answer this question by generating learning objectives that were measurable outcomes. Finally, once the participants had completed these tasks, they planned a lesson that would allow them to achieve the measurable outcomes for what they wanted their students to learn. Each group then reported to the rest of the participants: they read their scenario, explained what sorts of materials they had been given in facsimile, and walked everyone through their proposed lesson plan. The session concluded with an open discussion about the lesson plans, which naturally evolved into a productive conversation about the practicalities of teaching undergraduates about primary sources within the context of the archives.

Overall, the experience was a positive one. Because the brief version of the workshop was designed using backward design strategy as well as the active learning principles promoted by LALI, it was easy for the presenters to determine that their intended objectives for the session were met. The shortened session at Michigan also allowed participants an opportunity to reflect on whether or not they wanted to learn more about the LALI-ASC program at Dartmouth and gain more teaching tools at the onsite immersive workshop. At the very least, the symposium workshop allowed the presenters to reimagine how active learning pedagogy might be distributed more broadly than the confines of a twelve-person cohort, all while informing a larger audience about the value of this approach to teaching with archives and special collections.

REFLECTIONS AND FORECASTS

TEACHING UNDERGRADUATES WITH ARCHIVES: PAST, PRESENT, AND FUTURES

Elizabeth Yakel

University of Michigan

When I began fifteen years ago to think about what it takes for students to make meaningful use of primary sources and how to measure the impact of primary sources, I never imagined that I would be part of such a large community of educators interested in teaching with primary sources and engaging students with questions about history-making, evidence, and critical thinking. In 2003, I urged archivists to more "fully envision archival user education to include all aspects of archival intelligence" and to envision more "targeted ways to foster the development of expertise in novices and to reinforce and extend the archival intelligence of expert users of primary sources."[1] Since then, teaching with archives has blossomed. Not only is there now an actual position of instructional archivist, but there has been substantial

---

1. Elizabeth Yakel and Deborah Torres, "AI: Archival Intelligence and User Expertise," *American Archivist* 66 no. 1 (Spring/Summer 2003): 78. DOI: 10.17723/aarc.66.1.q022h85pn51n5800.

experimentation with pedagogy. There is even a term for this activity: teaching with primary sources. According to the Society of American Archivists Reference, Access, and Outreach Section, their committee on teaching with/about primary sources was established in 2010.[2] The development of professional labels and job descriptions for teaching with primary sources has helped to solidify the nascent community and give legitimacy to the activity. Elsewhere in this volume, Anne Bahde, Matt Herbison, Robin M. Katz, Heather Smedberg, and Marissa Vassari discuss the history of teaching with primary sources and the future of the community.[3] I will discuss some of the changes over time in the thinking and practices of this community.

As a community, we have moved from thinking in terms of one-shot classes to thinking about curricular interventions over time to increase student learning around both content knowledge and critical thinking skills. We are now beginning to consider how we might evaluate the impact of our work on students in more robust ways. We have also seen the development of standards around teaching with primary sources, an annual pre-conference before the Society of American Archivists (SAA) meeting, and working groups to better our practice at SAA and the Rare Books and Manuscripts Section (RBMS) of the Association of College and Research Libraries (ACRL), a division of the American Library Association. In this essay, I will focus on four important transitions I have observed in teaching with primary sources over the past fifteen years, and where I think the greatest effort and attention should now be focused. These four transitions are from 1) tour guide to teacher, 2) archival orientation to primary sources curricula, 3) showing greatest hits to crafting activities aimed at developing critical thinking skills, and 4) measuring satisfaction to assessing learning.

---

2. See Society of American Archivists, Reference, Access, and Outreach Section, Teaching with/about Primary Sources Committee, https://www2.archivists.org/groups/reference-access-and-outreach-section/teaching-withabout-primary-sources-committee.

3. Anne Bahde, Heather Smedberg, Matt Herbison, Robin M. Katz, and Marissa Vassari, "This Is Where We Go from Here: Constructing a Community of Teaching with Primary Sources Educators," in this volume.

From Tour Guide to Teacher

Moving from being an archives' greatest hits tour guide to an instructor teaching in the archives and engaging students with primary sources is an important conceptual shift for several reasons. First, it allows archival and special collections instructors to shift from thinking about this as students' only exposure to the archives to thinking about the tour as a first step: using it to set up potential future visits and interactions with archives. Second, it transitions us from highlighting the flashy items to thinking more deeply about archival records and the construction of the archives themselves—both what is documented as well as what is not (known as "the silences in the stacks"). Finally, it necessitates that archivists think of themselves as teachers and not tour guides. I will consider the first two shifts in the subsequent sections. Here, I want to discuss the archivist as teacher and focus on pedagogy; I will talk about assessment of teaching in a later section.

Teaching with primary sources signals a shift that the instructor is not just "showing off" the archives but is actively engaged in pedagogy. This includes the process of designing the teaching interaction by consciously developing lessons, creating learning objectives, and carrying out the lesson (either in the archives or in the classroom setting, perhaps even collaboratively with faculty). This means that archivists and special collections librarians now need to have different types of expertise regarding pedagogy and knowledge of learning theory. It also suggests a relationship with faculty as teaching peers and potentially a role that is integral rather than peripheral to the course.

The 2016 Society of American Archivists' Guidelines for a Graduate Program in Archival Studies (GPAS) included instruction for the first time as an area to be covered in an archival graduate program. Section F of the curriculum now calls for outreach, instruction, and advocacy.[4] GPAS goes on to state, "Includes primary source and information literacy as well as methods of promoting the value of archives to the

---

4. Society of American Archivists, "Guidelines for a Graduate Program in Archival Studies" (GPAS), Chicago: Society of American Archivists, 2016. https://www2.archivists.org/prof-education/graduate/gpas.

public and other audiences."[5] While GPAS does acknowledge instruction, it does not directly address pedagogical skills as central to the archival knowledge base. Full disclosure: I commented on this section and argued for more concrete attention to pedagogy and teaching. I have studied archival curricula in the past, but not recently.[6] My current impression, supported by a study done in 2015 and 2016, is that in-depth education on teaching pedagogy and learning theory related to primary sources is not common in archival graduate programs.[7] Conferences—such as the regular Teaching with Primary Sources Unconference prior to SAA, the individual Teaching Undergraduates with Archives symposium sponsored by the Bentley Historical Library at the University of Michigan, and most notably the recurring Librarians Active Learning Institute (LALI) created by Peter Carini at Dartmouth—have moved in to fill in this gap.[8] As a result, teaching and learning expertise is increasing among archivists.

This new expertise is all the more important given the growth in instructional positions in archives. Table 1 demonstrates the yearly trends in demand for instructional archivists from March 2014 to March 2019 based on the website Archives Gig (https://archivesgig.com/). The forty-seven positions listed since 2014 represent institutions across the United States—primarily colleges and universities (forty-two of the positions). Overall, the trend for these positions appears to have increased, although there may be some signs that it is leveling out.

Typical job titles paired instruction and outreach, research and

---

5. Society of American Archivists, "Guidelines for a Graduate Program in Archival Studies," https://www2.archivists.org/prof-education/graduate/gpas/curriculum.

6. Jeannette Bastian and Elizabeth Yakel, "Towards the Development of an Archival Core Curriculum: The United States and Canada," *Archival Science* 6 (2006): 133–150. DOI: 10.1007/s10502-006-9024-4.

7. Lindsay Anderberg, Robin M. Katz, Shaun Hayes, Alison Stankrauff, Morgen MacIntosh Hodgetts, Josué Hurtado, Abigail Nye, and Ashley Todd-Diaz, "Teaching the Teacher: Primary Source Instruction in American and Canadian Archives Graduate Programs," *American Archivist*, 81/1 (Spring/Summer 2018): 188–215. DOI:10.17723/0360-9081-81.1.188.

8. Peter Carini and Morgan Swan, "Active Learning with Primary Sources," in this volume.

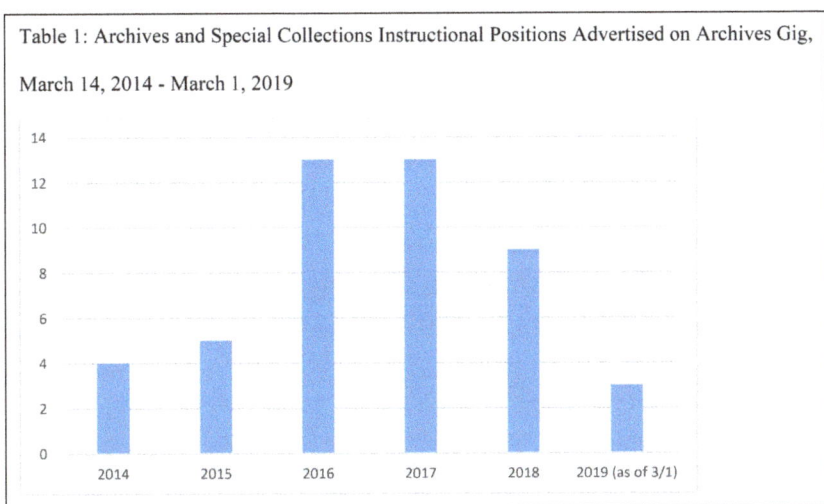

Table 1: Archives and Special Collections Instructional Positions Advertised on Archives Gig, March 14, 2014–March 1, 2019. This chronological graph shows a yearly breakdown of the archives and special collections instructional archivist positions advertised on the website Archives Gig between March 2014 and March 2019. The yearly counts are four in 2014, five in 2015, thirteen in 2016, thirteen in 2017, nine in 2018, and three as of March 1, 2019.

instruction, instruction and public services. Job requirements include teaching proficiency, commitment to student learning, and most recently delivery of instruction "in accordance with ACRL standards for primary source literary in the classroom . . . and through faculty partnerships and partnerships with other on-campus organizations".[9] Given this increased emphasis on teaching and teaching skills, for what types of activities and knowledge should archivists and special collections librarians be preparing? To answer this question, I turn to curricula building.

---

9. University of Pittsburgh, Archives & Special Collections Instruction and Outreach Librarian, accessed March 1, 2019. https://cfopitt.taleo.net/careersection/pitt_faculty_external/jobdetail.ftl?job=19000585&tz=GMT-06%3A00.

From an Archival Orientation to Creating Primary Sources Curricula

A second conceptual shift concerns the type of instruction to be offered. This is evident in the change in terminology from archival orientation to teaching with primary sources. This change opens archivists and special collections librarians up to a more expansive conceptualization of what teaching with primary sources entails. Teaching with primary sources makes us think about instruction not just as a one-time activity but as a curriculum built around primary sources. In this section, I will discuss the possibilities of a curriculum-centered approach. There are two aspects of this: 1) archivists partnering with instructors to enhance others' curricula, and 2) archivists creating curricula. Both of these aspects are important, although archivists have had more gains in the former type of curricular engagement.

The recent literature[10] and many of the presentations at the Teaching Undergraduates with Archives Symposium[11] demonstrated the tremendous gains that have been accomplished by partnering with faculty to co-create learning objectives based on primary sources. Moving away from the past, when students were parked in the archives while a professor was out, these models show us how student learning can be enhanced through collaboration. In these cases, the primary sources component is less about show and tell and more about an engaged and interactive learning exercise. This is a positive change, not only for faculty, archivists, and special collections librarians, but also for students.

Taking this a step further, I propose that archives and special collections develop their own learning objectives for teaching with primary sources. Curricula have rationale and coherence. Those rationale are often expressed as high-level learning objectives. What might be the

---

10. E.g. Anne Bahde, Heather Smedberg, and Mattie Taormina, eds. *Using Primary Sources: Hands-On Instructional Exercises* (Santa Barbara, California: Libraries Unlimited, 2014).

11. Cinda Nofziger, "More than Managing a Calendar: Reflections on the Role of an Academic Archivist," in this volume and Jill Severn, "Everything You Ever Wanted to Know about Starting and Running an Archives-Centered Faculty Teaching Fellows Program," paper presented at the Teaching Undergraduates with Archives Symposium, Ann Arbor, Michigan: November 7–8, 2018.

learning objectives for a repository to implement regarding their educational programs? Do repository staff even now think of themselves as capable of creating full-fledged learning objectives? In the Teaching Undergraduates with Archives Symposium, Jaime Burton, Matthew Strandmark, Julie Porterfield, and Kate Town provided examples of what a comprehensive curriculum might look like and accomplish.[12]

Curricula contain breadth and depth. Depth is achieved through interrelationships among the learning activities and learners' ability to follow from exposure to competency and potentially even to mastery. A curriculum might begin with an orientation, but would definitely not end there. At the K-12 level, the Common Core attempts to build knowledge and competency with primary sources over the course of one's elementary and secondary school career.[13] This is evident on the Library of Congress Teachers site, which allows teachers to search an educational standard (such as the Common Core Standards), a grade level, and a subject for materials to use in the classroom.[14] If one looks at the social studies curriculum over time, one sees increasingly sophisticated exercises building on core skills of reading primary source texts and images and evidential thinking.

From Showing Greatest Hits to Teaching Critical Thinking

What then is the content of the primary sources curriculum? Peter Carini has argued that archivists and special collections librarians should not use library bibliographic instruction as a model but should think more in terms of methods.[15] The joint SAA-ACRL/RBMS Guidelines for Primary

---

12. Jaime Marie Burton and Matthew Strandmark, "Applying Golinkoff and Hirsh-Pasek's Science of Learning to Undergraduate Primary Source Instruction and Assessment," and Julie M. Porterfield and Kate Dion Town, "Beyond Primary Sources: A Pedagogical Approach to Building at a Teaching and Learning Program in Special Collections," papers presented at the Teaching Undergraduates with Archives Symposium, Ann Arbor, Michigan: November 7–8, 2018.

13. Common Core State Standards Initiative, http://www.corestandards.org/about-the-standards/.

14. Library of Congress, http://www.loc.gov/teachers/standards/.

15. Peter Carini, "Archivists as Educators: Integrating Primary Sources into

Source Literacy, which became the standard in 2018, "articulate the range of knowledge, skills, and abilities required to effectively use primary sources."[16] These guidelines highlight the analytical, ethical, and theoretical concepts, as well as practical or logistical considerations related to the use of primary sources. The five areas of competency in the guidelines are: conceptualize; find and access; read, understand, and summarize; interpret, analyze, and evaluate; and use and incorporate. These align with other conceptualizations of primary source literacy (working with documents) as well as archival literacy (understanding and working in the archives) in the literature.[17] Carini notes that archivists and special collections librarians should definitely teach archival literacy; however, he also argues that they should teach primary source literacy along with historians and other disciplinary instructors.

> Archivists are experts in the evidentiary value of documents, texts, and objects. Part of the archival process is the appraisal of historical records for their evidentiary value. Archivists make decisions on a daily basis about what should and should not be kept, thus shaping the historical record from which historians work. In addition, archivists are versed in a breadth of historical documentation with an understanding of how the record has changed and evolved over time.[18]

Carini proposed a set of primary source literacy standards similar to the SAA/ACRL/RBMS Guidelines. However, most interestingly, he went a step further and presented a curriculum moving from the introductory

---

the Curriculum," *Journal of Archival Organization* 7/1–2 (2009): 41–50. DOI: 10.1080/15332740902892619.

16. SAA-ACRL/RBMS Joint Task Force on the Development of Guidelines for Primary Source Literacy (JTF-PSL), "Guidelines for Primary Source Literacy," Chicago: Society of American Archivists—Association for College and Research Libraries/Rare Books and Manuscripts Section: 1.

17. Elizabeth Yakel and Doris Malkmus, *Contextualizing Archival Literacy*, Chicago: Society of American Archivists, 2016.

18. Peter Carini, "Information Literacy for Archives and Special Collections: Defining Outcomes," *portal: Libraries and the Academy*, 16/1 (January 2016): 195. DOI: 10.1353/pla.2016.0006.

to advanced levels of archival expertise. Through the course of this exercise, he demonstrated which standards would apply and how the learning outcomes would adjust to the level of student expertise.[19] Burton and Strandmark described a similarly staged approach to curricular content at the Teaching Undergraduates with Archives Symposium.[20] Their curriculum featured four levels of increasing expertise: exposure, literacy, competency, and mastery. Furthermore, while the topical focus of the curriculum was the Civil War, Burton and Strandmark noted that, in addition to building expertise in subject matter, primary source, and the archives, they were also teaching higher level learning objectives that could be characterized as life-skills, such as collaboration, communication, content, critical thinking, creativity, confidence, and cross-cultural competence.

Ryan Bean and Linnea Anderson developed an archives curriculum around three modules.[21] The first module looks critically at the archives and considers topics and learning objectives around acquisition practices and the inherent biases therein. The second module concerns the archives as building and agency. The learning objectives focus on understanding the physical space and functions, and they place the policies and procedures in context. The third module is a hands-on documentary exercise with learning objectives of increasing careful reading and critical thinking skills. The modules build on one another and have generalizable learning objectives. Bean and Anderson conclude: "We identified that the three modules develop the student's ability to *"locate and critically evaluate information"* and *"master a body of knowledge and mode of inquiry"* and *"understand diverse philosophies and cultures* (italics original)."[22]

---

19. Carini, "Information Literacy for Archives and Special Collections," 200–205.

20. Burton and Strandmark, "Applying Golinkoff and Hirsh-Pasek's Science of Learning to Undergraduate Primary Source Instruction and Assessment."

21. Ryan Bean and Linnea M. Anderson, "Teaching Research and Learning Skills with Primary Sources: Three Modules," in *Past or Portal? Enhancing Undergraduate Learning through Special Collections and Archives,* Eleanor Mitchell, Peggy Anne Seiden, and Suzy Taraba eds., Chicago: Association of College and Research Libraries, 2012: 156–162.

22. Bean and Anderson, "Teaching Research and Learning Skills with Primary Sources," 160.

What we see from these examples are the emergence of two parallel streams in thinking about curricular content for teaching with primary sources. Both are important directions for instructional archivists. The first stream represents a sophisticated approach to teaching the more traditional content areas of domain, primary source, and archival literacies. This stream also problematizes the archives: what is there and why; what is not there and why not? The second stream represents a latent goal in the first, which has now emerged in its own right as archivists and special collections librarians attempt to show relevance and tie into the teaching and learning missions of the larger university. In this stream, archivists and special collections librarians create exercises that require critical thinking, the ability to judge evidence and use it to make claims, and the ability to develop arguments.

From Measuring Satisfaction to Assessing Learning

The flip side of teaching is learning, and learning objectives should lead to learning outcomes. A final transformation, and one that is ongoing in teaching with primary sources, is increased focus on assessment. In 2008, Magia Krause noted, "assessment of learning is an important part of any pedagogical approach because it provides feedback about what knowledge has transferred to the learner as well as the impact and effectiveness of the instruction."[23] In her survey of 208 members of the Society of American Archivists, Reference, Access and Outreach section, she found that although 66.3% of the respondents taught more than five instructional sessions per year, only 25.8% did any formal evaluation of their teaching or student learning. Perhaps more shocking, 33.1% did no formal or informal evaluation. Assessment is the next challenge in teaching with primary sources. Carini noted that the object of assessment can take many forms, from the success of the primary sources activity in the context of the larger class to assessment of the session in the archives. He also argued that assessments should be designed to

---

23. Magia G. Krause, "Learning in the Archives: A Report on Instructional Practices," *Journal of Archival Organization*, 6/4 (2008): 248. DOI: 10.1080/15332740802533263.

support the curriculum and therefore be at different levels, depending on the expertise.[24] I would characterize the assessment process a bit differently. One can assess teaching; one can assess content knowledge at the literacy, competency, or mastery levels; or one can assess (longer term?) impact outcomes, such as critical thinking, increased confidence in evaluating evidence, or greater cultural appreciation. What we need now is experimentation to determine what works best in what pedagogical circumstances.

Learning is an ephemeral activity to measure, and while some types of learning can be measured at the time of the lesson, behavioral and cognitive changes may occur over time. Various archival researchers have proposed ways to think about assessment, but we have yet to devise any generalizable assessment tool. As far back as 2002, Eilean Hooper-Greenhill and her colleagues piloted an assessment model, generic learning outcomes (GLOs), to measure the impact of learning in museums, archives, and libraries. The five GLOs were:

1. Increase in knowledge and understanding
2. Increase in skills
3. Change in attitudes or values
4. Evidence of enjoyment, inspiration, and creativity
5. Evidence of activity, behavior, and progression[25]

Increasing knowledge in the archives means learning new facts or information through primary sources. Increasing skills means learning how to do careful reading or managing archival research notes. Changing attitudes or values might be measured by increased empathy for

---

24. Carini, "Information Literacy for Archives and Special Collections," 197.

25. Eilean Hooper-Greenhill, Jocelyn Dodd, Theano Moussouri, Ceri Jones, Chris Pickford, Catherine Herman, Marlene Morrison, John Vincent, and Richard Toon, *Learning Impact Research Project (LIRP): Developing a Scheme for Finding Evidence of the Outcomes and Impact of Learning in Museums, Archives and Libraries: The Conceptual Framework* (Leichester, UK: Research Centre for Museums and Galleries (RCMG), 2003), 12. https://www2.le.ac.uk/departments/museumstudies/rcmg/projects/lirp-1-2/LIRP%20end%20of%20project%20paper.pdf.

some group of people as a result of exposure to primary sources. This echoes Chauncey Monte-Santo's keynote at the University of Michigan symposium in 2018 and her work on the cognitive and behavioral aspects of learning needed to engage with primary sources.[26] Evidence of enjoyment, inspiration, and creativity might be measured through the application of knowledge to other projects. Finally, evidence of activity, behavior, or progression would be identified through changes in how people act—for example, better time management, application of sourcing archival documents to seeking information about oneself or one's house in government records, or careful reading of other types of information.[27]

Others have attempted to measure more specific cognitive or behavioral changes. In a pre-post test design experiment, Wendy Duff and Joan Cherry measured confidence in using primary sources (changing attitude) and level of use of primary sources (change in behavior). They found increases in both.[28] In a post-test methodology, Morgan Daniels and I measured students' perceptions of their ability to accomplish specific skills related to research with primary sources.[29] Students perceived that their skills had increased in terms of archival search, asking for help, study skills and time management, research skills preparation for the visit, archival procedures, and interpretation of primary sources.[30] Similar to Duff and Cherry, we found that confidence increased among those who used primary sources in more substantive class projects (as opposed to those who just attended an archival orientation).[31]

---

26. Chauncey Monte-Santo, "Argumentation in History Classrooms: A Key Path to Understanding the Discipline and Preparing Citizens," *Theory Into Practice* 55/4, 2016: 311–319. DOI: 10.1080/00405841.2016.1208068.

27. Hooper-Greenhill et al., *Learning Impact Research Project*, 12–17.

28. Wendy M. Duff and Joan M. Cherry, "Archival Orientation for Undergraduate Students: An Exploratory Study of Impact," *American Archivist* 71 (Fall/Winter 2008): 499–529. DOI: 10.17723/aarc.71.2.p6lt385r7556743h.

29. Morgan Daniels and Elizabeth Yakel, "Uncovering Impact: The Influence of Archives on Student Learning," *Journal of Academic Librarianship* 39 (2013): 414–422. DOI: 10.1016/j.acalib.2013.03.017.

30. Daniels and Yakel, "Uncovering Impact," 417–419.

31. Daniels and Yakel, "Uncovering Impact," 418.

Other studies have shown negative results after exposure/using primary sources. For example, in 2015, Sarah Horowitz observed a decrease in four of five scores (observation, interpretation, evaluation, and engagement; although only engagement was statistically significant).[32] Furthermore, she completed a content analysis of students' final papers and saw no difference in scores between those who had used special collections and those who did not. However, those who used primary sources did score higher than those who did not.[33] Clearly, instructional archivists have a long way to go to assess learning.

As part of the University of Michigan's Third Century Initiative, which focuses on enhancing teaching and learning, the Bentley Historical Library received funds for the Engaging the Archives: Encouraging Students to Discover the Past Project.[34] The Bentley Historical Library adapted an assessment using the following learning outcomes promoted by the Third Century Initiative: intercultural engagement; creativity; self-agency and the ability to innovate and take risks; communication, collaboration, and teamwork; and civic/social responsibility and ethical reasoning.[35] In a separate article, Patricia Garcia, Joseph

---

32. Sarah M. Horowitz, "Hands-On Learning in Special Collections: A Pilot Assessment Project," *Journal of Archival Organization* 12/3-4 (2015): 221. DOI: 10.1080/15332748.2015.1118948.

33. Horowitz, "Hands-On Learning in Special Collections," 222–223.

34. http://thirdcentury.umich.edu/engaging-the-archives/

35. Stephanie M. Kusano, Amy J. Conger, and Mary C. Wright, *Development and Assessment of Intercultural Engagement*, Engaged Learning: Transforming Learning for a Third Century, no. 1, Center for Research on Learning and Teaching, Occasional Paper 32, 2016; Samantha K. Hallman, Mary C. Wright, and Amy J. Conger, *Development and Assessment of Student Creativity*, Engaged Learning: Transforming Learning for a Third Century, no. 2, Center for Research on Learning and Teaching, Occasional Paper 33, 2016; Stephanie M. Kusano, Mary C. Wright, and Amy J. Conger, *Development and Assessment of Self-Agency and the Ability to Innovate and Take Risks*, Engaged Learning: Transforming Learning for a Third Century, no. 3, Center for Research on Learning and Teaching, Occasional Paper 34, 2016; Stephanie M. Kusano, Amy J. Conger, and Mary C. Wright, *Development and Assessment of Collaboration, Teamwork, and Communication*, Engaged Learning: Transforming Learning for a Third Century, no. 4, Center for Research on Learning and Teaching, Occasional Paper 35, 2016; Samantha K. Hallman, *Development and Assessment of Student Social/Civic Responsibility and Ethical Reasoning*, Engaged Learning: Transforming Learning for a Third Century, no.

Lueck, and I discussed a number of other potential learning models that might be employed to frame learning assessment when teaching with primary sources.[36]

In our assessment of teaching with primary sources, we need to move from a satisfaction-based approach to one that focuses more on learning. But we need to be prepared for negative and ambiguous results. I suggest another model of evaluation: one that is staged similar to Carini's curriculum but that encompasses the skill assessments suggested by Garcia et al. and the GLO model. I propose an assessment model that encompasses three different types of learning input (cognitive, affective, behavioral) but also stages the potential outcomes by skill level (exposure, literacy, competency, and mastery). While this may seem like too many models of assessment for primary sources that overlap and conflict, this is the current state of affairs. There is lots of work to be done, but this represents the work we need to expect of the next generation of instructional archivists. In a span of fifteen years, we have made immense strides as a profession to embrace teaching with primary sources. While assessment may seem difficult, it can also be rewarding.

Conclusions

I have discussed four transitions: 1) from tour guide to teacher, 2) from archival orientation to primary sources curricula, 3) from showing the greatest hits to crafting activities to develop critical thinking skills, and 4) from measuring satisfaction to assessing learning. The first three are further along than the fourth. But all require continued attention and advocacy. We need to nurture new instructional archivists, hone our pedagogical skills, and be bold in proposing learning objectives for our students. Most of all, we need to be fearless in our assessments and accept complexity, inconclusive findings, and negative results. We

---

5, Center for Research on Learning and Teaching, Occasional Paper 36, 2016. http://www.crlt.umich.edu/engaged-learning/goals.

36. Patricia Garcia, Joseph Lueck, and Elizabeth Yakel, "The Pedagogical Promise of Primary Sources: Research Trends, Persistent Gaps, and New Directions," *Journal of Academic Librarianship*, 45 (2019): 94–101. DOI:/10.1016/j.acalib.2019.01.004.

Table 2: Ways of Learning and Types of Learning Input

	Literacy	Competency	Exposure	Mastery
Cognitive	Able to read primary sources and apply basic artifactual literacy techniques (Sourcing: Monte-Santo). Understands that documents have meaning beyond their informational content (Bean and Anderson)	Artifactual literacy techniques are second nature (Sensemaking)	Knows that primary sources relate to historical events. Information value/facts (GLO-1).	Critical/evidential /historical thinking are strong. Student is able to argue both sides of a question. (Critique: Monte-Santo)
Affective	Views historical events through personal experience (Ego-centric /Presentism: Monte-Santo)	Able to situate oneself in the cultural/temporal mode of people in the primary sources (Garcia – Intercultural engagement)	Awe factor when exposed to primary sources	Empathy with historical figures and confidence in assessment of the cultural/social environment of the historical figures/events (GLO-3; Duff and Cherry)
Behavioral	Understands concept and function of finding aids, fluent with the structure and information found in different sections	Can search individual finding aids and across finding aids to locate information (GLO-2)	Search extends to Google 1st page	Able to identify and evaluate primary sources through finding aids (understands representations) and make initial decisions about what primary sources to request for inspection (Yakel and Torres: Intellective skills)

need to better understand the dimensions of primary sources that have impact and what we as archivists and special collections librarians can do to activate these dimensions for learners. Only then can we measure learning impacts and demonstrate the value of teaching with primary sources beyond their physicality and content.

Acknowledgments

Ideas in this paper were developed, in part, through funding from the University of Michigan Mcubed Grant Program for the project Engaging the Archives: Researching Best Practices for Student Success in the Archives.

FACULTY PERSPECTIVES ON TEACHING UNDERGRADUATES WITH PRIMARY SOURCES: RESULTS OF AN ONLINE SURVEY

Sean Noel

Simmons University

Introduction

The use of primary sources in undergraduate instruction can be exciting for students and allow them to better understand the subject matter.[1] The idea of archivists and special collections librarians as instructors is not new; library and information science literature has been investigating the subject for years. Yet much primary source instruction is not done solely by archivists, but by faculty, in the context of college and university classes. Where do the subject experts—the faculty of higher education—fit into the dynamic partnership of teaching undergraduates with archives?

---

1. Krause, Magia, ""It Makes History Alive for Them": The Role of Archivists and Special Collections Librarians in Instructing Undergraduates," *The Journal of Academic Librarianship* 36, no. 5 (2010): 401–411.

In her 2007 survey, Doris Malkmus queried college and university history faculty on what kinds of primary sources they used, where they found those sources, and their thoughts on how archivists could help them.[2] Using Malkmus as an inspiration, this study provides a look at how faculty teach with primary sources today. This chapter will report findings of an online survey of faculty from Association of Research Libraries (ARL) member colleges and universities, who were asked to respond to questions about teaching undergraduates with primary sources. Specifically, the survey targeted the subgroup of faculty who 1) taught undergraduates, 2) with primary sources in a class session, 3) in partnership or collaboration with an archivist. Survey questions were designed to collect data on faculty members' perceptions and perspectives of their role in the process of primary source instruction.

Literature

In 2009, Peter Carini's "Archivists as Educators" explored the possibility of archivists embracing more complex pedagogy, with primary sources at the center of instruction. His work has become part of the modern canon on the subject. While focused on archivists specifically, this work provides key subjects for investigation of faculty participation as well.[3] A year later, and very much in that same line of inquiry, Magia Krause queried archivists on their role in teaching students with primary sources, as well as best practices for strategies of instruction and assessment. Krause explicitly asked, "What role do faculty and instructors play in helping undergraduates use primary sources?"[4]

Beyond instruction, assessment of learning has also been an important subject of research. The Archival Metrics Project has provided instructors with tools for "user based evaluation,"[5] Magia Krause (2010)

---

2. Malkmus, Doris J., "Teaching History to Undergraduates with Primary Sources: Survey of Current Practices," *Archival Issues* 31, no. 1 (2007): 25–82.

3. Carini, Peter, "Archivists as Educators: Integrating Primary Sources into the Curriculum," *Journal of Archival Organization* 7, no. 1–2 (2009): 41–50.

4. Krause, "It Makes History Alive for Them," 403.

5. "Archival Metrics: Archival Metrics Toolkits," Google Sites.

pursued rubrics as further methods of assessment.[6] That Malkmus excluded assessment from her survey may be an indication of the challenges of the subject; this argues for its inclusion in the current study.

Much of the literature is derived by, and focuses on, the archivist, yet college and university faculty are often the instigators of primary source instruction; they teach the courses filled with tuition-paying students. As such, faculty participation in primary source instruction must be scrutinized.

Methodology

The survey was built in Qualtrics and consisted of twenty-three questions, pretested by six independent readers and approved by the Simmons University Institutional Review Board. Email addresses were collected from public websites for a total of 10,929 faculty in departments of history and English from ARL institutions in the United States; Canadian institutions were excluded. The survey was available in January and February 2018, and combined single-choice and Likert-scale ratings, with some open text fields for more expansive responses to some questions.

After opt-outs and dead addresses were cleared, there were 10,417 potential respondents, of which 1,078 completed the survey. After filtering responses to find faculty who met the three criteria, the final total of faculty was 397. This total represents 3.81% of total possible respondents (10,417) and 36.83% of all returned results (1,078). Considering the population of 10,417 and the final sample size of 397, the survey results are potentially statistically significant, with a margin of error of 5% and a confidence level of 95%.

---

6. Krause, Magia, "Undergraduates in the Archives: Using an Assessment Rubric to Measure Learning," *The American Archivist* 73, no. 2 (2010): 507–534.

Results of Survey

The 397 faculty were from public institutions (64%) and private schools (36%). Almost 72% were tenured faculty. Respondents were distributed across disciplines: 50% history faculty, 40% English faculty, and 10% another discipline.

Partnership with archivists
Prior to filtering the faculty by the three main criteria, the initial results of the 1,078 respondents indicated that 61% who used primary sources to teach undergraduates did so without collaborating with an archivist. To access faculty perceptions of those who did collaborate with archivists, faculty were asked a series of questions that began, "Archivists with whom I work...". They responded on a five-point Likert scale from Strongly Agree to Strongly Disagree.

Overwhelmingly, faculty perceive archivists as valuable partners in both developing and teaching class sessions with primary sources, with 78% and 58% respectively in strong agreement with the question (Chart 1). When aggregating the positive responses, agreement increases to 96% in developing class sessions and 84% in teaching them. Likewise, respondents were strong in their disagreement with questions that asked them to articulate any feelings that archivists might overreach in their interest to plan or to teach class sessions with students; 64% strongly disagreed that archivists tried to be too involved in developing classes, and 68% strongly disagreed about archivists trying to be too involved in teaching. Aggregates of disagreement were at 81% in both categories (Chart 2).

Further, faculty strongly disagreed that archivists should limit their involvement to only providing a space for the class, at 77%, and strongly disagreed, at 66%, that archivists should only be involved with their classes by selecting material. The aggregates of disagreement totaled 89% and 82% respectively (Chart 3).

Faculty Perspectives on Teaching Undergraduates with Primary Sources 299

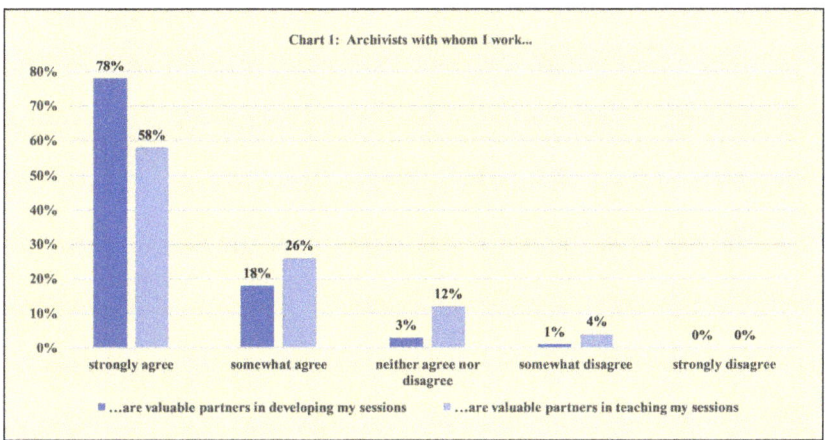

Chart 1: Archivists with whom I work . . . . The color bar graph shows the results of the five level Likert scale responses to the questions about archivists being valuable partners in either developing or teaching class sessions with the faculty member taking the survey.

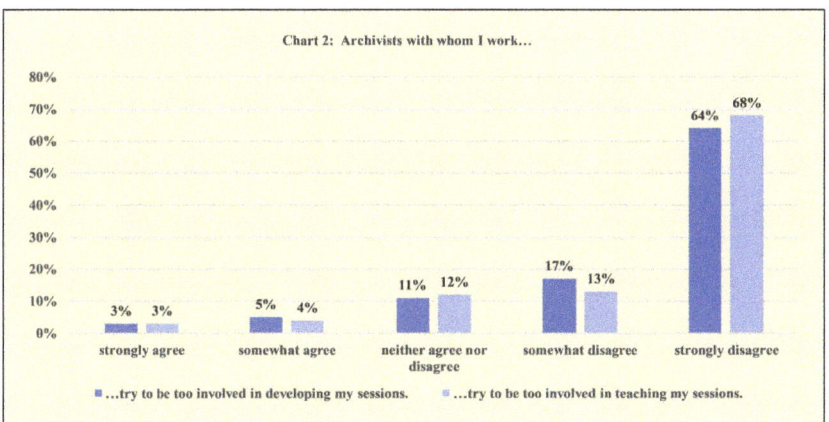

Chart 2: Archivists with whom I work . . . . The color bar graph shows the results of the five level Likert scale responses to the questions about archivists trying to be too involved in either developing or teaching sessions with the faculty member taking the survey.

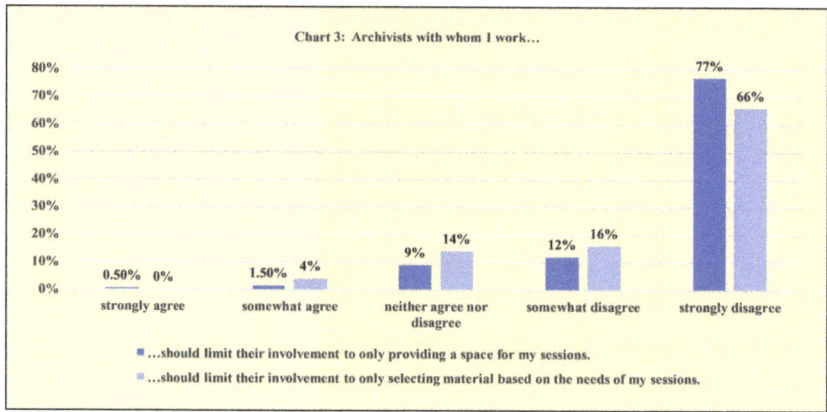

Chart 3: Archivists with whom I work . . . . The color bar graph shows the results of the five level Likert scale responses to the questions about whether archivists should limit their involvement to only providing space or to only selecting material for the faculty member taking the survey.

Selection of material and learning objectives

The survey asked the extent to which faculty saw their work with archivists as a collaboration, and within which tasks that collaboration occurred. Faculty responded that they take sole responsibility to select material for classes at the same rate that archivists solely selected that material, at 15% and 14% respectively; 71% responded that they collaborated with the archivist to select the exact archival material that was to be used to teach the lesson. However, faculty took the lead in determining the learning objectives for each session, with 65% responding that they alone determined the learning objectives, and 32% saying they collaborated with the archivist to create those learning objectives.

When asked to rate how important certain learning objectives were to them (Chart 4), faculty indicated the most important objective was that students "will have developed and demonstrated critical thinking skills" (60%), followed closely by students "will feel comfortable returning to the archive for another assignment" (59%). Only 1–2% of the responses rated the learning objectives as "Of Little Importance" and "Unimportant," and these are not represented in the chart.

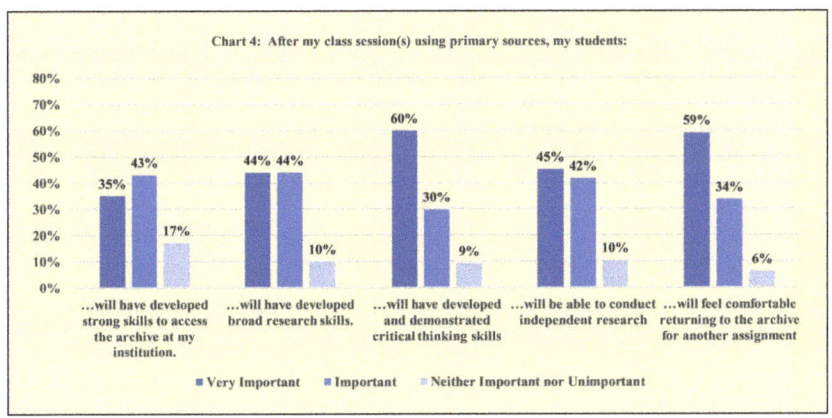

Chart 4: After my class session(s) using primary sources, my students . . . .
The color bar graph shows the results of the Likert scale responses to the questions of how faculty rate the importance of given outcomes when teaching with primary sources.

Number of class sessions

Much archival instruction happens in a single lesson, known colloquially as the "one-shot" class. When faculty were asked to describe the type of sessions they organized, one-shot classes accounted for 54% of all classes, with a one-time visit by the archivist to the class accounting for 8%, and a one-time visit with their students to the archive accounting for 46%. Multiple sessions accounted for the remaining 46%: either multiple visits by the archivist to the classroom (1%); multiple class sessions in the archives (19%); or a combination of these visits (26%). In a follow-up question, faculty indicated a number of reasons why they might limit archival instruction to a one-shot session:

34%	We could accomplish my learning objectives in one visit
23%	There is not enough time in the semester for more than one visit
22%	I want my students to interact with archival sources but do not plan for students to complete a project with those sources
19%	Other
2%	The archivist does not have time for multiple visits

Nearly half of the faculty who chose "Other" as a response (22 of 48) indicated that the class session with the archivist was meant to be introductory, and students would return on their own to do research. As one respondent put it, "The archivist's visit was an introduction to the collections; beyond that, I wanted students to go to the archives for further guidance." Another stated, "The archivist introduced them to the rules for using the archives and showed them sources. They then visited the archives on their own to research a collection on a specified topic." More "Other" responses included distance from the repository; different research priorities for different classes (some classes did have more than one session); and class size exceeding the special collections teaching space.

Assessment

Overwhelmingly, faculty responded that they assess how well students had met the learning objectives established for their class session. Faculty assessed formally, informally, or a combination of both methods in 84% of the responses. The 16% who responded that they did not assess student learning were asked for more detail with both set responses and open text opportunities to explain. "Please select the response that best fits your reason for not assessing your sessions where primary sources are used":

43%	Other
37%	I want students to be exposed to primary sources, but do not plan for students to complete a project with those sources
17%	There is not enough time to assess these sessions
3%	There are no good assessment tools for sessions with primary sources

The open text "Other" responses indicated that most faculty are, in fact, assessing some aspect of the classes but that, in most cases, they were distinguishing between assessing the specific session taught with an archivist from the assessment of the broader learning objectives set out for the course. Comments helped to clarify their practice of assessment. One wrote, "The students had to complete a paper based entirely on primary sources, which was assessed," while others noted, "I assess them in other ways. They write formal analyses on primary sources but these are not necessarily connected to the archival sessions and materials seen/used there," and "I assess at the end of the project, not after each session." Some responses seemed to suggest there are faculty who view assessment as unnecessary: "Micro-assessment is a waste of everyone's time and energy," and "The proof is in the pudding." This is a possible theme that a further study might probe more deeply.

How archivists could be helpful in the classroom
In an attempt to elicit more details from the survey respondents, a final open-text question was asked, which yielded responses from 65% of participants. The question was, "In what ways might your archivist be helpful to your classroom teaching?" Examples of responses allow authentic faculty voices to explain their thoughts and insights. These statements show that faculty see potential value in collaborating with archivists but also see specific roles for archivists in the classroom and can identify some areas for improvement. There is a broad continuum of perspectives reflected in these faculty comments.

One perspective valued archivists' knowledge but critiques instructional capability:

> *The archivist has the knowledge base but could use better teaching methods, working on tactics to involve the students more and get them more excited about the materials.*

Another faculty voice lauded both the archivists' knowledge *and* teaching skill:

> *The archivist is important in terms of their research and teaching insights. In collaborating with archivists in classes I've taught over the past several years, I have learned new ways of introducing primary source materials and have learned infinitely more about how to teach students to locate this material though finding guides and other means.*

The variety of faculty perspectives included what we might call "stay in your lane":

> *I have an excellent, long-standing relationship with this librarian, who often comes to do a session in my courses, graduate and undergraduate, on finding materials. . . . I don't rely on him to teach my classes though. I've had a lot more experience in archives in my field than anyone in the library system here. I need them to help me, not do my job for me.*

Still another stressed what the archivist should value and take away from the collaboration with faculty:

> *An archivist should see my teaching as an opportunity to discover and develop underappreciated or even new dimensions of their collections. My teaching is a bridge between scholarship and the archive, and archivists can learn what future research interests may be from the experience.*

Finally, there are faculty who viewed "their" archivist's knowledge base as valuable in a comprehensive sense, from identification of material to instruction and presentation:

> *ID of collections relevant to student/class focus; development of hands-on strategies to engage and learn to analyze select documents; development of research strategies to enhance student research; development of tools for storing research (Zoetrope, for ex) and presenting its analysis (Omeka, for ex).*

These few faculty comments are indicative of the broad spectrum of experiences across the academic landscape. Studies like this, and others in the domain, can help to map the variety of these relationships and help to build an understanding of best practices in the field.

Significance of the Data

Survey data describes faculty perceptions across a vast spectrum of experiences with archivists. Neither group is monolithic; each has competing priorities. Instruction is often only one part of an archivist's duties: other duties might include the arrangement, preservation, and description of archival collections; reference work; public service; and a variety of other tasks. Likewise, undergraduate instruction may be only a part of a faculty member's duties. As teaching with primary sources becomes more popular and prevalent, details of the collaboration between faculty and archivists become more valuable.

Relative to the selection of participants, history and English faculty were selected based on anecdotal experience. While Malkmus' study focused exclusively on history faculty[7], my experience with faculty from a variety of disciplines led to the inclusion of English faculty. The 10% of "other" faculty disciplines identified by respondents indicates a limitation of the study. I did not account for dual appointments or adjunct faculty who might teach in different schools within a university. The substantial 10% of "other" faculty opens the door to future research that would include a broader base of disciplines.

Relative to responses, faculty were overwhelmingly positive in their assessments of archivists as valuable partners. However, they described archivists as valuable partners in planning class sessions with considerably stronger emphasis than they did in identifying them as partners in teaching those lessons. Responses to both questions were overwhelmingly positive, but the discrepancy in the degree of agreement suggests a possible distinction between faculty perceptions of those two roles. Likewise, faculty established learning objectives independently two-to-one over collaborating with archivists to establish those objectives. These two results are not evidence of a trend, but they do suggest that while faculty value archivists as partners, they seem to put more value in archivists' expertise of the collections, and probably expect them to limit their participation in the planning process to helping to identify relevant collections and how they might be used.

---

7. Malkmus, "Teaching History," 25.

There are areas in which the responses to different questions correlate. For example, 71% of faculty responded that they collaborate with archivists in the selection of archival material for their class sessions. At the same time, many of the open text responses to "How can archivists be helpful in the classroom" note the importance of the archivists' knowledge of holdings in selecting material (e.g. "ID of collection relevant to student/class focus"). These responses complement each other, and, according to Magia Krause's study, they represent one of the two main strengths that archivists bring to the table: "Knowledge of primary sources and collections."[8]

Faculty responses seem contradictory in other areas. The learning objective most identified by faculty as "very important" (60%), is that students "will have developed and demonstrated critical thinking skills" in the class session. However, the most employed style of class was not a multiple-session class, but a one-shot lesson. Do faculty expect that critical thinking skills can be developed and demonstrated in a single session?

The specific responses relative to assessment allude to faculty perceptions that, while assessment is overwhelmingly part of their instruction, they are focused on assessing student learning as specifically related to the objectives of the entire course, and not necessarily the efficacy of the lesson where primary sources were employed, or the performance of archivists in participating with those lessons. This is another potential area for future research.

Conclusions

Instructing undergraduate students with archives is a growing practice; the evidence is in the explosion of literature in the last decade; the high profile of projects at Society of American Archivists (SAA) conferences, such as the Guidelines for Primary Source Literacy recently distributed by the Rare Books and Manuscripts Section (RBMS) of the Association

---

8. Krause, "It Makes History Alive for Them," 404.

of College and Research Libraries (ACRL)[9]; and the presentation of conferences like Teaching Undergraduates with Archives. We need to analyze the complicated system of teaching undergraduates with primary sources to uncover limitations, exploit successes, and proliferate best practices across the domain.

Much of the existing literature on teaching undergraduates with primary sources focuses on only a single aspect of the instruction: assessment and development of assessment tools, or practical approaches, or case studies, etc. Doris Malkmus presented a survey of faculty in an attempt to better understand the types of primary sources they use, how they locate those sources, and some of the challenges with employing those sources with their students. The current study stands apart in that it approaches faculty in the context of their partnership with archivists in teaching undergraduates.

The current study shows that a substantial number of faculty are interested in collaborating with archivists; at the same time, it shows how most faculty seem to have specific ideas about the role of each in the collaboration. Faculty value the archivist's expertise and knowledge of archival holdings, and they appreciate how the archivists can assist them in broad planning for educational sessions. They are not necessarily looking for archivists to teach per se, or to assess student learning or student response to the part of the class using primary sources. Of course, archivists may have their own interests in assessing their lessons, and the priority gap between faculty and archivists relative to assessment is a possible area for future study.

The archival domain is not monolithic. It encompasses a vast continuum of staffing models, instructional practices, and competing priorities. This study adds to the understanding of the paradigm of teaching undergraduates with archives by elucidating one element of the tripartite instructional partnership of faculty-archivist-student.

---

9. Guidelines for Primary Source Literacy: Final Draft, SAA-ACRL/RBMS Joint Task Force on Primary Source Literacy, Society of American Archivists, Summer 2017.

Bibliography

"Archival Metrics." Google Sites. Accessed August 01, 2018. https://sites.google.com/a/umich.edu/archival-metrics/.

Carini, Peter. "Archivists as Educators: Integrating Primary Sources into the Curriculum." *Journal of Archival Organization* 7, no. 1–2 (2009): 41–50. Accessed August 1, 2018. doi:10.1080/15332740902892619.

Krause, Magia. ""It Makes History Alive for Them": The Role of Archivists and Special Collections Librarians in Instructing Undergraduates." *The Journal of Academic Librarianship* 36, no. 5 (2010): 401–411. doi:10.1016/j.acalib.2010.06.004.

Krause, Magia. "Undergraduates in the Archives: Using an Assessment Rubric to Measure Learning." *The American Archivist* 73, no. 2 (2010): 507–534. doi:10.17723/aarc.73.2.72176h742v20l115.

Malkmus, Doris J. "Teaching History to Undergraduates with Primary Sources: Survey of Current Practices." *Archival Issues* 31, no. 1 (2007): 25–82. http://www.jstor.org/stable/41102141.

SAA-ACRL/RBMS Joint Task Force on Primary Source Literacy. Guidelines for Primary Source Literacy: Final Draft. Society of American Archivists, Summer 2017. Accessed August 01, 2018. https://www2.archivists.org/groups/saa-acrlrbms-joint-task-force-on-primary-source-literacy/guidelines-for-primary-source-lite-0

ABOUT "THAT PHONE CALL" AND THE FUTURE OF TEACHING UNDERGRADUATES WITH ARCHIVES

Terrence J. McDonald
University of Michigan

About "That Phone Call"

Every academic term, for the last seventy years or so, just about every college- or university-based archivist has experienced a phone call like the one below:

"Hello, Jan, it's Dean, over in the history department. How are you?"

"I'm fine, Dean."

"Well, it's about that time again this term for you to work your magic with my students. I'd like to bring them over next week and I'm sorry for the short notice but I've been working on my paper for the meeting of the International Society for the Study of (something), and so I'm behind on everything."

"Yes, Dean, I think we can accommodate you next week."

"Fantastic, Jan, you're a miracle worker in addition to being an archival wizard. I'm sorry that I won't be able to come over with the class, though, since that's the day when I'll be traveling to the conference where I'll be giving my paper."

"I understand."

"I know you'll work your customary magic and you know how great the students always think you are!"

Brief contemplation of this conversation reveals its remarkably patronizing subtexts: research is more important than teaching, archivists are obviously less busy and less important than departmental teaching faculty, and the encounter with the archives is irrelevant to the progress of a course (the absence of the course instructor from these sessions sends the students a powerful message). The cherry on top is the cheerful false praise: the archivist is an irrelevant wonderworker!

To begin to unwind and replace this conversation, we must recognize that for many years, for a variety of reasons, it has "worked" for those on both sides of it. The patronizing obliviousness of the departmental faculty member is familiar to the archivist, of course, as is the trivialization of the archival visit, derisively known by archivists as the "drive-by." But the exchange has worked for the archivist, too, because it encompasses in one visit the responsibility of most undergraduate teaching, thereby saving the archivist's time for supportive work with what has traditionally been the university's most important function: research by nonstudent researchers. In an academic world in which no one in most college- or university-based archives was specifically hired to do outreach to faculty and students, the drive-by, it turns out, was not only functional, but for many years produced the only type of praise that the archival faculty received from local departmental faculty.

As the movement for teaching undergraduates with archives gathers steam, its prospects are defined to some extent by the prospects of the institution in which it exists: the college and university. For a long time, that structure undervalued undergraduate teaching and upheld a "single standard of honor" that involved only research. In those days, a movement focused on undergraduate teaching in the archives stood little chance, and no one was proposing one. Indeed, as we will see, it would have been completely counterproductive for archivists to do so. But today, ironically, as colleges and universities deal with multiple challenges, the chances for a genuine change in the status of undergraduate teaching may be greater than ever before. In particular, the increasing price of undergraduate degrees and the shrinkage of graduate cohorts and teaching may produce one of the most important openings for such change in recent decades.

Archivists under the "Single Standard of Honor"

The American university was born as a college but rapidly shifted to being a place for research and graduate teaching (with undergraduate tuition paying the bills) in the last quarter of the nineteenth century. The Association of American Universities (AAU) was organized in 1900 solely to rationalize and control graduate education and faculty research (with two of its founding members, Johns Hopkins and Chicago, having no undergraduates at all). The research universities were full of ambition: their goal was to become the place where faculty research was highly valued and to usurp Germany's reputation as the best place for graduate students to receive their training. However, being short of resources, the research universities struggled until the post-World War II period, when resources from both federal and state governments flowed in a way that is unimaginable today.[1]

Research universities set the standard for prestige, and in the postwar years, their number increased. Although Carnegie classifications have shifted over time, typically about 125 American universities have been in the research-intensive or R-1 category, including the sixty-two American members of the even more prestigious AAU. Because there were so many R-1 universities and because they served as an aspirational goal for many others, the emphasis on research in those places had a huge effect, extending even to the smaller liberal arts colleges, who began requiring research for tenure, too.

From about 1955 to about 1969, resource availability brought the R-1

---

1. Roger Geiger has written the standard histories on the rise of the research university. See Geiger, *To Advance Knowledge: The Growth of American Research Universities, 1900–1940* (New Brunswick, New Jersey: Transaction Publishers, 2008) and *Research and Relevant Knowledge: American Research Universities Since World War II* (New Brunswick, New Jersey: Transaction Publishers, 2009). The fate of undergraduates in the research university is not a central focus of these works.

campuses close to the ideal of simple graduate production. Small or no undergraduate teaching loads were accompanied by large graduate cohorts: in many R-1 departments there were more graduate students than there are history majors today. The demand for faculty in the ever-increasing number of R-1 aspirants led to frequent moves by faculty and continuous negotiation aimed at reducing undergraduate teaching loads to zero or close to it.

In this context (the rising funding for and near realization of the fully fledged research university) the much-analyzed split between researchers—especially historians—and archivists, which some have called the "archival divide," had little or no impact on the question of the significance of undergraduate teaching. On this question, there was no divide between archivists and researchers: both sides were constituted by the postwar university as engaged in support for graduate and professional research. No one on either side received appropriate resources for undergraduate teaching or credit for deep concern about the lack of it.

In another context, Terry Cook has thoughtfully reviewed the relationship between historians and archivists, noting that through the 1980s, at least, the professional mindset among the latter was "curatorial, neutered, and self-deprecating." Archivists were satisfied to be the invisible "handmaidens of historians," in service to research. But precisely because archival work was connected with the one thing that the research university honored and rewarded— research—this was a high-status position, if in a subordinated role.[2]

This relative priority of research over undergraduate teaching can be seen in various aspects of archival work:

- The architectural dimensions of most university-based archives feature large-scale storage for materials, relatively small-scale public spaces, and no undergraduate teaching space.

---

2. Terry Cook, "The Archive(s) is a Foreign Country: Historians, Archivists, and the Changing Archival Landscape(s)," *The American Archivist*, 74, no. 2 (Fall/Winter 2011): 600–632. Undergraduate teaching does not figure into his analysis.

- The royal treatment for visiting researchers: obsessive counting of volumes produced from each archive and competitive reviews of acknowledgments in prefaces.
- Finding aids and websites designed to serve the search purposes of archivists rather than the needs of more "amateur" users.
- Nearly complete lack of archival positions designed to focus on undergraduate outreach or teaching.

Under this regime, an undergraduate class of any size would receive less time and attention in the archives than a visiting researcher in town for a week. And, importantly, there was nothing wrong with this behavior in its context. This is not a moral critique, but a review of how a university structured in one way led to behavior structured similarly. Moreover, this review is in no way intended to diminish or ignore the various other issues on the table between archivists and researchers (especially historians), which have been well outlined by Cook, Francis Blouin and William Rosenberg, and Randall Jimerson.[3]

Historians, for example, had no incentive to question the status of undergraduate education and so they did not. This is in part because the American Historical Association was formed in 1884 and, therefore, antedated the research university. In addition, it always supported research. Given that many of the other research-oriented disciplines—economics, political science, etc.—emerged out of it, history was "grandfathered" into the research university and never really had to establish its credentials. History would have its own issues to solve over the twentieth century—significantly, for example, those involving "objectivity"—but it would not face the same challenge of establishing professional respectability through more widespread development of

---

3. Cook, "Archive," 608. Francis X. Blouin, Jr. and William Rosenberg discuss the "archival divide" in *Processing the Past: Contesting Authority in History and the Archives* (New York: Oxford University Press, 2011), 91–93. Randall C. Jimerson provides a useful overview of the development of the archival profession in his introduction, "American Archivists and the Search for Professional Identity," in Jimerson, ed. *American Archival Studies: Readings in Theory and Practice* (Chicago: Society of American Archivists, 2000), 1–20. None of these authors discusses the issues of undergraduate teaching.

theory and research, as was required for archivists, as Jimerson has pointed out. And, importantly, as Cook has observed, researchers (again, especially historians) did not want archivists to change their behavior in any way, certainly not by taking on more undergraduate instruction, which might subtract time for service for historical research.

The Opening: Threats to the "Single Standard"

It would be nice to report that research universities awoke to the significance of undergraduate teaching on their own, but the effect of countless calls for this to happen—such as Ernest Boyer's important 1987 book, *College: The Undergraduate Experience in America*—was minimal. Instead, as was the case in the heyday of the R-1 university, it has been external resources (in recent years, the lack of the same) that began to promote change in the status of undergraduate teaching on R-1 campuses. Beginning in the 1970s, resource restrictions, periodic deep economic recessions, and neoliberal restructuring of universities themselves led to two relevant outcomes. First, university education became remarkably more expensive for undergraduates and online alternatives began to be a real threat. Meanwhile, storm clouds in the 1970s predicting decreased demand for university faculty finally became fully fledged storms in the 1990s and early 2000s, punctuated by the devastating recession of 2008. In many places, graduate cohorts shrunk drastically; in all places undergraduate enrollment rose significantly, if for no other purpose than to pay the bills, and the fractionating of tenure-track faculty lines led to fewer and fewer of those on the instructional track being eligible for tenure and thus being required to do research.

The revaluing of undergraduate education is a reality now. In twenty-first century America, the number of professional researchers is shrinking, prospects for graduate level education are dimming, and the value of the traditional four-year undergraduate residential experience is under serious question. In this context of quite radical structural change, ironically, the deep cultural resources of the residential campuses, including their archives, take on extraordinary significance. Undergraduate student work in the archives with primary sources that are available only there will not soon be replaced by online courses from Coursera.

In fact, in his 2013 book, *Higher Education in the Digital Age*, the late William G. Bowen called for the strengthening of "central aspects of life on our traditional campuses that must be retained" in the face of online modes of teaching. Certainly archival and other so-called cultural collections are a crucial part of the process he calls "minds rubbing against minds," and the "genuine learning [that] occurs more or less continually, and is often, or more often, out of the classroom as in it."[4]

How Change Might Happen

Calls to improve undergraduate education have been made before—indeed, many times before. How do we go from calls to change? In their classic work on how social movements achieve change, *Poor People's Movements*, Frances Fox Piven and Richard A. Cloward said that change occurs after a transformation of both "consciousness" and "behavior." First, "the system," or those aspects of the system that people experience and perceive, loses legitimacy. Second, those who have been fatalistic about change begin to assert rights for it. And third, there is a new sense of efficacy that leads to collective defiance: "they violate the traditions and laws to which they ordinarily acquiesce."[5]

The external pressures on traditional higher education mentioned above—increasing costs and multiplying alternatives—are real, and now, almost ten years after the historic recession and with the economy booming, appear to be secular and not cyclical forces. The old system, wherein undergraduate education was an afterthought, is collapsing. If anything, peak experiences, with resources available only on

---

4. William G. Bowen, *Higher Education in the Digital Age* (Princeton: Princeton University Press, 2013), 67–68.

5. Frances Fox Piven and Richard Cloward, *Poor Peoples' Movements: Why They Succeed, How They Fail* (New York: Random House Vintage, 1979), 3–4.

residential campuses (such as libraries, archives, museums, botanical gardens, etc.), are an important part of the argument for the value of the very high cost of an undergraduate degree.

Just as important, the appropriate relationship between archival and other teaching faculty has been called into question—mostly by archivists. Within the last ten years, there has been an outpouring of writing by and for archivists about ways to improve teaching with primary sources. Conferences, "unconferences," workshops, and panels at professional meetings have produced a loose network of archival alliances proposing the violation of the traditional relationship between archives and courses.[6]

Unwinding the pre-existing relationship between archival and teaching faculty requires both admitting the historical advantages of both and building a new and more productive relationship. There will be both social and economic impacts of this change. Reacquainting archival and teaching faculty with one another and restructuring their relationships will require time and resources. But aligning the effort with widespread calls for a more "experiential" undergraduate education, and more possibilities for outreach, will help with the resource issues.

The "anthropological" work of redefining the culture will take time and patience.

One of the great ironies of the old regime was that neither side knew exactly what it could ask for from the other. And neither side necessarily got what it wanted. Well-intentioned teaching faculty might have wanted more than a drive-by archival experience for their students, but they honestly did not know if busy archivists could accommodate such a request. Meanwhile, countless archivists wanted to "just say no" to the drive-by, but they did not want to risk the relationships they had

---

6. See essays by pioneers in this field: Robin M. Katz and Elizabeth Yakel in this volume, and also Patricia Garcia, Joseph Lueck, and Elizabeth Yakel, "The Pedagogical Promise of Primary Sources: Research Trends, Persistent Gaps, and New Directions," *Journal of Academic Librarianship*, 45 (2019), 94–101. Elizabeth Yakel and Doris Malkmus, "Contextualizing Archival Literacy," in *Teaching with Primary Sources* (Chicago: Society of American Archivists, 2016), 8–38, date the increasing attention to undergraduate teaching to the 1980s.

with teaching faculty, in spite of all the ways in which they were full of patronizing mixed messages.

If we assume that teaching students how to do research with primary sources is a good thing for both pedagogy and democracy, and we accept the utilitarian argument that this kind of experiential undergraduate education is now more valuable than ever—especially if it results in outreach products (websites, blogs, etc.) that both empower students and inform citizens—the place to start may be with the assumption of goodwill on both sides. This requires change on both sides.

Some Paths Forward

Archivists need to take outreach for undergraduate education seriously. For all the published exhortations to do this, the number of archives that have designated and funded a position for outreach and education (as opposed to simply adding these duties to someone's full-time schedule) is small. Second, archives need to take the lead on changing the conversation by redefining the partnership. Fifty years of rewarding if counterproductive relationships have produced a culture in which archival and teaching faculty rarely know one another, and that is why calling the drive-by into question needs to be preceded by a reasonable period of "getting to know you."

At the symposium from which these essays have evolved, several institutions (Michigan, Georgia, and Rochester, for example) reported on their experiences with funded seminars, in which departmental faculty worked with archivists to improve their courses. The results of these experiences—all of which required stipends to attract the departmental faculty—was extraordinary. In each case, users familiar with the archives came to see it in a new way, and a wide array of new disciplines and practitioners showed interest in the process. At the end of these experiences, the departmental faculty were likely to become proselytizers for teaching undergraduates with archives.[7]

---

7. See essays in this volume by Cinda Nofziger and Elizabeth Call, Kimberly Davies Hoffman, and Kristen Totleben.

But what, exactly, is "the process?" As those who run the training seminars report, the magic starts with simply getting archival and teaching faculty in the same room for some serious period of time. From there, simply getting to know each other—building respect for the training and talent that each can bring to a course—and establishing expectations for simple collegiality are the first steps. (Would any member of the departmental faculty in his/her right mind actually expect a departmental colleague to perform "wizardry" in a course on short notice?)

Keeping in mind that few departmental or archival faculty have ever been trained to teach, the next step is simple pedagogy. Allies in schools of education and/or information can play an important role here. On most campuses, there is a vast field of research and teaching on effective ways to teach the social sciences in K-12 schools, the schools that will provide all members of the freshman class at every college and university in America. Because most archival graduate training programs do not include training in teaching and because most departmental faculty who have worked in archives were simply dumped there by their own advisers, both sides have a lot to learn from the fields concerned with teaching undergraduates with primary sources.[8]

Luckily, the lessons from this research are straightforward: teach students what you want them to know (for example, model the way an instructor might read a primary source), and deconstruct assignments. Recognize that, for undergraduate students, the first archival encounter is like a trip to a foreign country: scary rules at the border and a foreign language inside. (How exactly do you read a finding aid?) Add time, lots of it, at every stage in the course, beginning when students have their first contact with the archives.

True partnership between departmental and archival faculty begins with the very long lead time for planning that genuine collegiality

---

8. Those who train K-12 teachers have developed many web-based platforms encouraging the use of primary sources, for example, Stanford History Education Group, https://sheg.stanford.edu/history-lessons; Read, Inquire, Write project, http://readinquirewrite.umich.edu/; and Library of Congress, http://www.loc.gov/teachers/usingprimarysources/.

would predict. Archivists can visit classrooms in advance of a trip to the archives; teaching faculty can participate in the selection of appropriate sources and assignments side by side with the archivists. In some cases—exemplified by the extraordinary team-teaching effort between archival and departmental faculty at Princeton, among other places—actual team teaching, between equals, will be the result.[9]

Good teaching of undergraduates always takes time—more time than anyone can imagine at the outset, and at some points in every semester, more time than anyone has. But in this case the rewards are extraordinary. For those few students who have had this experience—for example, on many campuses, those students who have written an archivally based senior honors thesis—the experience is life-changing. For all of us, for all our institutions, and for our society as a whole, changing lives must be what we are about today.

In his book, *The Internet of Us*, Michael Patrick Lynch applauds institutions that facilitate and encourage the construction of "grounded belief" as "doing the work of democracy," because "knowing is having a correct belief (getting it right, having a true opinion) that is grounded or justified and which can therefore guide our action." Teaching undergraduate students how to develop a grounded belief about an historical situation through the use of archival primary sources is surely a crucial type of this work and one that will be done best when archival and departmental faculty are both partners as members of the teaching faculty.[10]

And then, one day, there will be this phone call:

"Hello, Jan, this is Dean over in history. Good to talk with you again. I'm planning to offer my course based in the archives again next year and I wonder when you might have time for a cup of coffee so we can start planning."

---

9. See essays in this volume by Martha A. Sandweiss and Daniel J. Linke.
10. Michael Patrick Lynch, *The Internet of Us* (New York: W. W. Norton, 2016), 60–61.

THIS IS WHERE WE GO FROM HERE: CONSTRUCTING A COMMUNITY OF TEACHING WITH PRIMARY SOURCES EDUCATORS

Anne Bahde
Oregon State University

Heather Smedberg
University of California San Diego

Matt Herbison
Drexel University College of Medicine

Robin M. Katz
University of California Riverside

Marissa Vassari
Rockefeller Archive Center

The Teaching with Primary Sources (TPS) Community has grown and become more active over the past decade, through a number of publications, online resources, meetings large and small, and loose networks of individuals with the shared goal of wanting to improve their ability to teach with archives and other cultural heritage materials. This community is broadly composed of archivists, librarians, college faculty, museum educators, K-12 teachers, and others who teach with primary sources in numerous ways. Each of these groups is represented by separate professional organizations, with varying approaches to supporting growth on this topic. But as this community has expanded, members have increasingly voiced the desire to bring some unity and professionalization to the activities and growth of the TPS collective. The Reference, Access, and Outreach (RAO) section of the Society of American Archivists (SAA) took important early steps, forming a TPS working group (later a committee), which conducted a 2013 survey that identified professional support needs for archivists doing instruction[1]. As a result of their findings, RAO TPS working group members developed a cumulative bibliography of literature on teaching with primary sources in 2011–2012,[2] a pilot site for sharing teaching resources in 2015–2016, and an unconference that has occurred annually since 2015. The Rare Books and Manuscripts Section (RBMS) of the Association of College & Research Libraries (ACRL) joined with SAA in 2016 to develop the Guidelines for Primary Source Literacy.[3] RBMS established the Instruction & Outreach Committee (IOC) in 2017, and this group has since made concerted efforts to support TPS practitioners as well. These efforts, in addition to numerous statewide, local, or institutional initiatives, such as those at the Library of Congress and the Brooklyn Historical Society, have laid a foundation for the extraordinary growth TPS has seen in recent years. However, these efforts lack cohesion, and sometimes result in duplicative efforts, while other needs are left unmet. Members of the community can also find it difficult to identify a clear path to professional opportunity and growth in this environment.

---

1. Teaching with Primary Sources Working Group Survey Findings and Recommendations, August 2, 2013: www2.archivists.org/sites/all/files/TPS_survey_final_report_080513.pdf.

2. Teaching with Primary Sources Bibliography: https://www2.archivists.org/groups/reference-access-and-outreach-section/teaching-with-primary-sources-bibliography.

3. Approved standard available at: https://www2.archivists.org/standards/guidelines-for-primary-source-literacy.

The University of Michigan Teaching Undergraduates with Archives Symposium in 2018 afforded an unprecedented opportunity to bring the TPS Community face-to-face to discuss shared desires to work more effectively and confidently in the TPS realm. Recent years have seen a marked increase in instruction and outreach programming at national and regional conferences, but the University of Michigan symposium was the first national gathering (that we know of) solely dedicated to teaching with primary sources that welcomed archivists, librarians, faculty, and students. As well-established practitioners and thinkers who have each been involved with many early efforts, and who have devoted much time and attention to the collective development of the profession, the authors of this chapter seized this opportunity to tap into the energetic gathering of engaged TPS minds from multiple professional and organizational "homes," eager to work toward a blueprint for how to build a better-connected and better-supported community. Recognizing that the profession has plentiful case studies, we instead wanted to take advantage of this unique opportunity to have strategic and practical discussions about how to best organize these efforts moving forward. To this end, we designed the participatory session, "Where Do We Go From Here? Constructing a Community of Archives Educators," around what we see as five key issues shaping the future of TPS: 1) professional development; 2) assessment; 3) promotion and visibility; 4) products and resources; and 5) communication and community support. The authors kicked off the session with a structured conversation about our own experiences in these areas, then led all participants in facilitated subgroups to further brainstorm on these themes.[4] The goal was to elucidate which concrete, actionable next steps might help develop a roadmap for the TPS Community over the next several years. These group discussions were intended to identify challenges and solutions, tap into community knowledge, and pool ideas.

While the larger event drew faculty and students as well, nearly all of the participants in our session were librarians or archivists based at

---

4. For detailed notes from these discussions, including nuts-and-bolts suggestions, see the publicly accessible session notes document: see https://bit.ly/2LmlO9Y.

campuses. The symposium focused solely on undergraduate learning, and surveys indicate the biggest audience reached by teaching archivists is undergraduates.[5] But the TPS Community is broader. Because our learning environments reach graduate students, K-12 schools, lifelong learners, and beyond, the solutions we propose and support going forward should be more inclusive.

The collaborative session was full of lively exchanges; the fluid and high-energy brainstorming of ideas was exhilarating for seemingly everyone in the room. As subgroups reported out, participants offered further comments from their own experiences, bounced off each other's ideas, and suggested interesting tangents; this made for animated yet difficult-to-attribute conversations. The following sections blend these collectively generated ideas with themes from the authors' initial conversation. The authors thank the approximately 50 participants whose ideas and energy contributed to the spirit of unlimited potential in the session, and we hope they will recreate that energy in actions moving the TPS Community forward.

Professional Development

How do we bridge the gap between the various professions within the TPS Community, in order to build skill sets, increase confidence, and work towards similar goals? More and more often, archivists and librarians are asked to lead instruction despite not having previous teaching experience, and they want to develop a better understanding of pedagogy; others have a natural interest in teaching and want to know where to start. Observing and hearing students work with archival

---

5. See Anna Elise Allison, "Connecting Undergraduates with Primary Sources: A Study of Undergraduate Instruction in Archives, Manuscripts, and Special Collections," (master's thesis, University of North Carolina at Chapel Hill, 2005); Brian Dietz, "Getting Undergraduates into Archives: Educational Outreach Efforts of University Archives, Manuscript Departments, and Special Collections," (master's thesis, University of North Carolina at Chapel Hill, 2005); and Magia Krause, "Learning in the Archives: A Report on Instructional Practices," *Journal of Archival Organization*, 6, no. 4 (2008): 233–268.

material encourages archivists who are reticent to dive into instruction to make the jump. Educators often remark on students' excitement and investment in lessons and projects grounded in archival material, and archivists are aware that education with primary source materials is an excellent form of outreach and a powerful way to instruct—it is also increasingly mandated by curricula, standards, and disciplinary trends.

Participants in this subgroup discussed how to level the playing field and figure out what archivists need in order to instruct effectively. Common threads throughout the subgroup discussion included many archivists feeling they lack several crucial proficiencies: classroom management skills and pedagogical grounding, successful methods for how to reach out to educators, and training in how to frame the materials in a way that they can be seamlessly implemented in an instructional setting.

Just as archivists feel there are challenges, so do teachers and instructors. Often, they are unsure of where and how to find primary source material and rely on a few published readers and curated websites. Archivists have a better understanding of the collections, which can be of help when primary source projects are being developed and integrated into syllabi. Providing professional opportunities that develop and hone the skills needed to teach with primary sources for all those involved inside and outside the classroom walls will ensure that the community as a whole is stronger and more transparent. Five overarching possibilities for supporting archivists in instruction roles became apparent during the subgroup discussion: graduate courses, professional development intensives, certificate programs, workshops and webinars, and a mentorship program.

Offering students in library and archives degree programs graduate courses in classroom management, instruction design, and other areas of pedagogy would be the ideal way to equip future archivists with the necessary skill set for teaching and would build the confidence of budding archivists early on in their career. Pedagogy is not learned overnight, and archival best practices cannot be communicated and digested in an effective manner without understanding the nature of work in each profession, whether librarians, archivists, instructors, or other members of the community. And professional development focused on teaching with special collections is limited. Having a structured set of classes that focus on pedagogy would provide a firm foundation for moving into instruction. While there are intensive programs available through various institutions (such as Dartmouth's Librarians' Active Learning Institute–Archives and Special Collections track (LALI–ASC), Rare Book School, or California Rare Book School), they tend to have limited spots available and to be on the more expensive side. It has become evident that we need more (and more affordable) educational offerings, and, ideally, options for funding individuals interested in participating.[6]

Similarly, a continuing education certificate could be established through a professional organization that offers classes focused on instruction in archives. Several of the participants in the subgroup cited other certificate programs that are available to archivists, and participants felt a certificate in instruction would acknowledge that it is no longer a niche part of the archival profession, but a robust area of education and outreach.

The participants referenced separate professional development opportunities focused on fusing archives and education, such as workshops and webinars, as another solution for professionals who do not have a formal background in instruction or education. These less time-intensive options are often more accessible to more professionals at this time. Making resources and local workshops more widely known through listservs, social media, and conferences allows archivists who do not have the time to dedicate to a graduate or certificate program to seek out new skills and build a network of supportive individuals in the field.

A mentorship program could also be an option for supporting

---

6. The lack of pedagogical training in the SAA directory and ALA-accredited archival education programs is addressed in Lindsay Anderberg, Robin M. Katz, Shaun Hayes, Alison Stankrauff, Morgen MacIntosh Hodgetts, Josué Hurtado, Abigail Nye, and Ashley Todd-Diaz, "Teaching the Teacher: Primary Source Instruction in American and Canadian Archives Graduate Programs," *The American Archivist* 81, no. 1 (2018): 188–215, https://americanarchivist.org/doi/full/10.17723/0360-9081-81.1.188

archivists new to instruction. Pairing such an archivist with an established teaching archivist or an experienced educator would allow for more flexible and personalized communication. In-person meetings and conversations over email could lead to sharing strategies, offering feedback, and perhaps hands-on experiences in a classroom setting.

By acknowledging the gaps, listening to the TPS Community, and working to consolidate and strengthen existing opportunities, the archival field will benefit from continued learning and professional growth in instruction.

Assessment of Programs and Learning

The assessment subgroup focused on concerns surrounding assessment of student learning, teaching effectiveness, and performance of instruction programs within special collections and archives settings. Beginning with the question, "What do you need in your assessment toolbox?" participants generated several ideas; these were mostly borne from the anxiety, confusion, and frustration surrounding this topic. Throughout the discussion, participants touched on crucial considerations about the purposes of assessment, exploring questions of how to know whether students are learning, how to act on the results of assessment, and how to identify and focus on what the instructor personally wants to know for improvement.

The group was fortunate to have participants who are grappling with assessment issues from a variety of roles in archives and libraries—instructors, program coordinators, and administrators—and many expressed frustration with multiple elements, including the processes, outcomes, and uses of assessment. At every level, assessment is about time: time for preparation, data gathering, reflection, analysis, resultant actions, and further responses. Tellingly, however, nearly all participants in the group felt their current position duties and departmental settings do not allow the necessary time for successful, meaningful, and actionable instructional assessment.

Despite this, most agreed that assessment can be a crucial activity that enables all parties to demonstrate to a variety of important audiences the importance and impact of instruction using special collections and archives. The group explored several ideas to move the TPS Community into a new era of assessment in our classrooms. A comprehensive training program (perhaps presented via formal graduate or professional development programs, tailored to the particular concerns of special collections and archives instructional environments) would be a way to prepare instructors to confidently engage in the mechanics of assessment, methods of data gathering and analysis, techniques for interpretation and evaluation, and effective systems of implementing change. Further, administrative support for release time for instructors to complete and implement such training is critical.

This last observation prompted a deeper discussion of the need for shared professional values surrounding instructional assessment. Many participants noted that within their departments, various staff with multiple (and often competing) roles and identities are tasked with instruction duties but may have little training in (or sometimes, concern for) emerging best practices in this field. This often leads to notable variation in the approaches to and quality of instruction. Leaders of instruction programs who do not supervise or otherwise lack influence over their peers' instructional styles must then struggle with assessment evidence showing limited student learning and compromised teaching effectiveness in these classes. When one is building an instruction program based on high-impact, pedagogically grounded experiences with unique materials, anchored in best practices and standards in the field, the support of administrators is essential. This support can be manifested in department- or even library-wide discussions about the reasons for setting high standards for instructional quality; the intended results of such an approach for students, instructors, and the institution; and an established, enforced set of performance expectations for instructional activities (as well as the necessary training to accomplish this). Elevating high-quality instructional practices, including assessment, to a collective department goal, and promoting this as a shared mutual value across the department, is a necessary action from administrators if programs are to achieve their full potential.

The primary need expressed by participants was for high-yield, low-cost, repurposable, scalable, shared, and easily adaptable tools and models for both classroom and program assessment. Tools such as rubrics, crosswalks to the ACRL Framework, formative classroom techniques, and program toolkits, each adjustable for different levels of expertise and time, emerged as a central priority for the TPS Community. Increasing engagement with campus centers for teaching and learning, campus assessment offices, campus institutional review boards, or similar campus teaching and research support resources may be an easy way to expand one's personal assessment toolkit (for university-based practitioners). Increasing partnerships with non-archives and special collections instruction colleagues in the library or with nearby institutions is another. Several participants inspired us with stories of individual assessment successes that began by starting with small efforts, such as establishing personal reflective practices, and recommitting themselves to their own values about the difference assessment work can make in individual approaches to teaching. This commitment can spur further growth both at the personal and program levels, but it requires a personal examination of values and circumstances: What do I want to know? What is important to me? What do my administrators and peers require? And perhaps most importantly, how can this investment of time be maximized for greatest effectiveness?

Many expressed hope that as the TPS Community begins to increase communication, build a united body of practice, and foster sharing, we will naturally begin to identify consistently useful assessment techniques and methods, dispel some of these shared frustrations, and build collective confidence in the value of assessment to show why what we do is so very valuable in today's educational landscape.

Promotion and Visibility

We asked participants in this subgroup to discuss how to best advocate for the work we are all doing. Although teaching is easily understood by others (as opposed to, say, archival processing) and (in some settings) student learning is considered a "hot button" topic, participants who chose this subgroup felt a need to better highlight and demonstrate the value of this work. Participants were eager to brainstorm concrete, practical ideas that could be put in place easily by an individual or a department.

The conversation quickly turned to the nitty gritty details of publicity, from e-newsletters to social media strategies to major national media outlets. Participants shared some tips for developing a publicity plan or a media kit, but a more lasting and accessible place to harness this kind of collective knowledge might be helpful to this community. The conversation then turned to how big of a role TPSers should play in publicity. Should this be work we do and skills we build, or should we try to encourage or require specialists within our organizations (say, from marketing, communications, design, or development units) to get this work covered?

Questions about broad-based media or social media exposure inevitably lead to existential questions about the purpose of outreach, promotion, and visibility. Is the goal to expand services or programs (for example: to get more faculty partners or classes)? To lobby administrators or funders for more funding or resources? Or is the point recognition: for the department, unit, repository, or the organization? Or, as a community of educators, are we thinking about our own careers? Individual recognition, of course, often directly relates to promotions and/or compensation.

To create more local interest in our instruction services, participants generated ideas such as research prizes for undergraduates—a program already in place at many institutions. A more unique idea was to repeat successful instruction sessions for library/archives colleagues, other teachers/faculty, administrators, or even donors. Because word of mouth is the best advertising, this type of program felt simultaneously innovative, feasible, and effective, especially compared to more traditional outreach events such as orientation events and tabling. The subgroup was interested in exploring ways to make such "ambassadors" a more systematic program, as well.

Participants were also inspired by the handful of undergraduates who were invited to co-present at the Michigan symposium, and all present agreed that it is important to amplify the voices of collaborators and students. At the same time, however, the subgroup wrestled with wanting to share the spotlight with students and other partners (or even our institutions), and feeling that we actually need to center ourselves more in the narrative of our labor. For this reason, increasing visibility through celebratory events struck a chord among session participants because it would make visible the amount and type of labor that goes into our work.

To have the broadest possible reach within our profession, subgroup participants wanted to make our work available to others online. This echoes a long-heard desire for sharing our work, whether through institutional repositories, disciplinary repositories, pre-prints, or the much-anticipated TPS Collective "resource bank" (discussed in more detail below).

Products and Resources

This subgroup focused on prioritizing methods or tools for creating, reusing, and sharing the products of instructional work. We first spent some time considering what exactly we meant by "products": brainstorming teaching tools we as individuals produce, or those we wish we had the time to create. These include lesson plans, exercise worksheets, handouts, longer unit plans, and take-home assignments. Participants also identified teaching support materials like the outlines or prompts we prepare for ourselves, slides we show in class, and the specific prompts we give to students to foster discussion and facilitate effective, active learning experiences. Participants all wanted to have access to examples of assessment tools and instructions or guidance on effective use of those products, as discussed above, but are much less consistently creating these. We also discussed other intellectual work we would like to better document or have access to, like the selection of sources used in class, including specific openings or passages that worked well within the context of the class exercise. Other products with potential for reuse or sharing are descriptive labels created to accompany selected items, or those labels created by student exhibition assignments. In general, instructors seek windows into one another's classes sufficient to find ideas for organizing their own classes, as well as having readymade tools at their disposal to save time. One participant noted that having videos of actual classes would be the best way to see the nuance of how successful sessions are conducted, in a way that reading about a class through a lesson plan or case study does not. Videos also offer the opportunity for reflective learning at the individual level.

While participants universally wanted to see shared products, most of us tend to work independently or even in isolation and there was an underlying anxiety about sharing work for a variety of reasons. Some folks are territorial about intellectual and creative output, too. But our participants agreed these psychological barriers should not hold us back from developing community tools to promote the sharing of teaching products. Rather, the profession should actively support individuals in adapting to a model of sharing and encourage a culture of attribution and credit as we build practical solutions for sharing products. An easy step that individuals can take to start embracing this culture of sharing, with little additional time investment, is to create products using collaborative tools like Google Docs or make use of shared network drives or cloud storage options like Box or Google Drive. Even if at first an individual is only sharing with themselves, the next step—sharing with others—is technologically easy. One participant noted that using these types of collaborative tools with department colleagues is handy, but does feel like someone is "rifling through your underwear drawer." LibGuides can be useful tools for creating content for a more public audience, but participants agreed these are time consuming and questioned their value. But by focusing on creating LibGuides for classes that repeat, for content that duplicates across classes, or to document the list of items pulled for classes, this labor can simultaneously help students, our colleagues at the reference desk, and the community.

Participants see value in developing community connections to share products at institutional, local, regional, and national organization levels. As an example of an institutional approach to nurturing a culture of sharing, one participant described monthly gatherings of instruction and reference staff. Among other benefits, these events serve as a useful opportunity to reflect on the impact of recent instructional sessions on the reference desk, while providing useful feedback for future classes. It was suggested that local or regional networks are well suited for more informal sharing or workshopping products, while national organizations are better positioned to create guidelines, support platforms for community discussions, offer professional development support, and advocate for the importance of TPS work. In addition to a variety of intensive and shorter professional development opportunities offered by local, regional, and national groups, the new RBMS Instruction & Outreach Committee (IOC) newsletter, *Primary Source News and Notes,* was named as an interesting new product to watch.

The following section will pick up on this idea of community development support in more detail, but one thing was clear from our discussion: it is hard to separate strategies for sharing the products of our work from broader thinking about the way we each work and learn. Participants valued a blend of community opportunities, including those that can be accessed easily online at a low cost, with ample opportunities for in-person learning and sharing. While products may be shared remotely, knowledge might well need to be shared in person. Making space for each kind of connection is essential.

Communication and Community Support

The fifth subgroup focused on the question: What do you wish existed to improve communication and community? Participants quickly fixed attention on three ideas: resource sharing, communication, and creating face-to-face opportunities with other TPSers.

Participants felt that resource sharing could best be accomplished through development of an online resource bank: a website that would facilitate sharing the types of community products and resources discussed in the previous section. Second, communication can be facilitated by the creation and deliberate activity of some kind of virtual group (perhaps a listserv, Google Group, or subreddit) to allow various practitioners (regardless of professional affiliation) to all come together in a space for discussion and learning. Third, to support face-to-face opportunities, we should further develop regional support to encourage communities at that level. The model used by the Archival Educators Roundtable at Rockefeller Archive Center (AER-RAC, discussed below), is a particularly inspirational approach to regional community-building.

Since at least 2012, those in the TPS Community have discussed the idea of a community-driven online resource bank and forum/ listserv, with the SAA-driven TPS Bibliography as an early, narrow-scope foray. With the positive response to TeachArchives.org in early 2014, it became clearer that a resource bank could enable the entire TPS Community to freely provide sets of pedagogically sound how-to resources as well as sample exercises. The TPS Resource Bank pilot website, intended as a proof-of-concept by the SAA-TPS Committee, launched in 2016.[7]

Session participants expressed a keen interest in resource bank efforts moving forward. As enumerated in the previous section, people want easy and effective ways to communicate and share resources, news, and ideas. Following on the work of the TPS Resource Bank pilot site, this need has led to the renewed, currently in-process efforts to build the forthcoming "TPS Collective," driven primarily by the RBMS Instruction & Outreach Committee and supported by volunteers from SAA's Teaching with Primary Sources Committee (SAA-TPS). Launched in June 2019, the TPS Collective website[8] is designed to support resource sharing, in the form of lesson plans and other tools; news and notes from the field in themed, peer-reviewed series addressing practical how-tos, collaboration, reflective practice, and more; a community of practice discussion forum; and useful toolkits assembled by experts in the field, beginning with one on implementing and applying the Guidelines for Primary Source Literacy.

Participants expressed the need for more robust methods of communication across the TPS Community. As such, the discussion turned to mailing lists and forums. At the time of writing, there are at least two small email lists (SAA-TPS and Archival Educators Roundtable

---

7. The pilot website http://rb.teachwithstuff.org is no longer updated and will redirect to the TPS Collective website upon launch.

8. http://rbms.info/tpscollective.

at Rockefeller Archive Center (AER-RAC)) and one large forum (the Library of Congress' TPS Teachers Network) with a specific focus on teaching with primary sources. Other email lists and forums focus more broadly on library and archives public services or instruction, with some discussion threads aligned closely to interests of TPS Community members. Currently, none of these are actively used by a significant number of the TPS Community. While sessions participants expressed clear interest in these types of communication tools, some expressed doubt that they themselves would actually use them, simply due to personal preferences. However, most acknowledged that this sort of communication tool was still a "gimme" and important for those members of the community who are inclined to use them.

The question of the TPS Community's scope has recrudesced at intervals since at least 2012: who will share resources and who is likely to use them? In this vein, the existence of the Library of Congress' TPS Teachers Network (TPSTN) led to a lively side-discussion in the subgroup. While the TPSTN is an active online community resource with a K-12 audience, participants noted that the large majority of symposium participants work primarily with undergraduates, and are only a subset of the larger TPS Community. We discussed various approaches to ensuring the inclusion of the symposium's absent voices, including those of non-archivist/librarian educators. Some expressed a sense of urgency to develop a shared online community, even if non-archivists aren't yet included. Others were concerned that if the TPS Community gets an online resource and forum off the ground without including non-archivists, the community would risk perpetuating our history of exclusion, losing the benefit of the full breadth of experience and voices.

The third effort supported by session participants was encouragement of face-to-face opportunities. Participants acknowledged the value of large-scale periodic meetings (like the symposium itself, the 2018 Midwest Archives Conference Symposium[9], and the annual TPS Unconfer-

---

9. The October 2018 MAC Symposium ("From the Stacks to the Classroom") represents a TPS meeting at the regional-organization level. The previous MAC symposium with a TPS focus occurred in 2012.

ence[10]), but discussion focused on smaller and more responsive local or regional gatherings. A regional model for this discussion was the Archival Educators Roundtable (AER) meetings developed and hosted by Marissa Vassari at Rockefeller Archive Center, starting in 2016.[11]

AER meetings are guided by two principles: bring-a-buddy and bring-your-problem. The first encourages attendees to bring someone to the meeting who is not coming from the same type of workplace; e.g., an archivist might bring a high school teacher, or a higher education faculty member they've worked with, or a museum educator. This results in an impressively diverse group in a meeting of only 12–20 attendees. The second tenet, bring-your-problem, also sets these meetings apart from most others: rather than attendees reporting what they're working on, the focus is on group problem-solving around an immediate need. While most traditional conferences, and even some unconference sessions, are lecture-style and passive, AER meetings focus on small group, active learning through evidence-based and problem-based discussions. The meetings themselves are a model for how so many in the TPS Community are trying to change the way we teach with archives.

Details and ideas on setting up local AER meetings around the country will be featured on an upcoming AER website and in a future issue of the RBMS IOC *Primary Source News and Notes* newsletter. The model is very adaptable to different settings. The Rockefeller's AER meets twice yearly for six-hour meetings, drawing participants from two-hour-drive catchment, but in different regions they could readily be run as half-day meetings drawing from a group of closer, urban participants; or a full-day, annual meeting drawing from a wider, less populous area. In the waning moments of the subgroup discussion, participants expressed excitement about developing a number of

---

10. Since 2015, the TPS Unconferences have been run as daylong events held during the SAA national annual meeting. They offer both preprogrammed workshops and structured discussions. The discussion topics are decided upon by the attendees day-of (in traditional "unconference" style). More detail at TeachWithStuff.org.

11. These AER meetings are not to be confused with the SAA Archival Educators Section or the annual Archives Education Institutes run by the Archivists Round Table of Metropolitan New York.

regular AER meetings around the country and the opportunities that might arise when that network fed back into the larger national development of shared resources and communications.

Getting There from Here

The energy, excitement, and buzz of conversation following the subgroup discussions underlined the need to build on the momentum of the session and to take action based on the voiced needs of the Teaching with Primary Sources Community. This chapter is one step toward shaping these discussions into a framework that will rally members of the TPS Community and advocate for concrete next steps. Coordination is key for creating unified avenues of professional development, assessment, promotion and visibility, products and resources, and communication and community support. As we heard during the session, "the community is there, it just isn't wrangled in a collective way."

In fact, while session participants deeply appreciated efforts by SAA and RBMS to support TPS work, neither of these organizations sufficiently represents the full range of TPS professionals, and even archivists and special collections librarians often have to choose between the two. Further, the variety of issues relevant to collections-based teaching specifically and TPS more generally are sufficiently complex and multifaceted to benefit from a sustained level of support beyond what currently exists. One potentially effective, long-term solution for developing and carrying out these goals would be the creation of a new, dedicated, national professional organization. This step, along with the many exciting ideas generated by this session, will strengthen and empower the TPS Community to cohere into a discipline of our own, but success will rely on the energy and contributions from the full range of passionate TPS educators. We stand poised to shape this energy and coalesce these efforts. The best way to build the future of this professional community is together.

PRIORITIES FOR PROGRESS

Robin M. Katz
University of California Riverside

Accretion is the opposite of erosion. The ocean gently laps at the shore, imperceptibly depositing individual grains of sand. Stronger waves break and crash, noticeably leaving new sediment behind. Over time, the beach gets bigger. There is land where there wasn't any before.

It is an energizing and invigorating time to be someone who thinks carefully about teaching with archives. The November 2018 symposium at the University of Michigan, Teaching Undergraduates with Archives, was the first conference entirely dedicated to pedagogy in archives and special collections. An incredible roster of leading thinkers in this subfield gathered for the event, and it offered an opportunity to reflect on where we stand. Our bank has clearly widened.

Elizabeth Yakel's chapter reminds us to pay homage to the thinkers and teachers and students who paved the way, and the essays in this volume demonstrate the incredible activity happening on the ground at this very moment. But as we look forward, how do we make sure we are on firm ground?

Despite great strides, our gains are not guaranteed. We need to cement our progress so we can continue to have a positive impact on the lives of our students for years to come. If we do not come together as a cohesive discipline, we face the twin risks of inaction—stagnation or irrelevance.

Our current approach isn't quite working. Too much of our attention is placed on anecdotal reports that do not actually push this subfield forward. Our literature and our conference programs are chock full of case studies that show we deliver instruction through an impressive but set range of options. We welcome classes into our repositories for hands-on or skill-intensive sessions, lamenting the "one-offs" and pushing for multiple "touches" with the same group. We serve as guest lecturers or experts in the classroom, or we teach broader overviews or introductory how-tos. We partner with instructors to develop and support assignments that use our collections or primary sources elsewhere. We require students to make reading room visits and book research consultations. We are embedded in classes, we co-teach, or we lead our own term-length courses. We offer stand-alone workshops and master classes, and we offer out-of-term experiences like summer programs. We train and mentor student employees and interns, who we engage in doing our work (curation, digital humanities, processing, digitization); sometimes we partner with courses where students are given credit to participate in the labor of libraries and archives. We award prizes for undergraduate research through scholarly or creative projects, papers, or even book collecting. In rare cases, archives can serve as a client for students developing computer science projects, responding to a design or marketing brief, or offering translation services.

What we do not need are more case studies. The professional literature is already full of them. Sure, if truly new and innovative models are developed, we need to hear about them. Sometimes, the specifics of a local implementation are helpful and interesting and fun. But not every student-curated exhibition is significant.

If we are going to make any progress—instead of getting bogged down in minutiae about things that only happened one time—we have to tackle more challenging but meaningful questions. We need to develop frameworks for thinking about the work we do that would be useful to others. It is more important that we distill common questions and problems that need to be addressed. Those of us who teach undergraduates with archives must, in the coming years, apply our attention and talents to:

1. Establish shared identities and vocabularies
2. Facilitate an exchange of ideas
3. Solve problems of scale
4. Systematically target particular audiences
5. Get serious about assessment

Our community needs to come together to dramatically scale up our efforts, demonstrate real value, and make meaningful improvements. By intentionally reaching the right students at the right time, we will have broader and deeper impact. We must rise to these challenges to best reach our most fundamental goal of creating resonant and consequential learning experiences for our students.

1. Cohesion: Establish Shared Identities and Vocabularies

We will absolutely have to agree on some boundaries for our constituents, some definition of who we are, and some shared understanding of what we do if we want to build on the momentum that was palpable at the Michigan symposium.

The participants at the Michigan symposium reflect the diversity of librarians, archivists, curators, faculty members, adjunct instructors, teachers, administrators, and students who are invested in collections-based pedagogy. We work in a diversity of organizational contexts within academia, cultural heritage, the government, and the private sector. We have vastly different academic backgrounds and training, our rank and status and position vary, and we occupy different spaces. Our expertise varies from person to person, spanning pedagogical how-tos, collection specifics, niche subjects, complex research skills, and technical proficiencies. More importantly, we serve a wide range of audiences—primarily, but not entirely, undergraduates. While this interdisciplinarity is a strength, we need a unified identity to coalesce around.

We have also struggled to name what it is we even do. Is it teaching and learning, pedagogy, instruction, or education? We are also working with *stuff*, of course—collections, objects, artifacts, and archives. Some of us are preoccupied with materiality; others are concerned with the cultural or historical record of primary sources. The "collections" we refer to can be confused with those in museums, and the term "archival educator" can refer to ourselves or the faculty who train graduate students to become future archivists. "Teaching with primary sources" has gained currency; I like to say collections- or archives-based learning. Whatever we land on, we need to have a shared language that we own and can rally around.

We need to work with graduate programs and employers alike to better ready the people who will do what we do, now and in the future. Many of us did not intend to (or could never have foreseen that we would) end up with these intersecting professional and research interests, so it is no surprise that career pathways are not clearer, and that we do not adequately train or coach or mentor future leaders. Since we know this is a problem, it is our responsibility to act.

We will also inevitably have to keep using the lingo of our administrators and funders to continue to gain and maintain support. Of course, we've been employing object-based, inquiry-driven methodologies all along. But what is today a high-impact, student-centered, flipped classroom full of active learning will be called something else tomorrow. The trendiness of this language can appear to undermine cohesion, at times. But if we manage to stay relevant (and funded) as those trends change, we will be better poised to last.

2. Connection: Exchange of Ideas

We are eager for local, regional, and virtual communities of practice, where we can have ongoing discussions and share resources. Existing professional organizations either fail to fully encompass our entire community (because of barriers ranging from discipline to cost) or remain hidden among/mired in bureaucratic trappings. To create meaningful relationships and engaged interactions, new venues or traditions may be required. Our discipline should establish new modes of organizing to problem-solve and innovate.

We constantly tell ourselves not to reinvent the wheel. There has been a longstanding desire for and slow march towards a "resource bank" or a "collective" —an online exchange where we can cut to the chase and share the practical information: activities, worksheets, lesson plans, learning objects, citations, and scripts. In this context, we can use technology to our advantage—tag and group and sort and link the collective wisdom of our peers. It is important to note that some of our colleagues in the academy will rightfully feel more proprietary towards their instruction materials. This is one of the cultural questions our community—once we are better defined—will have to explore and resolve.

Since our work is undervalued or misunderstood by the people who hire and review us, we need to do what we can to acknowledge and reward our successes within our community. We could establish honors and awards not just for research, publications, and presentations but for the creation of learning objects, for individual achievement in teaching, and for successful education programs by organizations. We can use peer review and competitive application processes to our advantage. We might even one day develop training credentials or continuing education expectations. It is necessary to find ways to celebrate, recognize, and reward each other for the work that we do.

3. Expansion: Solving Scale

The question of how to scale is probably the most pressing issue facing every instructor at every program interested in teaching with archives. Hands-on, small-group experiences have been the central focus of what we do. But with every major gain—a full-time educator, a dedicated classroom—we still run up against new limits. There are only so many hours in a day and seats in a building. Capacity for this kind of customized experience can and should grow—we need teams of instructors, and whole suites available to serve as the laboratories of transformative learning experiences—but it will always be finite. And for those of us based at even the smallest of liberal arts colleges, our potential audience dwarfs our capacity.

Large lecture courses with multiple discussion sections are a good fit for scaling up through repetition. A single experience can be designed and prepared with the intention of delivering it any number of times. To maximize our impact, we should be thinking about the number of "preps" versus "sessions" that we have each week.

This will involve relinquishing some control over collections, spaces, or class time. Collaborators such as archivists, librarians, and staff in other units; student employees; faculty partners; or graduate students can be trusted and deputized to facilitate and deliver the learning experience. New spaces (and the safe transfer of physical collections to those spaces) may need to be considered, but if we can loan exhibition materials across continents or make collections available in other reading rooms through interlibrary loan, we can certainly bring an archival box to the history department.

What if we created the demand for our services, instead of always reacting to inquiries? Instruction librarians have experimented with providing a "menu of options," but in practice, these served more as ideas for instruction possibilities than a set of experiences that could simply be "ordered." If we truly focused and developed instruction based on our various strengths—our collections, our staff's subject expertise, or the skills we are good at developing—we could scale much better.

We can look to our colleagues in museum education, who develop a curriculum for an exhibition and train teams of museum educators or volunteer docents to lead inquiry-based tours. The tour is advertised with clear learning objectives or content areas, and a wide range of groups decide whether or not they will sign up for the tour. Though most of us love the range of work we get to do, this approach scales much better than creating a customized experience for every 16 students who walk through the door.

I would love to see funded graduate teaching assistants routinely assigned to academic librarians. We teach hundreds of students per term, in between other intensive demands. Graduate students would gain useful experience in student-centered and object-based pedagogies. Teaching assistants for librarians and archivists might help to conduct research in a collection, propose item selections, find contextual materials, prepare materials, facilitate sessions, or provide drop-in consultation hours. This would require funds, of course, but the bigger challenge may actually be coordinating with academic departments and administrative units to ensure that this work can count towards the graduate student's funding package.

Don't think that hands-on is the only option—but it is certainly central to what we do. There are many tools available to us to maximize time in the archives—that is, to use time more efficiently. As much as we plan for what *should* happen in the reading room; we should also be asking what does *not* need to be done in the reading room. Cover this content in pre-visits to classrooms. What does not need to occur in a face-to-face setting? Homework is a tried and true instructional technology. Tasks or readings can be assigned ahead of time—even by librarians or archivists.

We should be enthusiastically investing in the creation of videos or online learning modules. These can be made publicly available on the open web or kept within learning management systems. This should become a standard practice, as much as using pencils and checking bags. It will take money, skills, labor, and most importantly, time. Administrators and funders, take note. The creation of lasting content, delivered remotely, will become a vital strategy for ensuring that our collections stay relevant through scalable, high-impact instruction services. It has to be a piece of the puzzle.

4. Intention: Systematically Targeting Particular Audiences

By running instruction programs that are request-driven, we are essentially giving the squeaky wheel the grease. Our regular customers may in fact turn out to be our most logical audiences and partners, but let's make sure.

How do we avoid the problem of seeing the same students multiple times but missing others entirely? We need to devise strategies for systematically interacting with our student bodies. The approach will have to be proactive and collaborative, engaging academic departments and administrative units alike. It will require careful thinking, meaningful reflection, and bold experimentation.

No matter the scale, the questions related to interacting with our student populations are the same. What are the crucial points? Where can we be of assistance? What should students learn over the course of their career? Curriculum mapping is a tool for understanding what is taught and how students move through programs. It helps to highlight the content and skills covered, and can help assess whether programs are meeting learning objectives. Curriculum mapping can be done in parts. Specific academic programs can be intentionally targeted in an incremental or focused approach. When looking at individual departments, consider how to provide a meaningful introduction to using primary sources for all incoming students. Decide which upper division courses present opportunities to build advanced, independent archival research skills. Is there a capstone experience for this major? If so, support and enrich that experience for all graduates.

Looking more broadly, when institution-wide curriculum mapping efforts exist (often prompted by reviews of accreditations or general education requirements), we need to make sure that we have a seat at the table. This can be accomplished via smaller scale outreach efforts by individuals and departments, but it will also require more systematic efforts to ensure representation in faculty senates and administrative committees.

5. Evaluation: Get Serious about Assessment

For a decade, we have heard calls for more assessment—but we are still waiting. Relatively few rigorous empirical or ethnographic studies exist. Assessment is vital to understanding our own work, to improving, and to making the case for resources to support our efforts. We assume that it is inherently a good idea to teach undergraduates with archives, but can we prove it? Do we even understand the value we add?

We will need money and skills and time to establish cultures of assessment. We will need to question our base assumptions and ask hard questions. We need to agree on a shared vocabulary for what it is that we are doing and on standard measures for our work, so that we can compare apples to apples and come to a consensus. We need to clearly articulate our goals and establish priorities. If we truly review everything that we do, we will likely need to stop doing things that do not meet our objectives and we will absolutely need to stop doing things that do not work. We will need to experiment, take risks, and fail. Most importantly, we will need to take action based on what we find; to implement the lessons learned.

Conclusion

We have made gains. The 2018 Michigan symposium, and this resulting volume, reveal that we have started to form a significant community of practice. Now is the time to build a firm foundation. None of this will happen overnight, and there are many obstacles, but if we can agree on shared priorities, we may be able to establish a more cohesive and connected discipline. By intentionally focusing on key audiences, we will take our emerging field to new heights. If we believe that what we do has value, we must commit to addressing challenges—such as the problem of scale—head on. The true markers of success will be a robust culture of assessment and resulting improvements that have an impact on generations of students.

Contributors

Anne Bahde is the Rare Books and History of Science Librarian in the Special Collections and Archives Research Center at Oregon State University. She concentrates on primary source literacy, digital humanities, and data visualization in her scholarship and practice, with special attention to the intersections of these areas. With Heather Smedberg and Mattie Taormina, she was the recipient of the 2016 Primary Source Award for Research from the Center for Research Libraries, awarded for their 2014 edited compilation *Using Primary Sources: Hands-On Instructional Exercises.*

Nancy Bartlett is associate director at the Bentley Historical Library, University of Michigan. A Fellow of the Society of American Archivists, she has written and edited extensively on archives and architecture, the cultural conditions of archives, and the history of archival principles. She is a member of the Bentley Historical Library research team investigating "Engaging the Archives: New Partnerships and Understandings of Teaching and Learning with Primary Sources." This five-year project, begun in 2015, is made possible by the University of Michigan Third Century Initiative. Nancy also served on the planning and program committee for the Teaching Undergraduates with Archives Symposium.

Caroline S. Boswell is an Associate Professor of History and Humanities at the University of Wisconsin–Green Bay, where she also directs the Center for the Advancement of Teaching and Learning. She is co-editor of the *Syllabus* journal, an online open access journal that publishes peer-reviewed critical syllabi, assignments, and articles on syllabus design. Her historical research examines the social history of politics in seventeenth-century England. She is author of *Disaffection and Everyday Life in Interregnum England* (2017), which explores the intersections between the politics of everyday life and the politics of revolution within communities and social relations. Among other courses, she teaches UW-Green Bay's gateway course on historical methods and a senior year practicum in digital and public humanities, both of which make extensive use of local and digital archives.

Elizabeth Call is currently the University Archivist at the Rochester Institute of Technology Libraries. Prior to this Elizabeth has held roles at the University of Rochester, Columbia University, and the Brooklyn Historical Society. Elizabeth holds a master's degree in library and information science from the Palmer School of Library and Information Science, Long Island University, and a master of arts degree in public history from New York University.

Peter Carini is the College Archivist for Dartmouth College and is a member of the teaching team in Rauner Special Collections Library, where more than 130 class sessions are taught each year using archival documents, rare books and manuscripts. Peter has been facilitating the use of primary source materials in the classroom for more than twenty years and writes and presents regularly on the subject.

Meghan Clark graduated from the University of Michigan in May 2019 with a degree in history and a minor in environment. While at U-M, she participated in two Michigan in the World digital projects. Her published work, "Give Earth a Chance: Environmental Activism in Michigan" and "Go Blue: Competition, Controversy, and Community in Michigan Athletics," examines environmental and women's activism in the 1960s and 1970s. She is currently a research fellow at the Ecology Center of Ann Arbor and plans to move to Chicago to conduct legal research before starting law school in fall 2020.

Ashleigh D. Coren is the Special Collections Librarian for Teaching and Learning at the University of Maryland, College Park, and is also an adjunct lecturer in the College of Information Studies. She is also a Program Facilitator for the Association of College and Research Libraries Information Literacy Immersion Program, and in 2018 she was named an American Library Association Emerging Leader.

Shelby Daniels-Young received her master of science in information in May 2019 from the University of Michigan School of Information and is currently a Pauline A. Young Resident at the University of Delaware Library, Museums and Press. She loves the intimate interaction with history that archival materials can provide. Her goal as an archives professional is to bring more attention to the stories of individuals and groups who are underrepresented or marginalized in historical narratives.

Rachel C. S. Duke is the Rare Books Librarian at Florida State University Libraries, where she was previously an instructor in the History of Text Technologies program. She holds a master's degree in English literature from Rutgers University–Newark and is a doctoral candidate in medieval literature in Florida State University's English department. As Rare Books Librarian, Rachel co-leads the instruction task force of FSU's Special Collections and Archives. The team is currently working toward the following objectives: pre and post-session assessment of student outcomes; a collaborative model for session solicitation, planning, and execution; and strategic deployment of multi-visit assignments in curricular bottlenecks.

Shira Loev Eller is the Art and Design Librarian at George Washington University Libraries and chair of the libraries' Scholarly Communications team. She previously worked as a reference and instruction librarian for the Corcoran College of Art + Design. In her current role, Shira works closely with the Special Collections Research Center to teach with archives and rare books, and she curates the artists' books collection. Shira is active in the Art Libraries Society of North America and is currently co-coordinator of the Books Arts Special Interest Group.

Elizabeth Gadelha is the Archivist for Digitization Services at the Bentley Historical Library, University of Michigan. She served on the planning and program committee for the Teaching Undergraduates with Archives Symposium. Her interest in teaching with primary sources stems from assessing and researching arts integration programming in Chicago Public Schools. She holds a master of science degree in information from the University of Michigan and a bachelor of fine arts degree in photography from the University of Illinois at Chicago.

Andi Gustavson is Head of Instructional Services at the Harry Ransom Humanities Research Center, where she teaches classes that engage with primary source material from the collections. She has published on oral history in *The Journal of American Studies*. Her current book project, *What Comes Home: Vernacular Photography and the Cold War, 1945–1991*, considers personal snapshots, affect, and the visual representation of war. She received her doctorate from the Department of American Studies at The University of Texas at Austin.

Jonathan C. Hagel earned a bachelor's in history and a master's in American studies from Lehigh University before completing my PhD in history from Brown University in 2012. Since then, I have been teaching at the University of Kansas, where I am an Assistant Teaching Professor in the Department of History. I teach courses in American cultural history, the Great Depression, Kansas history, and the historian's craft. I am currently working on a book manuscript about the development of antiracist ideas and ideologies in the United States from the 1920s to the 1960s.

Matt Herbison is the Reference & Education Archivist at the Legacy Center Archives of Drexel University College of Medicine in Philadelphia. At work, he enjoys supporting archives users at all levels of inexperience or expertise. At work and beyond, he loves teaming with others throughout the burgeoning Teaching with Primary Sources Community, developing opportunities and resources to support the work and goals we all share.

Laura Hibbler is the Associate University Librarian for Research and Instruction at Brandeis University. She also serves as the library liaison to the university's departments of history and African and African-American studies. Laura has a bachelor's degree in history from Yale University, a master of science in library science degree from the University of North Carolina at Chapel Hill, and a master of science in instructional design & technology from Brandeis University.

Kimberly Davies Hoffman serves as the University of Rochester's Head of Outreach, Learning, and Research Services at the River Campus Libraries. With interests in engaging pedagogy, instructional design, assessment, and creating professional development opportunities, she has been a founding member for programs like LILAC (http://academy.libraryinstruction.org/), the 3Ts (http://threetees.weebly.com/), and RYSAG (https://www.geneseo.edu/xerox_center/rysag). Current projects include her participation in the ARL Digital Scholarship Institute, a grant-based digital collection of case studies highlighting faculty's teaching with technology (DigITaL, Digital Ideas in Teaching and Learning), and an openly published book tentatively titled *Open Pedagogy: Varied Definitions, Multiple Approaches*. This book aims to highlight faculty-library collaborations in adopting open educational practices. Kimberly earned her master of library science degree at the University at Buffalo and a bachelor of arts degree in French and international relations at the University of New Hampshire.

Ella Howard is Associate Professor of History at Wentworth Institute of Technology in Boston, an institution specializing in hands-on and applied learning. Her teaching and research interests include urban history, public history, digital history, and the history of poverty. She is author of *Homeless: Poverty and Place in Urban America* (University of Pennsylvania Press, 2013). She is currently researching a monograph on historic preservation, segregation, and gentrification.

Lae'l Hughes-Watkins is the University Archivist at the University of Maryland. Her research focuses on outreach to marginalized communities, documenting student activism within disenfranchised populations, and utilizing narratives of oppressed voices within the curricula of post-secondary education spaces. Her most recent article is "Moving Toward a Reparative Archive: A Roadmap for a Holistic Approach to Disrupting Homogenous Histories in Academic Repositories and Creating Inclusive Spaces for Marginalized Voices," in the *Journal of Contemporary Archival Studies*. Lae'l is the founder of Project STAND, a national consortium of sixty colleges and universities working to create a digitally centralized location for access to primary resources on the narratives of student activists and organizations from traditionally underrepresented communities. Project STAND was recently awarded a National Leadership grant for $92,000 by the Institute of Museums and Libraries. She is a 2019 LJ Movers & Shakers, an Academic Research Libraries Leadership and Career Development Program fellow, with an SOA Merit Award for her leadership in Project STAND.

Robin M. Katz is the world's first primary source literacy librarian. Her background is in archives and special collections, but she is currently based in the library's Teaching and Learning department at the University of California, Riverside. She co-created TeachArchives.org based on a groundbreaking US Department of Education grant she led at Brooklyn Historical Society. She has also worked at the University of Vermont, the Beinecke Rare Book and Manuscript Library, Kent State University Special Collections & Archives, and more. During her tenure as co-chair of the Society of American Archivists Teaching with Primary Sources committee, the group received a Council Exemplary Service Award. She served on the Society of American Archivists and the Association of College and Research Libraries joint task force, which authored the Guidelines for Primary Source Literacy. She is currently co-chairing the 2020 conference for the Rare Book and Manuscript Section of the American Library Association. She received her master's in library and information science from Kent State University and her bachelor of arts degree from Brandeis University.

Matthew D. Lassiter is Professor of History and Arthur F. Thurnau Professor at the University of Michigan. His publications include *The Silent Majority: Suburban Politics in the Sunbelt South* (Princeton, 2006), the coedited anthology *The Myth of Southern Exceptionalism* (Oxford, 2009), and the forthcoming book *The Suburban Crisis: Crime, Drugs, and White Middle-Class America* (Princeton). He has collaborated with undergraduates and the Bentley Historical Library to produce four digital exhibits through the Michigan in the World program (https://lsa.umich.edu/history/history-at-work/programs/michigan-in-the-world.html) and is the primary investigator of the Policing and Social Justice HistoryLab, a new initiative to involve undergraduate and graduate students in archival research and production of digital exhibits mapping histories of police violence and social protest in Detroit and the state of Michigan.

Daniel J. Linke received bachelor's and master's degrees from Case Western Reserve University in Cleveland, Ohio, and worked at three archival repositories (Cleveland History Center, the University of Oklahoma, and the New York State Archives) before arriving at Princeton University in 1994. First serving as the Seeley G. Mudd Manuscript Library's (https://rbsc.princeton.edu/mudd/) assistant archivist for technical services, he was promoted in July 2002 to his current position, the University Archivist and Curator of Public Policy Papers. As head of the Mudd Library, he is responsible for collection development, and he oversees the library's public services and technical services work, as well as University records management. Since April 2019, he has served as the interim head of the Department of Rare Books and Special Collections.

Analú María López is the Ayer Indigenous Studies Librarian at the Newberry Library in Chicago and of Xi'úi (Pame)-Guachichil descent. Interested in underrepresented Indigenous narratives dealing with identity, language, and decolonization, she writes and creates photographic-based projects exploring these topics. A student of the Nahuatl language for more than ten years, she is also interested in Indigenous language preservation efforts. She holds a master of library and information sciences degree with a certificate in archives and cultural heritage resources and services from Dominican University and a bachelor of arts in photography with a minor in Latin-American studies from Columbia College Chicago.

Holly Luetkenhaus is the First Year Experience Librarian at Oklahoma State University. She holds a master of science in library science degree and a master of arts in English. Her research interests include information literacy and intersectional studies. She has presented at the Association of College and Research Libraries' Conference, Library Instruction West, and the Annual Conference on the First Year Experience about her work in teaching information literacy skills to first-year students and incorporating critical pedagogy into library instruction.

Terrence J. McDonald became the director of the Bentley Historical Library in September 2013 after serving for ten years as dean of the University of Michigan's College of Literature, Science, and the Arts. He earned a bachelor's degree from Marquette University and joined the U-M faculty after receiving his doctorate from Stanford University. Professor McDonald specializes in United States history in the nineteenth and twentieth centuries, the same period covered by the archival holdings at the Bentley. He has received a Guggenheim Fellowship for his research and holds an Arthur F. Thurnau Professorship, which is awarded to the University's most outstanding undergraduate teachers.

Chloe Morse-Harding is the Reference and Instruction Archivist at Brandeis University. Prior to working as an archivist, she taught high school English. She holds a bachelor of fine arts in creative writing from Emerson College, a master of arts in teaching in English education from Tufts University, and a master of science in library sciences with a concentration in archival management from Simmons College.

Sean Noel is a PhD candidate at Simmons University interested in the use of primary sources in the undergraduate curriculum. Originally from Maine, Sean Noel has lived and worked in Boston for more than twenty-five years. In 1994, he received his bachelor of arts in English literature from Boston University, Phi Beta Kappa, followed by two years in Aomori, Japan, teaching English and studying Kendo. Sean has spent twenty-two years at Boston University's Howard Gotlieb Archival Research Center in several positions focusing on public service, educational outreach, and administration. He is now Associate Director. He lives in Waltham, Massachusetts, with his wife and daughter.

Cinda Nofziger is the Archivist for Academic Programs and Outreach at the Bentley Historical Library, University of Michigan. She manages a robust instructional program, collaborating with faculty to engage students. She co-organizes a semester-long teaching seminar bringing together faculty and archivists and is a member of the Bentley's research initiative "Engaging the Archives: New Partnerships and Understandings of Teaching and Learning with Primary Sources." She also served on the planning and program committee for the Teaching Undergraduates with Archives Symposium. She holds a master of science in information degree from the University of Michigan and a PhD in American studies from the University of Iowa.

David Peters is the Head of the Archives Department at Oklahoma State University; he has had a thirty-three-year career there. Peters is a Certified Archivist and has a master's in library and information science with a specialization in archives from the University of Oklahoma. He attended Tabor College and OSU before serving in the Peace Corps. Peters has authored and co-authored books on the OSU campus and has a running article in the university's STATE magazine highlighting OSU's archival collections. Peters has a long history of serving in leadership positions in local historical and service organizations and well as state and regional archival societies.

Leah Richardson is Research and Instruction Librarian for Special Collections at George Washington University and an active member of the Libraries' Scholarly Communications team. She has more than ten years of experience working and teaching with archives and rare books in academic libraries. Her research focuses on archival pedagogy, critical librarianship, and labor. Leah was part of the SAA/ACRL-RBMS Joint Task Force that developed the Guidelines for Primary Source Literacy, published in 2018.

Martha A. Sandweiss, Professor of History at Princeton University, began her professional career as a museum curator and director, and taught at Amherst College for twenty years before moving to Princeton in 2009. Archives and special collections have long been central to her classroom teaching. Her work focuses on the history of photography, the history of the American West, and the history of race in American life, and her many publications include *Print the Legend: Photography and the American West* (2002) and *Passing Strange: A Gilded Age Tale of Love and Deception Across the Color Line* (2009). Most recently, she has served as founder and director of The Princeton & Slavery Project (https://www.slavery.princeton.edu).

Heather Smedberg is the Reference & Instruction Coordinator for Special Collections & Archives at the University of California San Diego Library, where she regularly engages with students, faculty, and other librarians to teach primary source literacy and related topics. Along with Anne Bahde, she served as the founding co-chair of the Instruction & Outreach Committee of the Rare Books and Manuscripts section of the Association of College and Research Libraries (RBMS). With Bill Landis, she served as co-chair of the RBMS/Society of American Archivists Joint Task Force on the development of Guidelines for Primary Source Literacy. And with Anne Bahde and Mattie Taormina, she is co-editor of the book *Using Primary Sources: Hands on Instructional Exercises*.

Elizabeth Smith-Pryor is an associate professor in the Department of History at Kent State University, who specializes in African American history. She is completing her second monograph, tentatively titled *Equal Opportunity is Not Enough: The Urban League's New Thrust in Cleveland, Ohio, 1968–1975.* In 2016, she was awarded the Ford Foundation Senior Fellowship for this project, which explores a key moment when one mainstream African American organization—the Urban League—contested normative definitions of equality and opportunity in an era of racialized inequality. She is the author of *Property Rites: The Rhinelander Trial, Passing, and the Protection of Whiteness* (2009). As a teacher of undergraduates and graduate students, Smith-Pryor thinks archives and archivists are wonderful! Working with Kent State's university archivist, she has twice taught a course on Civil Rights and Black Power where students created a digital history project based on the university archives' holdings.

Sarah Stanley is the Digital Humanities Librarian at Florida State University. She received a master's in English literature from Northeastern University in 2015, where she studied early modern women's writing. In her capacity as Digital Humanities Librarian, Sarah teaches digital literacy and digital research methodologies to faculty and students alike. Sarah uses text encoding and the creation of digital editions as a pedagogical tool to teach students about critical engagement with texts. She currently serves on the Text Encoding Initiative Technical Council, where she edits and maintains the TEI guidelines. Sarah is currently pursuing a master's of science in information from Florida State University.

Naomi J. Stubbs is Professor of English at LaGuardia Community College, City University of New York. Stubbs's areas of research include nineteenth-century American theatre and popular entertainments. She is the author of *Cultivating National Identity Through Performance: American Pleasure Gardens and Entertainment* (Palgrave, 2012) and co-editor of both *A Player and a Gentleman: The Diary of Harry Watkins, Nineteenth-Century American Actor* (University of Michigan Press,

2018) and *The Harry Watkins Diary: The Digital Edition* (https://quod.lib.umich.edu/h/hwatkins/). Stubbs is also the co-editor of the *Journal of American Drama and Theatre* and coordinator of learning communities and English internships at LaGuardia, and her current research centers on undergraduate research opportunities in the humanities.

Morgan Swan has served as the Special Collections Education and Outreach Librarian at Dartmouth College for more than seven years. His duties include teaching more than one hundred one-shot sessions in Rauner Special Collections Library every year, supervising Rauner Special Collections Library's Reader Services department, directing the special collections fellowship program, and coordinating outreach efforts via public programming and social media. Before coming to Dartmouth, he worked at the Beinecke Rare Book & Manuscript Library at Yale University for nearly five years. Morgan has a PhD in English literature from Yale University and a master's in library and information science with a concentration in archival studies from the University of Wisconsin-Milwaukee.

Camila Zorrilla Tessler is the only archivist at Yale's Manuscript and Archives department who does not have a qualifier in front of her title. She spends her time doing a little of everything at work, and in her free time she knits, sews, and weaves. She has a master of letters from Newcastle University in Newcastle-upon-Tyne in Children's Literature and a master of library and information science from the University of Arizona. Her archival research interests are archival ethics, as well as diversity and cultural competency.

Hannah Thoms graduated from the University of Michigan in May 2019 with a degree in anthropology and minors in history and museum studies. After working in the collections departments of several history museums, she co-created the digital exhibit, "Give Earth a Chance: Environmental Activism in Michigan" in fall 2017. She later worked as a research fellow at the Ecology Center of Ann Arbor and co-produced another public history website, "Detroit Under Fire: Police Violence,

Crime Politics, and the Struggle for Racial Justice in the Civil Rights Era." Her senior thesis, "Collecting New Guinea: Transformations in the Lives of Four Ethnographic Collections, 1875–1988," received the Terrence McDonald Prize for Archival Research from the U-M Honors Program. Hannah currently works as a Collection Assistant at Motown Museum in Detroit.

Kristen Totleben is Modern Languages and Cultures Librarian at the University of Rochester. She is the collections and outreach librarian for nine languages, comparative literature, and literary translation studies. Her research interests include working with special collections, digital scholarship practices, and organizational culture. Co-editor of the Association of College and Research Libraries book *Collaborating for Impact: Special Collections and Liaison Librarian Partnerships*, she is particularly interested in the combinatory use, application, and holistic integration of primary and secondary sources in research workshops, collection development, and analysis and research services.

Matt Upson is the Director of Undergraduate Instruction and Outreach Services at Oklahoma State University's Edmon Low Library. He enjoys finding opportunities for innovative instruction and interaction with students, including co-authoring a comic book guide to basic library research skills and information literacy titled *Information Now*. Matt earned a master's of library science from Emporia State University and a bachelor of science degree in secondary education from Oklahoma State University.

Marissa Vassari is the Archivist & Educator in the Research and Education division of the Rockefeller Archive Center (RAC). She develops educational outreach projects, coordinates the RAC-City College of New York Internship Program, oversees the exhibit creation process for a wide range of audiences, and facilitates outgoing loans. She has presented her education work at the Mid-Atlantic Regional Archives Conference and written an article about developing policies and procedures for temporary exhibits in archives in *Collections: A Journal* *for Museum and Archives Professionals*. In 2016, Marissa founded the Archival Educators Roundtable, which facilitates communication among professionals who use primary sources in public outreach and teaching. Marissa earned a bachelor of arts in psychology and special education from Marist College, a master of arts in childhood education from New York University, and a master of library and information science degree with an archival studies specialization from the University of California Los Angeles.

Christine Weideman has been Director of Manuscripts and Archives in the Yale University Library since 2008. She has published and presented widely on core archival functions and is a Distinguished Fellow of the Society of American Archivists. She has served as the Yale University Library point person for the Yale History Keeper's Program since its inception in 2017.

Brian A. Williams is Assistant Director and Archivist for University History at the University of Michigan's Bentley Historical Library. He joined the Bentley Historical Library as an assistant archivist in 1994 after starting his archival career at the Oberlin College Archives. Williams studied history at Muskingum College and Hope College, earning a bachelor of arts in 1988, and earned his master of library and information science degree from the University of Michigan in 1990. He is currently leading the Bentley Library's project to identify every African American student who attended the University of Michigan from its founding in 1817 to the Black Action Movement in 1970.

Elizabeth Yakel, PhD, is a Professor and Senior Associate Dean for Academic Affairs at the University of Michigan School of Information. Her teaching and research foci are in the areas of access to digital archives and curation. Throughout her career, she has researched how users discover, analyze, and use primary sources and the repositories that hold them. She is active in the Society of American Archivists (SAA), where she served on the governing council and was elected a Fellow in 1999.

Joshua Youngblood is Rare Books Librarian and Instruction and Outreach Unit Head for the Special Collections of the University of Arkansas Libraries. An active member of several professional organizations, Joshua currently serves as President of the Society of Southwest Archivists and is a past steering committee member of the Society of American Archivists Research, Access, and Outreach Section. In addition to numerous conference presentations, he has published on archival curation of digital exhibits, undergraduate research with primary sources, and the history of Arkansas and the American South. As a faculty member of the University of Arkansas, Joshua works on campus-wide issues such as academic integrity policy and supports interdisciplinary research through service work for several campus programs and community organizations. Before coming to Arkansas, he worked in cultural resource management for the Florida Department of State including as Archives Historian for the Florida Memory Program.

www.ingramcontent.com/pod-product-compliance
Lightning Source LLC
Chambersburg PA
CBHW042141160426
43201CB00022B/2366